LIVING

═══ ON THE ═══

FAULT LINE

REVISED EDITION

Also by Geoffrey A. Moore

Crossing the Chasm

The Gorilla Game

Inside the Tornado

The Gorilla Game Revised

LIVING

ON THE

FAULT LINE

REVISED EDITION

Managing for Shareholder Value in <u>Any</u> Economy

GEOFFREY A. MOORE

HarperBusiness

An Imprint of HarperCollins*Publishers*

A PREVIOUS EDITION OF THIS BOOK WAS PUBLISHED IN 2000 BY HARPER-
BUSINESS, AN IMPRINT OF HARPERCOLLINS PUBLISHERS.

HarperCollins books may be purchased for educational, business, or
sales promotional use. For information please write: Special Markets
Department, HarperCollins Publishers Inc., 10 East 53rd Street, New
York, NY 10022.

FIRST EDITION

Designed by Nancy Singer Olaguera

Library of Congress Cataloging-in-Publication Data

Moore, Geoffrey A., 1946–
    Living on the fault line : managing for shareholder value in any
economy / Geoffrey A. Moore.—Rev. ed.
        p.   cm.
    Includes index.
    ISBN 0-06-008676-9
    1. Industrial management. 2. Stocks—Prices. 3. Competition. I.
Title.

    HD31 .M625 2002
    658.15'5—dc21
                                                            2002023059

02 03 04 05 06 ❖/QW 10 9 8 7 6 5 4 3 2 1

To George Moore,
who has spent his entire life putting
his humor, intelligence, and compassion
in service to others,
and
to Peter Moore,
who has the gift of inspiring others
to be their best selves.
Thanks for all the love and encouragement.

ACKNOWLEDGMENTS

This book had its beginning in a moment of customer dissatisfaction. It was back in 1996, and I was consulting with the Boise divisions of Hewlett-Packard using the models laid out in *Crossing the Chasm* and *Inside the Tornado* and was placing particular emphasis on how the technology adoption life cycle created a unique marketing challenge. Specifically, what I said was: *At every stage of the life cycle, the strategy that causes success in that stage causes failure in the next.*

It was then that I began to hear the grumbling. *Wait a minute. We are a global company. We are managing offerings at every stage in the life cycle all at the same time. Indeed, in some countries the offering is at one stage of adoption, and in other countries at another. We have teams around the world trying to work together from a common basis. You cannot just switch strategies every ten minutes. So now what, smart guy?*

Now what, indeed. How could a large enterprise manage the amount of change that technology-enabled markets demand? Start-ups, by virtue of their small size, could perhaps make the adjustments I was calling for, but what could global organizations hope to accomplish? The more I thought about it, the more it came down to a single question: *What could management do to overcome the inertia of large organizations?* If I could answer that question, clearly it was time to write the next book.

But before I could find that answer, my agent, Jim Levine, suggested I write a different book, this one on high-tech investing, and that in turn led to a collaboration with Tom Kippola of The Chasm Group and Paul Johnson of Robertson Stephens called *The Gorilla*

Game. That intervention was fortuitous because it brought to light a connection between stock price and competitive advantage that became the basis for tackling the problem of corporate inertia described in Chapter 2 of this book.

So at the outset I would like to acknowledge my dissatisfied clients in the Boise divisions of Hewlett-Packard—thank you, for without your prodding this book would never have happened, and sorry for it being so late. And I would like to thank Jim, Tom, and Paul for the wonderful detour into the realm of high-tech stock valuations and the value that has added to this book.

To these I need to add several people who made direct contributions to the ideas and models that populate these pages. On coming to grips with stock price and the valuation of technology stocks, Michael Mauboussin of Crédit Suisse First Boston has been a continual inspiration and help. He continues to write some of the best essays on this subject, and I encourage interested readers to track them down. On the issue of value disciplines and their impact on competitive advantage, I continue to profit from the work of Michael Treacy and Fred Wiersema as described in their book *The Value Disciplines of Market Leaders.* And on the issue of culture, I am deeply grateful for and dependent upon the work and assistance of Bill Schneider, whose work I cite and whose models I have taken more than a few liberties with. I am also indebted to Brad Spencer, an organizational development consultant and friend, who helped me bridge the thinking between Schneider's work and Treacy and Wiersema's.

Those are some of the most explicit influences I can acknowledge that supported the development of this book. But there is also the implicit influence of colleagues, and here I am blessed with two sets. For the past decade I have been a part of The Chasm Group along with Mark Cavender, Tom Kippola, Philip Lay, Mike Tanner, and Paul Wiefels, all of whom, like myself, spend most of their days consulting with high-tech executives on the challenges of developing technology-enabled markets. The result has been a community of intellectual exchange that has contributed to every idea on every page of this book. At the same time, for the past two years I have been a venture partner at Mohr Davidow Ventures.

Here my colleagues include Bill Davidow, Jon Feiber, Nancy Schoendorf, Rob Chaplinsky, George Zachary, Michael Solomon, Randy Strahan, Donna Novitsky, Mo Virani, Jim Smith, and Erik Straser. What they have all brought to my thinking is a continual focus on shareholder value—what creates it, what enhances it, what destroys it—all of which has been instrumental in the development of this book.

Then there have been the readers of this manuscript in its earlier drafts. These brave souls deserve special acknowledgment, particularly because they were able to get comments back after a ludicrously brief interval in order to influence the final draft. Needless to say, they should not be held accountable for any defects therein, but instead be acknowledged for contributing to whatever coherence there is. These include Michael Eckhardt, Chris Meyer, Jim Fawcette, Greg Ruff, Dennis Hunter, Russell Redenbaugh, Stan Leopard, Tom Kendra, Al Magid, and Mel Lemberger. Two additional readers I would like to especially acknowledge. The first is Nicholas Carr at *The Harvard Business Review* who rightly took me to task for flaws in an early version of Chapter 2. I don't know that they have all been addressed, but the chapter benefited greatly from his critique. And the second is Bill Meade, a friend and colleague at Hewlett-Packard, who, in addition to managing the on-line investment chat community that has formed around *The Gorilla Game,* has continually participated in and helped shaped the ideas that frame this book, including giving me mini-lectures via e-mail on the work of Joseph Schumpeter.

That leaves a small cadre of people without whom any author is hopelessly adrift. These include my literary agent, Jim Levine, my editor, David Conti, and my business manager and aide-de-camp, Angelynn Hanley. All three of these individuals live with me behind the scenes where the work is anything but polished. Yet all three retain a cheerful optimism in the face of any number of pending calamities, reminding me of the character Henslowe in the recent movie, *Shakespeare in Love,* who when faced with similar circumstances repeatedly asserts, "It all works out. I don't know how exactly, but it just does." Thanks to all three of you for keeping the faith.

And that brings me to one final person to acknowledge, Marie, who has kept her faith in me for more than thirty years of marriage and has been "the wind beneath my wings." (There is a story about that line, but I will leave it for another time.) It is hard to explain how much I draw from and depend upon our relationship. On the surface our careers appear so different—she teaching third-graders, me high-tech executives (well, perhaps not *that* different)—but at the core we come together in common values and in a common strategy for living. And so we continually exchange ideas and perceptions, anecdotes and incidents, laughter and love, and in so doing come away so much the stronger. To the degree that there is balance in this work, that there is any stability beneath its constant dealings with change, it has its roots here. For this and so much more I am deeply and forever thankful.

Postscript

In revising this book in 2002, in addition to all of the above, I would like to acknowledge the extraordinary contribution and support of Pat Granger, my assistant for the last year and a half. To use the parlance of this book, my context is her core, and by outsourcing to her all the thousand acts of organization, administration, and communication that are the very stuff of business life, I am freed to work on projects such as this. Pat, one thousand thank-yous.

CONTENTS

PREFACE

They say that confession is good for the soul, so let me begin with one. So much has changed since this book was first written that I hesitated even to revise it. So many assumptions baked into the original text have proven to be false or unreliable, so much of the rhetoric now exposed to be slick or hollow, that as an author, I just wanted to run and hide. Well, the good news is there is no place to hide, and if managers and CEOs are expected to take their lumps, why shouldn't authors and consultants as well? So be it.

That said, when I thought about writing *another* book—the "right book," that mythical creature that tantalizes and eludes us all—I found that much of what I intended to include was in fact part of this current book. To be sure, our consulting practice at the Chasm Group has matured considerably since 1999, and there are updates to several of the frameworks presented in the original edition, and they are included in this revision. But for the most part, the underlying thinking and models have held up well despite the drastic changes in the economy. That is because, at the end of the day, managing for shareholder value really is about managing for competitive advantage, whether one is sailing with the wind or into it.

What I did find myself wanting to swap out was the surrounding set of economic assumptions that had driven the earlier text. The dotcom threat that I posed as bogeyman, the force that would drive corporate America to become more adaptive to change, has instead been exposed as an investment mania. The whole notion of disruptive innovations riding into power on the back of increasing returns, while real, is nowhere near as commonplace as I had once assumed. Valuing time over money, as a strategy, works only when you are riding a big investment bubble; once the wave crashes, and capital returns to prudence, then the balance between the two reasserts itself. In sum, much of my celebration of a new economy was just a lot of old baloney.

So let us strip all that talk away. Let us look at the world through the eyes of a chastened technology sector, an America no longer untouched by terrorist attack, and a global economy more challenged than it has been in a long time. In light of all this, does it make any sense at all to still be talking about a *new economy?*

I think it does. Indeed, I believe it is more crucial than ever that we do so. Managing for shareholder value going forward is going to require ever more effective utilization of financial capital. We can't succeed in this without a clear appreciation of the demands of that capital. And the first demand of capital is that it be deployed in efforts that can raise the value of the company it is invested in.

In the economy of the twentieth century, the path to increased valuation was scale. Capital was used to grow the company. More and more tasks were brought inside the corporation where they could be handled more cheaply, and smaller companies, unable to scale, got squeezed out through marketplace power plays and massive efficiencies. Such forces led inexorably to the formation of the *Fortune* 500, in which the greatest honor goes to the largest institution.

At the turn of the century, however, the tables are turning. As work becomes more technologically enabled, more and more investment is required to keep pace with competitive performance. This plays into the hands of companies who specialize in a specific form of work. It does not play into the hands of large, all-purpose corporations. For those companies to match the specialist company's investment creates redundant consumption of capital with no material advantage gained. A small company outsourcing to that specialist can duplicate the large company's performance, perhaps by paying a small markup, *but with no capital outlay.* Instead it can use its capital to further differentiate its offers from its larger competitors, thereby creating market advantage without creating extra bulk. Shareholders monitoring ROIC (return on invested capital) have been quick to appreciate this difference.

As we shall discuss at length, the economy is changing in ways that let virtually any company deconstruct its offerings to trade off using inside versus outside resources to its best advantage. This is a relatively new outcome in large part enabled by the rise of the Internet. By providing a communications backbone that permits more and more work to be distributed across corporate—and even continental—boundaries, the Internet is redefining how the world manages its supply chains. To be sure, Internet-enabled e-commerce is still in its infancy, and much of its promise has yet to be realized, but no one believes that it is directionally off course. The only argument is over how far it can go and how soon to commit.

Over time I believe that the age of the Internet and the age of outsourcing will become synonymous, and that together they will make for a truly new economy. Outsourcing manufacturing in the electronics industry is the poster child for this change. It is now clear that, with few exceptions, an electronics company cannot compete without adopting this tactic: it simply takes too much capital garnering too little return to sustain the sophisticated capabilities required. Only specialists can raise such capital because by their focus they can create enough business throughput to generate an attractive return. Thus the contract manufacturers have coevolved with the original equipment manufacturers to create a whole new ecosystem.

Where manufacturing has led, I believe, the services industries will eventually follow. If it makes no sense to manufacture in-house, what sense does it make to run your employee benefits in-house? Payroll? Facilities? Data center? E-mail? As capital puts more and more pressure on management to generate better and better returns, we are all being forced to focus more and more on our key differentiating capabilities, what in this book we call *core*, and leaving all the rest, what we call *context*, to others.

Let us not underestimate the disruptiveness of this change. First of all, it is proving hugely challenging to bring about. Much of the infrastructure and many of the systems required are today still woefully immature, and the stories of failed efforts are legion and chastening. But even more important in my view, we must not underestimate the change in management thinking needed to take advantage of this new world. It is no longer enough to make a profit. In this world, the question is, given the resources you used,

did you make *enough profit?* And going forward, can you distin-
guish between your high-return and low-return business processes,
and can you arrange for the former to be your focus, and the latter
to be delegated to someone else in the supply chain?

It is the goal of this book to give managers a framework for
tackling these issues and setting strategy to take best advantage of
the capital entrusted to them. This is what we mean by managing
for shareholder value. It does not replace the need to manage to
the P&L, but it does transcend it, meaning it represents a superset
of concerns of which the P&L is a component. Without this larger
frame of reference, managers will continue to beat their heads
against a wall of investor unresponsiveness, continue to accuse
Wall Street of shortsightedness, continue to believe their stock
price is at the mercy of some analyst's whims. With this frame of
reference, they may still find reasons to complain, but they will do
so with a much better appreciation for the forces driving the
investment community to act as it does.

In the end, the new economy is about creating a breakthrough
in the efficient deployment of capital. It implies a world in which
work is redistributed across a vast network of specialists inter-
linked by information and logistic systems that allow for a raft of
just-in-time processes to unfold. In such a network, the return on
capital reaches unprecedented levels because every company is
deploying the bulk of its capital against its high-return core
processes and little or no capital against its low-return "me too"
context processes. The total return on capital in such a system far
exceeds any other alternative.

To be sure, this new economy today is still more vision than
reality, but we can begin to approximate it and by so doing create
superior shareholder returns in the present. At the same time, if we
really are able to distribute work into nations that have yet to share
in global prosperity, if we really can give the people of those
nations a stake in the global economy, then perhaps by so doing we
really can make the world a better and safer place for all of us.

So both in the short term and in the long there are attractive
targets for this discipline of managing for shareholder value to aim
at, and with that, let us get on with the business of setting it forth.

LIVING

═══ ON THE ═══

FAULT LINE

REVISED EDITION

1

THE INVESTOR PERSPECTIVE

Management must serve four primary constituencies in a capitalist system: customers, partners, employees, and investors. Of these, investors have the least visible presence, yet their influence is both deep and pervasive. Without investment capital and equity liquidity, companies cannot transcend the limits of local, owner-operated businesses.

Thus we embrace investors—often, however, without fully understanding their motives. Too often indeed we learn about these motives in the negative sense, when we violate unspoken covenants and expectations, leading to a deteriorating stock price and plummeting market capitalization, accompanied by loss of marketplace prestige and acquisition currency. The sad part of all this is that investor perspective is a hugely useful guide to management decision-making both in good times and bad, and keeping it in view is critical to navigating the uncertain waters of technology-enabled markets.

The key notion we will explore in this chapter is simple: investors are always looking for your company's future prospects to brighten. *That is, when they sell, they want the buying investor to see a brighter prospect than they did back when they bought. That, and only that, raises the value of your stock and creates a positive return for their investment. When they judge your company and your executive performance, all your decisions will be filtered through this lens: are you brightening the prospects?*

From a management point of view, this means that investors want your company to become more powerful under your watch. Increasing power—not revenue, not earnings, not dividends—is what increases stock price. Conversely, any action that diminishes power will sooner or later result in disappointing investors. Stock price tracks to investor perceptions around this issue. Thus it is that stock price over time acts as an information system to management about marketplace power. It is a grade on your strategy and execution, and if you learn to use it as such, you can improve your team's performance as well as create a powerful equity-based war chest for future growth in power.

STOCK PRICE AS AN INFORMATION SYSTEM

Stock price is a consequence of an impersonal force—investment—supplying capital to the sources of greatest risk-adjusted return. Investors in the aggregate are representatives of that force. As such they will never lie. They may get confused in the short term, but as soon as the true lay of the land comes clear, they will adjust their investments accordingly. In other words, you can trust investment to be unflaggingly self-interested.

More importantly, however, you can trust investment to be right. To be sure, as individuals, investors are often wrong, but collectively over time, they cannot be. That is, because investing is an inherently Darwinian exercise, poor investors lose capital and lose the ability to raise more, whereas good investors increase the capital they have under management and get pressed into investing additional capital as well. Over time capital ends up in the hands of those fittest to generate more capital. (As a society we may choose to enforce redistribution of that capital—that's a decision that lies outside the purview of this book—but regardless of that decision, it is in everyone's interest first to accumulate it.)

These successful investors pursue a single, simple end: to gain the best risk-adjusted return on capital they can. As we shall explain in more detail shortly, this is primarily a function of investing in entities that demonstrate the strongest competitive advantage in the markets they serve. Capital, in other words, flows to competitive advantage and abandons competitive disadvantage.

Your stock price is a measure of your attractiveness as an investment destination. Day to day, or even month to month, it is subject to so many distorting effects that it is virtually impossible to extract a meaningful signal from all the noise. But over time the effects of random noise cancel out, and a reliable signal does emerge. This long-term "noise-free" price establishes your "normal" market capitalization, a valuation by the investment community of your future earnings prospects relative to all the other sources of investment available. Even in the short term, although the absolute value of your market cap may be distorted, your valuation relative to your direct competitors is not likely to be. That is, if you rank companies in a given sector by market cap, you will almost always be ranking them by competitive advantage status.

Now when we are on the winning end of this exchange, we like to praise the wisdom of our shareholders for seeing our true value. When we are on the losing end, on the other hand, we are more likely to grouse about disloyal or impatient investors who are too short-term in their orientation. Neither reaction, however, is truly appropriate because both personalize the transaction. It is not personal. Capital is like water—it does not flow uphill against the gravity of competitive advantage. It can be pumped uphill, to be sure—that is what governments do all the time—but that is not its natural tendency. Therefore, wherever capital is allowed to follow its natural course, you can count on it to point out where competitive advantage lies.

This has huge implications for all kinds of executive decisions. Because stock price is in effect an information system about competitive advantage, it can help you sort through which markets to attack, which strategies to pursue, which partners to endorse, and which tactics to execute. It can teach you to abandon the familiar and embrace the strange—or vice versa. It can tell you where to invest and where to divest—or to put it in Kenny Rogers's vernacular, it can let you "know when to hold 'em and know when to fold 'em."

Capital in this sense functions like a canary in a coal mine. It is often your best leading indicator about your future competitive advantage as well as that of your partners and your competitors. It is thus a great counselor. Now to be sure, there are times when true leaders, like great chess players, choose to go against the wisdom of others and disregard the advice of counsel. It is not the goal of this book to make you or your company a slave to capital's dictates, particularly given the noisy environment in which they are communicated. But it is a goal that you should learn how to take counsel from capital markets, and to that end, the first step is learning how to decode stock price, beginning with your own.

1

UNDERSTANDING SHAREHOLDER VALUE

What is a share of your stock worth? By definition a share entitles its owner to a percentage of the future returns of your business. Owning all the stock in your company would entitle one to 100 percent of all your future earnings forever. What, exactly, should that be worth? And how would or could one know?

The challenge lies in the word *future*—how to value what is essentially a bird in the bush, not a bird in the hand. Investors and analysts must find some way to understand your business and its future trajectory so that, at any given price, they can decide whether to buy, sell, or hold your stock.

This has led to something of a consensus around the following as the fundamental valuation formula:

The total value of a company, its market capitalization, is equal to the present value of its forecastable future earnings from current and planned operations, discounted for risk.

Let's parse this sentence one phrase at a time. We're interested in the *present value* because the initial competition for all investment is cash—investors keeping their cash in hand and not parting with it to anyone. How much of this cash in hand today is your company really worth? Only a buyer and a seller agreeing to trade shares for cash at a given price can truly testify to that amount, with each new trade bearing witness to a new act of valuation. The stock market continuously reports on the fluctuations in this ongoing stream of cash-equivalent valuations in the form of a running series of stock price quotes. Multiplying any given quote by the number of shares outstanding, you can calculate your company's current total value, or *market capitalization*, at any time.

The price of the last trade sets the historical value for your company. It is a benchmark for the next trade, but it does not set the value of that trade. Instead, future considerations do. Specifically investors focus on *forecastable future earnings* for the following reasons:

- It is earnings, not revenues, that are tracked because that is what an investor is entitled to a share of.*

- They are *future* earnings because investors are not entitled to past earnings, only those coming up. When these earnings move from a future promise to a present achieved reality, they can either be distributed to investors in the form of some kind of a dividend or they can be reinvested in the company. If they are reinvested, the investor defers their reward in hopes of future additional earnings that such reinvestment might generate.

- And finally, they must be *forecastable* earnings because investors need some current foundation for incorporating the future into their present calculations.

Forecastability is fundamental to *investability* in that the higher the probability of the forecast, the lower the risk of investment.

---

*I am thoroughly indebted to Michael Mauboussin of Crédit Suisse First Boston for guidance in writing much of this section, although he should not be held accountable for any errors I make in trying to translate financial theory into everyday management language. As a case in point take the sentence footnoted here. Technically, it's not earnings but cash flow that the stock market tracks. For most technology companies, the numbers are similar—but not always. The challenge is that earnings can be defined by accounting practices in multiple ways, not all of which are of interest to or in the interests of investors. Cash in and cash out, on the other hand, leaves an unmistakable trace of value created. Nonetheless, I will continue to use everyday language and concepts despite their susceptibility to technical correction.

Companies with high forecastability are typically market leaders in robust markets, such as IBM in enterprise systems, Microsoft in PC software, and Intel in microprocessors. When a company is a market leader in a weak market, such as American Airlines or United Airlines, or when they are in a strong market but not the market leader, such as Motorola or Ericsson in the mobile phone handset market, then forecastability becomes a much greater challenge, and stock price suffers.

The forecastable future earnings investors focus on must come from the company's ongoing *current and planned operations*. That is, although investors are entitled to a percentage of any bonanza earnings the company gets—say by finding gold on its corporate site or, more likely, by investing in a strategic partner whose stock subsequently appreciates—they have no practical basis for incorporating the chance of such gains into their valuation of the stock. Thus, although Adobe made over $300 million when it sold its investment in Netscape, the windfall had no appreciable impact on its stock. Moreover, although a company can indeed create earnings outside of operations—say, via the actions of its corporate treasury, by investing in derivatives, for example—it will not please its investors by so doing because it is inherently changing the risk to which the earnings stream is exposed. Indeed, in the 1990s the CFO of Dell Computers was taken to task precisely for such actions. If investors want to take derivative risk, they would like do so on their own time; they don't want someone else to do it for them.

And that leads directly to the last phrase, *discounted for risk*. This discount is what compensates investors for the use of their capital. After all, in committing their capital to your company, investors are taking a risk that it may be consumed without a return, or that it may generate a substandard return, or that had they invested it somewhere else they could have earned a better return. You pay for that risk by promising to return them more money than they invest. The question is, how much of a premium would be fair?

Risk is the true wild card in all investment decisions. It can never be known, only probabilistically assigned. Moreover, perceived risk changes dynamically with new information about any of the myriad of variables incorporated in its view. So rather than try to calculate it,

free markets use the mechanism of many investors buying and selling to let the price seek its own level. That is why the stock market is
so jittery. It is continually rebalancing its equations to account for
streams of information that may have bearing on risk. The market
does this not through some grand mathematics but rather through
the simple expedient of free exchanges, some right, some wrong, but
all having the effect of automatically rebuilding the new equation.
We may never be able to write this equation down, but with the ticker
tape we have its output before us at all times.

To recap then, your market capitalization is equal to the present
value of your company's forecastable future earnings from current
and planned operations, discounted for risk. That's the definition, if
you will. But it is one thing to define a concept and another to really
get it. To really get shareholder value, I think you have to visualize it.

VISUALIZING SHAREHOLDER VALUE

To put all the foregoing words into a single picture, consider the
following figure:

Valuing Future Earnings

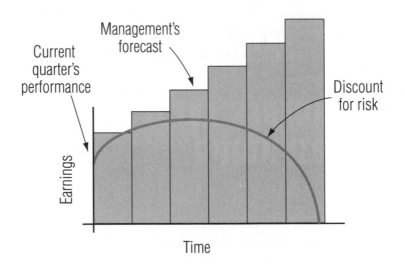

Figure 1.1

The *Y*-axis in this graph represents earnings. It is benchmarked by the operation's latest earnings report—that sets the value of *Y* on the left side of the curve. The *X*-axis represents future time. The bars represent management's forecast of future earnings over the next several years. The curve represents an investment analyst's attempt to discount management's forecast to incorporate appropriate risk.

Every quarter this graph gets redrawn based on a new benchmark and a new forecast. That is, you can think of each of the bars shifting one space to the left, the leftmost bar now being replaced by the new quarterly report, and a new bar appearing on the right representing a future quarter just coming into view. This results in the projection of a new curve, representing a revised assessment of the present value of future returns discounted for risk.

Any point on the curve is to some degree speculative, and the farther out to the right it is, the more speculative it becomes. That is, earnings forecasts near to the *Y*-axis tend to track closely to management's guidance. That is because sales pipelines, work-in-process, and backlog all help make the next few quarters more visible and predictable. As a result, this part of the curve is not subject to significant discount for risk unless management's credibility is at stake.

Farther out on the curve, however, it is a different story. Forecasts that extend beyond the sales pipeline are necessarily little more than extrapolations of investments and trends. The risk in these forecasts increases directly with time, and thus the discount for risk must also increase over time as well. Thus, even though future earnings forecasts increase indefinitely, the present value placed on them decreases. Eventually this value is set to zero—at the far right of the curve where it meets the *X*-axis—meaning that beyond this point in time no forecasts of any size will alter the valuation investors are willing to support.

Each unit of time on the *X*-axis, therefore, implies an increasingly larger discount rate applied to management's forecast. Where *X* = 0, the discount rate = 100%, because that's the quarterly report's figure and that money is in the bank. Where *Y* = 0, the discount rate = 0%, meaning no promise has value regardless of size. At every point in between, the effective discount rate is set at some intermediate value by the judgment of the investor or investment analyst.

Now let's assume for the moment that this operation we are forecasting represents the total revenue stream of the company. This would be the case for a one-product, one-division enterprise. In that case we could make the following claim: The *area under the curve* represents this company's *market capitalization*.

Market Capitalization

Figure 1.2

That is, the area under the curve is a direct visualization of the present value of forecastable future earnings from current and planned operations discounted for risk. This is the pie that investors are buying a piece of. A share of stock, therefore, is valued as a percentage of this pie.

Now let's stop for a moment.

While there are still a number of additional modifications needed to make this figure actually correspond to any real-world situation, we can make one key point using the market capitalization figure simply as it stands. The job of the executive team of any corporation from an investor's point of view is to *grow the area under this curve*. Period. So how would you do that?

CREATING SHAREHOLDER VALUE

To enlarge the area under the curve you must move the curve itself either up or to the right. Effectively this means:

1. Make the forecastable earnings line go higher, or

2. Make the forecastable earnings line extend out farther, or better still

3. Do both.

In all these cases you are in effect creating that brighter future investors seek.

Now, it is not hard to do this in a presentation. PowerPoint is particularly good at making small areas bigger. The critical issue is how to manage this change in the real world. And the way to do that, quite simply, is to *increase your competitive advantage in your target markets:*

Competitive Advantage

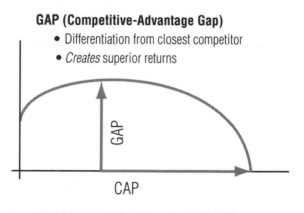

GAP (Competitive-Advantage Gap)
- Differentiation from closest competitor
- *Creates* superior returns

CAP (Competitive-Advantage Period)
- Barriers to competitor entry, customer exit
- *Sustains* superior returns

Figure 1.3

Competitive advantage has two dimensions—somewhat analogous to space and time. The dimension that corresponds to space has to do with the *competitive-advantage gap*, or just *GAP* for short. This is the distance (metaphorically) between your company's offerings and those of your closest competitors. It is a function of *differentiation*. You can increase this distance by any number of tactics—coming out with a new product, cost-reducing a current offering, building a coalition to add value to your existing offers, enhancing the service component of your current offer, or the like. When you do this, and your competitors do not, you increase the value gap between your offer and theirs.

Improving GAP shows up primarily on the vertical axis because it directly impacts both sales revenues and gross margins. That is, a larger GAP allows your company's offer to win a greater share of sales away from your competition, or it allows it to earn a higher price premium than it did before, or in many cases, both. Such increases in sales volume and gross margins, assuming they are made within your existing cost structure, go straight to the bottom line to create increased earnings, thereby pushing the curve higher on the *Y*-axis.

Competing on GAP is familiar to all management teams. Every time Ford introduces a new car, J.Crew a new line of shirts, or Compaq a new computer, they are competing on GAP. Every time your company rolls out a price promotion, adds a new feature, or cost-reduces a component assembly, it is competing on GAP. The intent in every case is to increase competitive advantage in the short term by differentiating the offer. Managers get it, investors get it, and we are all on the same page. The *Y*-axis, in sum, is not the hard one.

The same cannot be said of the *X*-axis. Here the goal is to change the length of the curve, measured in time. Here the question investors want answered is, *how long can your company sustain the competitive advantage it has just demonstrated?* We call this length of time the *competitive-advantage period*, or *CAP* for short. CAP represents the *sustainability* of GAP—the amount of time your company can hold on to your competitive advantage once the superior returns you are generating attract additional and more intense competition.

The essence of the CAP challenge is that most actions that change GAP are painfully short-lived, losing momentum the moment a competitor matches them, thereby removing the differentiation that was the source of enhanced revenues and margins. To secure a longer CAP, one must create barriers to entry against competition seeking a piece of your market, or high switching costs for customers and partners who might wish to defect to such a competitor, or both. In such cases the net result is that competition cannot readily match your changes, at least not in the near term, thereby lengthening your competitive-advantage period.

Long CAPs contribute to a higher stock price by increasing the length of the forecastable period for advantaged returns, allowing the projected earnings curve to extend farther out to the right before it finally touches down on the X-axis. In effect, they represent a reduction in long-term risk, which leads to a reduction in the discount rate applied for that risk, which in turn causes your stock price to go up.

Let's look at the impact of improving GAP and CAP in visual terms:

Increasing GAP and CAP

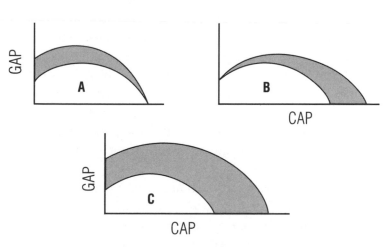

Figure 1.4

Compare the areas of increased valuation. In Figure A a modest improvement in quarterly performance has led investors to redraw the curve from a slightly higher point on the Y-axis. Having no reason to change their understanding of CAP, they simply trace a trajectory from that higher point to the same end point. By contrast, in Figure B quarterly performance has come in as expected, so the Y-axis remains the same, but a change in the competitive landscape has caused investors to reevaluate the attractiveness of essentially the same current performance in terms of now-improved longer-term prospects. Now note that the increase in area under the Figure B curve is substantially larger than that in Figure A. This represents a greater value being placed on sustainability than on short-term, short-lived improvements, due to the ability to leverage even a small percentage of the out years' much larger revenue expectations. This is the best argument there is to suggest that investment markets are not, in fact, short term in their thinking.

Of course, what the markets really want is the best of both worlds, which is Figure C. This represents a typical outcome wherever a company wins a market share leadership position in a rapidly growing market, causing it to gain both immediate returns (pragmatic customers like to jump on the winner's bandwagon almost regardless of how the product comparisons turn out) and long-term sustainability (pragmatic customers and industry partners alike prefer to stay with their existing relationships, even when they are not performing up to par, because switching costs is such a waste of time and money). The valuation of these companies, which coauthors Tom Kippola and Paul Johnson and I analyzed in *The Gorilla Game,* vastly exceeds that of their direct competitors and represents some of the highest-capitalized companies in the world, even after the technology stock bubble burst at the turn of the century.

Thus it is that *tall GAPs* and *long CAPs* become the focal point for the rest of this book. Or, to put it another way, time and management attention spent engineering *strong sustainable competitive advantages* (GAP times CAP) is the essence of what we mean by managing for shareholder value.

CATEGORY POWER VERSUS COMPANY POWER

Competitive advantage exists at two different levels in an economy. It is most visible when it is attached to specific companies. Here it is measured by comparing a set of companies in a given category with respect to their revenues, earnings, market shares, and most importantly, market caps. But competitive advantage also exists within *category*. Here the notion is that a given category of business is more attractive to investors than another category. How or why would that be?

Remember, investors are looking for prospects to brighten. That is what will allow them to sell your stock for more than they paid for it. So a category's attractiveness to investors is a function of its prospects for brightening. Considered in that light, for example, categories near the end of their life cycle are, generally, less attractive than categories near their beginnings, and categories that have high purchase velocity and high gross margins are more attractive than those that rank lower in these dimensions.

Here is a list of the most salient factors that impact category power:

- **Market size and saturation:** impacts revenue growth

- **Business cycle status:** impacts short-term performance, GAP

- **Typical gross margins:** impacts earnings potential, often implies CAP

- **Transaction velocity (frequency of purchases):** impacts return on capital

- **Capital requirements:** impacts return on capital

These factors lead investors to make investment decisions about the *categories* they want to invest in that precede their choice of which *companies* to invest in. And that in turn has huge implications for managing for shareholder value.

The key concept is simple: company power exists within category power. Or to put this another way, a company cannot be more powerful than its category. Or to put it a third way, a company's value is a function of its category's value factored by its position within that category.

Of course, most companies participate in multiple categories, and thus this effect is often blurred by the mix, but at the end of the day, the principle still holds. And this in turn leads to the first order of business in managing for shareholder value: managing the set of categories the company participates in. In particular, when companies are heavily invested in a particular category, and the power of that category is on the wane, management should contemplate a host of actions, including the following:

1. **Exit weak categories.** In the 1990s Texas Instruments exited a number of businesses including defense contracting, computers, and consumer products, to focus resources on its Digital Signal Processing chip business. It garnered a huge gain in stock price by so doing. Similarly, Nokia achieved comparable gains by exiting a number of other businesses to focus on their mobile telephony capabilities.

2. **Disaggregate.** Sometimes a corporation is active in multiple attractive categories with very different risk/reward profiles. Here investors are conflicted because they cannot get 100 percent of their capital into the profile they really want. That is, the high-risk folks want all their money to go there, the low-risk folks have the opposite agenda, and both raise their discount for the stock out of that frustration. Disaggregation, or spin-outs, is a strategy for increasing shareholder value in this situation, as Hewlett-Packard demonstrated, for example, when it spun out Agilent. Similarly General Motors spinning out Delco and Ford spinning out Visteon represent the same tactic.

3. **Consolidate.** Other times the category's power is waning but it is such a large part of the business mix that exiting is not an option. Here consolidation is the normal mode for increasing shareholder value by decreasing competition and increasing leverage on infrastructure. In high tech, Computer Associates has historically been a consolidator in categories of waning power.

4. **Focus on vertical markets.** While the generic value of a given category of offer may be waning, adaptations to particular vertical markets and their market-specific challenges often create opportunities to renew earnings and growth potential. In the 1980s and early 1990s virtually all what were then the Big Eight consultancies reorganized into vertical practices as a way of shoring up returns from what was becoming an increasingly commoditized set of tax and audit services. In high tech, companies like PeopleSoft and Lawson Software have taken horizontal financial and HR systems into specific verticals and gained power through compelling niche adaptations.

5. **Integrate horizontally.** In technical markets customers often struggle finding the in-house expertise to manage all the best-of-breed software and hardware purchases they have made. This slows down category growth and can lead to category devaluation. One response is to integrate a whole raft of these products into a mega-category delivered by a single vendor. Companies like Veritas and SAP have taken this approach in systems management software and enterprise resource planning software, respectively. As of this writing there is a similar phenomenon occurring around Internet application platforms with such companies as IBM, BEA, and Oracle all integrating a host of "software plumbing" functions into a single fabric.

6. **Integrate vertically.** When categories mature such that new customer acquisition is no longer as powerful a growth engine as existing customer development, it is often a winning strategy to vertically integrate. This increases both account control and share of the customer's wallet. In the 1990s and the current decade both IBM and Oracle have taken this approach to growing their presence further in enterprise systems, as did Apple in consumer products.

7. **Migrate within the value chain.** As categories mature and evolve, the locus of competitive advantage, and thus of advantaged earnings, often shifts, and companies that follow this shift can increase their shareholder value. Thus Kodak went

from being a camera company to a film company, Gillette from a focus on razors to razor blades, and Hewlett-Packard from instruments to computers to printers to ink!

8. **Transcend and transform the category.** More radically, companies under the pressure of waning category power can attack the problem through transforming themselves completely. Monsanto exited its traditional chemicals business to focus on bioengineered products. By merging with Time Warner, AOL completely changed its category dynamics and investment thesis. Microsoft, via its dot.NET initiative, promises an equally far-reaching self-reinvention, in this case from a purveyor of products to one of services.

9. **Disrupt and overthrow the category.** When all else fails, start the revolution! This is the approach taken by companies like Qualcomm in wireless telephony and Rambus in computer memory chips. It was also the thrust behind HMOs and the like reengineering the health-care industry, and Enron's much-chronicled attempt to transform its energy business into a series of financial hedging services.

To conclude, managing for shareholder value begins with managing one's relationship to category valuation. That said, however, categories take years to develop and cannot be changed easily or often. Most day-to-day management, therefore, focuses at the level of company power. That is where the bulk of this book will focus as well, and it is the topic to which we shall now return.

LOSING COMPANY POWER

While there are no laws of gravity in financial space, nonetheless it often happens that what goes up does come down. In a moment we are going to launch into a prolonged discussion of how management can raise stock price by increasing company power through focusing on GAP and CAP. Before doing so, however, it behooves us to understand what can cause valuation to go the other way. The simplest instance of this is when stock price falls after the release of a quarterly earnings report.

Recall that quarterly earnings represent a kind of variance report on last quarter's projected earnings, a rolling forward of the calendar one quarter that tests whether the company's actual performance lived up to its prior promises. Effectively this roll-forward resets the starting position of GAP at the *Y*-axis, placing it either higher, lower, or equal to the expectations implied by the prereport curve.

Impact of the Q2 Quarterly Report

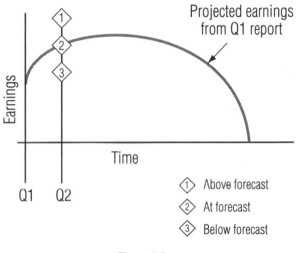

Figure 1.5

Depending on that outcome, investors then decide whether the company's value has increased, decreased, or remained the same, and the company's stock price moves accordingly.

The significance for the investor of reported quarterly earnings—indeed their only meaningful impact on stock price—is whether they confirm the market's existing valuation of the company. Did management execute its stated strategy and did it work? If the numbers confirm it did, the company's stock price will continue to move in lockstep with its category, keeping pace with its comparables as the market weighs the relative value of that category against other investable categories. If they do not confirm expectations, however, the market uses the quarterly report to adjust the value of the company's shares, often dramatically.

In making these corrections, the market performs a curiously asymmetrical operation, particularly in categories that are early in their life cycle. If earnings exceed estimates by a few cents per share, the stock price might not rise at all (it could even fall a bit). By contrast, if earnings miss those same estimates by a few cents, the company's stock could easily lose half its value in a single day. This seems neither rational nor fair, but in fact it is both. Here's why.

When actual performance exceeds estimates, these are typically the ones that appear in print. They are known to be conservative, if for no other reason than that it is in the interests of both management and investment analysts to keep them that way. This gives rise to a second estimate, sometimes called the whisper number, which savvy investors use as the real standard against which to calibrate the upcoming report. In an efficient market, valuation moves to accommodate this later projection and adjusts to the actual report from that vantage, hence the possibility of management beating its numbers and having its stock price go down. It may be that the whole category is off, but it may also be that the company missed its whisper number.

In either case, however, when earnings exceed published estimates by a few cents, the adjustments are modest. This is not the case, by contrast, when companies miss on the downside.

CORRECTIONS TO THE DOWNSIDE ARE SEVERE

Investors know how hard management teams work to set expectations that they will not miss. So, when that does happen, it means the team has exhausted all its reserves, activated all its safety valves, and has still come up short. This does not bode well for the future at all.

When companies miss their numbers, it usually reflects problems that are several quarters old and are likely to take several quarters or longer to correct. That is, although the team has made its numbers in all the preceding quarters, we can now surmise that they applied increasingly heroic efforts to do so. When the team eventually fails to pull out the quarter, investors infer, usually quite rightly, that a long-term erosion has occurred in the company's competitive-advantage position. Worse, this situation can be expected to worsen over the following quarters. Here's why.

Short-term problems are always attributable to GAP. The company's offers, for whatever reason, are no longer as compelling as they once were. Sales or gross margins or both are down. If the company could magically restore its GAP overnight, then all would be well. Sometimes this actually happens. For example, when a company is transitioning its product line from an old platform to a new one, they almost always have at least one bad quarter as customers stop buying the old in anticipation of getting the new. In that case, as soon as the new product line comes out, the backlog is released and a great quarter makes up for the previous poor one.

But in other cases the problems are not as fixable. New entrants may have confused the market. Some company may be trying to buy market share at ruinously low prices. Some other company may be able to give away the product to garner a lucrative service contract, or perhaps the company's offerings may be getting a bit long in the tooth and a competitor has come up with much better ones. In each of these cases, the company's GAP will be impacted for some time to come, perhaps even permanently. A reduced GAP projected forward in time creates a lower market cap.

But that's not the end of it. Consider what a deteriorating GAP does to CAP. As a company's overall power in its marketplace weakens, the other members of its value chain begin to reexamine their allegiances, pulling back some of their commitments to the company and reallocating them to other vendors. Observing this, competitors sense an opportunity and move in, often offering sweetheart deals to gain market share. Their gains in share undermine the company's previously secure position, leading investors to reduce their estimates of the company's CAP. Now a reduced GAP is being projected forward over a shortened CAP, further reducing market cap.

Worse still, that action, in turn, further reduces GAP! As stock prices go down, partners retreat further, and competitors increase their attacks. None of this is lost on customers. They experience an increase in their negotiating power and begin to press the company for better prices. This diminishes the company's ability to achieve differentiated earnings, thereby shrinking its GAP. And so it goes, decreases in GAP creating decreases in CAP, and vice versa, in a truly vicious circle.

When a company misses its forecast by a few cents, the market assumes that it may have lost its edge, and the market recalculates not only the height of its projected future earnings curve but its duration as well.

Impact of Missing Expectations

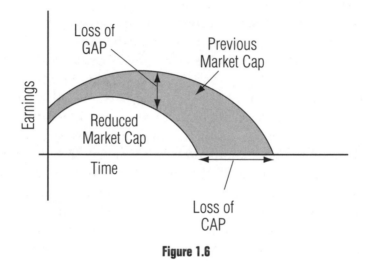

Figure 1.6

When GAP and CAP are corrected simultaneously, the area under the earnings curve is drastically reduced, as the diagram illustrates. This is the visualization that correlates to a 50 percent decrease in market cap, the sort of thing that happens in high tech routinely when quarterly numbers are missed.

Why is this effect largely confined to high tech? Actually, severe market-cap collapses—effectively, fault-line behavior—are an artifact of any market in which securities are being valued primarily for their long-term future growth opportunities rather than their near-term earnings. When the bulk of the value of an investment is based on the company's expected ability to dominate *the future acquisition of new customers,* the market is extremely sensitive to any changes in that company's current competitive-advantage position. This is where the volatility of the fault line comes from. It is just part of the lay of the land.

VOLATILITY CREATES CONFUSION

Because its effects are so violent, volatility in technology-enabled markets galvanizes investors to demand that management take immediate and drastic action. The simplest and most obvious response is to cut costs, often in wholesale fashion. Cutting costs is not necessarily a bad reaction. All companies build up unproductive processes over time, and every company's roster has a bottom 10 percent that is not contributing competitively. It is the *wholesale nature* of this response, however, that can so deeply damage shareholder value, often irrecoverably.

There are a number of problems with the wholesale response. The first is that it often cuts indiscriminately from fat and muscle. "Ten percent across the board" is the battle cry, implying that all operations make an equal contribution to shareholder value. This is simply never true. Thus the only justification for across-the-board cuts is when the time it would take to determine the right places and then to negotiate the right commitments exceeds the window in which action is demanded.

But that leads to a second problem, which is the impact of drastic surgery, both short and long term. In the short term, it creates huge amounts of anxiety until it is announced, then ongoing depression afterward—not, interestingly, among those laid off, but rather among those not. Their world becomes an amalgam of guilt for still having a job, fear of losing that job in the next layoff, and suppressed anger at having to work harder and harder to maintain what is showing itself to be a less and less viable operation. And in the long term, the effect is to destabilize key projects and customer relationships and to worry investors and partners, darkening all stakeholders' visions of the company's future prospects.

All of which leads to a third and final problem statement: why aren't these cuts being made systematically all along? Why do corporations have to get deep into the penalty box before they take action? To be sure, in boom times it is often more important to focus on the top line than the bottom, and when bubbles burst, even the best companies can get caught flat-footed. But that only accounts for the most egregious challenges. There is a deeper malaise being masked here, which I believe can be best stated as follows:

> **When it comes to systematic pruning and recycling of their most valuable resources—specifically, human capital and financial capital—most corporations lack any operating model whatsoever.**

This is a chilling statement for anyone to hear, but particularly so for investors, as it implies that over time their capital will, in aggregate, be put to less and less productive use. It is, of course, equally chilling to management because it suggests we are all flying blind, setting ourselves up for some future encounter with a guillotine. Employees upon first hearing this, on the other hand, might feel that in the absence of systematic pruning their jobs are more safe; but it takes only a moment's reflection to realize that the opposite is the case, that without renewal and refocus their jobs are inevitably going to deteriorate into increasingly less valuable services and eventually to extinction.

Why then is all this the case? In my view, it is because we lack an effective mental model that predicts how and when the value-creating properties of a given business process erode over time. Armed with such a model, executives should be able to exercise the needed attention during annual business planning cycles, thereby reducing the need for more drastic interventions during down times, and hopefully allowing them to skate past all but the worst declines relatively unscathed.

Not surprisingly, I have a candidate model in mind, called *core versus context*, which is the subject of the next chapter.

2

CORE VERSUS CONTEXT

When investors look at management's use of their capital, they have but one wish: please employ it in activities that have at least a chance of increasing stock price. From the investors' view those are the activities that are *core* to the company's operations. Everything else is *context*.

This is actually a somewhat radical view. Customers, for example, do not agree with it. They see *core* as anything that will impact their customer satisfaction. For them context might well be whatever the company has to do to make itself profitable. Management too often sees core differently, frequently in terms of *core competence,* what the company is distinctively good at, and employees often see it in terms of *what we have always done,* or *what we are best known for.*

All these definitions are legitimate in their own frame of reference, but none of them are appropriate if our goal is to manage for shareholder value. For that we must learn to adopt the investor's view.

CORE VERSUS CONTEXT: THE INVESTOR'S VIEW

As we saw in the first chapter, the factor under management control that has the biggest impact on stock price is competitive advantage. From an investor's point of view, it then follows, a business process is core when its outcome directly affects the competitive advantage of the company in its targeted markets. Here is the ground upon which companies must differentiate to win power, and the goal of core work is to create and sustain that differentiation. This observation results in a simple litmus test: *any behavior that can raise your stock price is core—everything else is context.*

For core activities, the goal is to *differentiate as much as possible* on any variable that impacts customers' purchase decisions and to assign one's best resources to that challenge. By contrast, every other activity in the corporation—and in an established company this is typically the overwhelming bulk of all activities—is not core. It is context. And the winning approach to *context* tasks is not to differentiate but rather to execute them effectively and efficiently in as standardized a manner as possible.

Differentiating on context is the single biggest waste of resources in *Fortune* 500 operations. In the case of tasks that used to differentiate, it is the result of our failing to intervene now that they no longer do. But in many other cases, we differentiate on tasks that could never increase shareholder value. This is the natural result of people wanting to make the best contribution they can and to get recognition for it. The problem is, such acts of differentiation soak up time, talent, and management attention with no opportunity to impact stock price. If the goal is to manage for shareholder value, then such an expenditure of scarce resources is simply wrong, and management needs to put an end to it.

In so doing, of course, we need to be careful not to throw out the baby with the bathwater. In any given category of business, one company's core may well be another company's context. Retail display is core to a boutique but context to a warehouse discounter, whereas price is core to the discounter but context to the boutique.

In the car business, the new Volkswagen Beetle is all about design. Everything else in the car is context. The same holds for the Apple Macintosh in the computer industry. In both cases the differentiating value is in the design (the bits) and not in the manufacturing (the atoms). For both, therefore, manufacturing is context, not core. The difference is, Apple is able to outsource its manufacturing whereas Volkswagen is not. That bodes well for Apple shareholders, but poorly for Volkswagen's.

Now let's be clear here. If some contract manufacturer introduces a widespread defect into Apple's computers, that can lower the company's stock price. That is, failure to execute context tasks properly can undermine a company's competitive advantage. Nonetheless, because such tasks cannot raise Apple's stock price, they are not core. Instead one might think of them as *hygiene*.

Hygiene refers to all the things that the marketplace expects you to do well but gives you no credit for doing *exceptionally well*. Do you bathe consistently? Good. If you didn't, someone might have to speak to you. But even if you bathe constantly, no one is going to give you a promotion. The same goes for companies that ship what the customer asked for, send them a bill that actually corresponds to what they ordered and received, and answer the phone when a customer calls for support. If they fail to do these things, they will be in trouble, but once they achieve a certain level of consistency in them, they get no premium for doing them better than that. In short, context tasks add value but do not contribute to competitive advantage.

Core and context, it is important to recognize, interoperate to create quality. Both are fundamental to any organization's effectiveness. The interaction between core and context determines how much core value gets through to the marketplace. Without careful management to the contrary, however, *context inevitably gets in the way of core*. It is simply a matter of absorbing time, talent, and management attention.

To test the degree to which your organization has the problem, ask yourself how much of your week is spent in context meetings. How much of your time, in other words, is spent on *hygiene?* Now apply that ratio to the company as a whole. In a start-up the ratio is typically 80/20. Eighty percent of the resources are being deployed against core tasks, things that truly differentiate the company's offerings. In the typical *Fortune* 500 company, on the other hand, it is closer to the opposite, 20/80. That means the latter has to allocate four times the number of resources to an initiative just to gain the same throughput.

But the actual situation is much worse than that. We focused on the 20 percent that was actively trying to do the core work. What about the other 80 percent? Well, they are hard at work on context tasks. What are they doing? Trying to add value, of course.

How do they do that? By differentiating their work, making it stand out, making it special. What does that take? Time, talent, and management attention, of course. Whose? Now here is the nasty part. It doesn't just take their own time, talent, and attention—it takes *everyone else's* as well! Wherever differentiation occurs, that is, it requires widespread interaction to make sure the desired novel effect is achieved.

Now we can see why failing to manage context can be so debilitating. This is where all those meetings that you don't really want to attend come from. Of course, there is a theoretical alternative. One could hire people and give them a mandate *not to differentiate*. But that is a hideous charter to give any human being, and even people who overtly agree to it—I am thinking of assembly-line workers in particular—will subvert it over time, consciously or unconsciously. And so whether we intend to or not, as we add context function after context function to our payroll, we spin a cocoon that eventually enwraps and immobilizes us all.

Now we might justify this course by saying we are creating jobs, and we are. But let's look a little more closely at the people in these jobs. They're not stupid. They know in the back of their minds that these jobs are not core and could thus be eliminated. So what kind of behavior does that perception generate? Conservative behavior, of course. Don't rock the boat, you might tip the boat over. Resistance to change inside established companies, in short, is primarily a function of too many resources deployed in *context* as opposed to *core* activities.

It is what one might call the Dilbert problem. Dilbert cartoons parody an organization that has become 100 percent context—it has no core. It is the contemporary version of theater of the absurd, an ongoing production of *Waiting for Godot* performed in cubicles. In such a world, individuals know their jobs are meaningless but struggle valiantly to retain them anyway for fear they can find nothing else. And so when some new disruptive technology comes to town, when aggressive change is clearly the order of the day, it runs headlong right into a *business-as-usual coalition*, not in any one department specifically, but in every department generally. Nothing can get done quickly, and in many cases, nothing can get done at all.

CLIMBING UP THE DOWN ESCALATOR

Where, we begin to wonder, is all this context coming from? Here is the ultimate irony. In technology-enabled markets, where technology itself is the basis of differentiation, core *becomes* context over time! That is, by virtue of competition, whatever differentiated last year's offerings is likely to become hygiene by next year. This is simply the inexorable progress of the technology-adoption life cycle.

Management teams in such markets find themselves perpetually trying to climb up a down escalator, as recent developments in e-commerce will illustrate:

E-Commerce Escalator

Figure 2.1

In 1995 Netscape shipped Navigator 1.0. In 1995, having a corporate Web site to present information about your company was differentiating. It meant you had access to prospects that your competitors simply did not see. Today, by contrast, my limousine service has a Web site (if you're traveling in the Bay Area, be sure to check it out, www.phl-limousine.com).

By 1997, as companies were getting on the Web site bandwagon, the rage was the intranet, not the Internet, but even then marketing was working to get its offers presented to prospects over the Web. If you could do that in 1997, you were differentiated. Today every company's site on the planet bombards you with this stuff.

In the same period, technology-based companies were driving their customer support operations to the Web, thinking to lower costs, not realizing they were also increasing customer satisfaction. (As ATM banking has taught us, often the best service is self-service.) Cisco was a leader in this effort. At the century's close every significant company in high tech did it.

And so it goes. Each of the lower steps on this escalator *was* core and then *became* context. And it does not take too much imagination to see even the highest step in view—should this structure indeed be embraced—will soon thereafter be next. It is the nature of competition. What else can our competitors do if they do not want to simply yield the field? Thus all the work we put into differentiation—because that is our core—will someday come to haunt us because it has become context. It just doesn't seem fair, but this is Darwin at work, improving the species by perpetually raising the bar.

This forced migration to higher orders of behavior has two dimensions we must address before we are done with this book:

1. Once they cease to differentiate, most custom processes are too complex to maintain given their eroding contribution to shareholder value. That is, as context, they require too much ongoing application of time, talent, and management attention. We need to find some way to dispose of them.

2. Executives who excelled at managing core processes in their day won promotions and are now running the company. Their greatest expertise, however, may now lie in what have become context functions. When met with an emerging competitive challenge, their instincts and experience may therefore lead them to push the wrong agenda, with the corollary that if the company fails to make progress, they are likely to push all the harder.

The second of these issues lies at the heart of a widespread critique of command-and-control management that has characterized the past ten to twenty years. Hierarchical organizations centralize decision-making in senior executives at the top, the very people most at risk of mistaking context for core. By contrast, people competing face-to-face in the marketplace daily have all such illusions stripped from them. It is critical that the seasoned judgment of the former be infused with the recent experience of the latter if good decisions are to be made. Going forward, therefore, companies must explore alternative management cultures and styles, a subject we will address at some length in the last section of this book, "Building to Last."

In the meantime, however, we need to attack the problem right in front of us: how are we going to get out of going to all these meetings?

OUTSOURCE THE CONTEXT, INSOURCE THE CORE

Fortunately, there is a bright side to all this core/context discussion: *there is no context that cannot become someone else's core.*

You make the hamburger? Great, I'll make the bun. Oh, the bun is core, too? Great, how about the condiments? How about the coffee? How about keeping the bathrooms clean? How about the uniforms, the hiring, the payroll, the benefits administration, the promotions, the marketing, the advertising, the facilities construction, the real estate planning, the financing? You decide what you think is core, and then let's talk about everything else.

This is the world of outsourcing. Today, with more and more of our business data accessible on-line, we have an exceptional communications infrastructure to support the coordination of such efforts. Moreover, phalanxes of new service providers are lining up outside our doors anxious to do this kind of business. The question to ask is, why should these people do any better at our context work than we would ourselves?

The simple answer is, this is where they are putting their A team. It's context to you, but it is core to them. Take your copy room. What is the career path for someone working in it? What kind of a player are you going to recruit? But outsource that same copy room to Ikon or someone like them, and now the person running the operation can aspire to become president. Why? Because that's what Ikon does for a living. Who's going to attract the better person to do the job—you or Ikon? Who is going to come up with more efficient procedures, additional value-adding service offerings, higher-quality processes?

Well, maybe they are, you grudgingly reply, but I bet it will cost a bundle. Will it? Will *the marginal cost* of that company adding another customer truly exceed *the total cost* your company must bear if you do it in-house? The service economy bets the opposite way. It says we cannot only do it better than you, we can do it cheaper than you. Why? Again, it's our core, it's what we do for a living—give us some credit. If we think about this all day every day, and you try to think about it never at all, don't you think we might be able to outperform you? Moreover, it is a competitive economy. If you don't like our price performance, take the other guy's bid.

But if this is such a good idea, you still ask, why has it been so long in coming? And why isn't everybody doing it? These are both great questions, and each deserves a section of this chapter to answer it. In regards to the first, the short answer is, until recently, it really was cheaper to do most processes in-house. Here's how to look at it.

COASE'S THEORY OF TRANSACTION COSTS

The economist who best sheds light on this issue is R. H. Coase, who in the 1930s wrote an article entitled "The Nature of the Firm." Coase asked himself a few simple questions that are as compelling now as they were then: What exactly is a firm? Why does it grow to a given size and then level out? Why doesn't it grow larger? Why doesn't it level out sooner?

He framed his answers around the notion of *transaction costs*. Coase proposed that conducting transactions inside a company, where one can eliminate paying off the middleman, avoid sales taxes, and secure privileged access to scarce commodities, was inherently more efficient than doing so outside the company, and so over time, such transactions would migrate inside. At some point in this growth, however, he noted that the infrastructure needed to keep the internal value chains communicating efficiently and responsively would become bureaucratized to the point that it would become less responsive than the external market. At this size, increases in the company's competitive advantage from additional scale would be diluted, and other companies would be able to win and hold market share against it, causing the firm to cease to expand further. Thus a point of equilibrium would be reached that "explains" a company's given size.

This theory maps well to the history of the blue-chip companies that have made up the *Fortune* 500 for most of the past century. However, with the rise in business usage of the Internet, particularly in the U.S. economy, intercompany communications and commerce systems have become increasingly efficient, such that Coase's theory of transaction costs *has now begun to operate in reverse!* That is, the free market has become the low-cost provider of more and more transactions, and thus they are now migrating from *inside* to *outside* the corporation, with outsourcing, not insourcing, being the new low-cost play.

The reasons are the ones we have already reviewed:

- Any task your company is doing in-house to save money is one for which you must bear the *total cost*. But if another company is doing that same activity for other customers, then to do it for your business as well, that company need only bear the *marginal cost* of the effort. Marginal costs will always be lower than total costs.

- Add to this the idea that the bulk of all tasks needed to complete a whole product are not core to your company's competitive advantage. They are hygiene factors, not differentiators, in your offer: if they are missing, your offer is unacceptable, but you do not gain any competitive advantage from doing them well. Now ask yourself, if some other company does this task for a living, so that they do gain competitive advantage for doing it well, and you do it because you have to, which organization is going to have the more efficient methods and the more progressive approach?

- Finally, realize that anyone you employ on these tasks in your company is in a dead-end job—this isn't your added value, it is just a necessary evil for you. That same person employed in a company dedicated to this type of work can be on a career path to be president. So who is going to get the best employees with the best motivation?

All the bulleted arguments above are compelling in their own right, but there is one final argument lurking in the background behind them all: *Context work provides a lousy return on invested capital.* If you commit twenty or fifty or two hundred people to work that is context, and your only reward is a few pennies' difference in cost between your in-house effort and an outsourced one, look how much financial capital, human capital, and opportunity cost you have tied up for such a paltry gain.

What investor would applaud that? The answer is none. If that is all you promise, you will not be able to raise capital in the first place. Or conversely, if you have raised capital, you have promised much more than this. But if that is the case, and you subsequently divert great chunks of that capital to low-return activities such as this, how much more work must be done elsewhere to create a balancing hyperreturn on the remaining capital? It is just a losing game, and management teams that let context get the best of them are big losers.

The conclusion from all of the above is simple in theory: outsourcing strategies rule! But let's not go off the deep end here. Outsourcing can only deliver its value in economies and societies where intercompany commerce and communication is on par with or superior to intracompany processes for the same tasks. This is a relatively new state of affairs in the U.S. economy, and for much of the rest of the world it is not yet true, although one can see the changes coming.

Specifically, success with outsourced value chains requires companies to significantly reengineer both culture and systems. On the culture side, they must come to terms with being both a supplier to and a customer of their direct competitors. Business values, in other words, must migrate from win/lose to win/win ideas. Thus IBM is now supplying disc drives to its archrival EMC and personal computers to its archrival Dell Computers—but only after fifteen years of struggling with its corporate values and culture to get there. And on the systems side, without significant investment in supply chain applications and without the Internet, one could not coordinate a virtual value chain to make the just-in-time responses needed to win new markets and customers. That is why it is only just now, and only largely in the United States, that this new ecosystem is performing optimally, and even here it is operational only in a few sectors of our economy.

But wherever these requisite conditions can be met, low-cost transactions must inevitably migrate outside the corporation. And that in turn explains why it is that small businesses, and not the traditional *Fortune* 500 companies, continue to generate the bulk of the new jobs in our economy. The giant corporations that built themselves up to a given size via the traditional approach to managing transaction costs will be downsizing for a long time to come. Indeed many of them can be expected to downsize to death. They simply will not be able to make the cultural and systems adjustments needed and will instead watch helplessly as their stock price decomposes to the point where investment bankers parcel them out for absorption into more adaptive enterprises.

SPIN OUT CONTEXT, NOT CORE!

But suppose, nonetheless, that for some class of context work the company cannot find a qualified outsourcer. Suppose, for example, that you want a specialized kind of condiments, or a particular approach to recruiting, hiring, or training—something you have been doing in-house for some time, in a differentiated way. Now, despite its attractive features, you realize it is not core, but as it is also not standard, no service provider wants to touch it. Yet for you to change to a more standard approach would be disruptive and expensive. Nonetheless, unless you can come up with a better alternative, that is what you will have to do. What else could one do?

There is another possibility. You could try calling together the internal organization that is responsible for this body of work and making them an offer they can't refuse. That offer would be to create their own service company, independent of your company, with your company as their first customer and with a guarantee of some period of business and a promise to be an active customer reference. The alternative to this offer is that the company will go with a standard outsourcer, eliminating the in-house function anyway, but with nowhere near as happy an outcome for either the group or the company.

If the group goes forward with your offer, now when it differentiates, it will be doing the right thing, because it will be improving *its* competitive advantage, and thus such changes will deserve *its* time, talent, and management attention. To be sure, these same resources will now also start serving your competitors. That's why it is important that you be sure this is context, not core, that you are outsourcing. But if it is context, then just as you don't mind your competitors using your plumbing contractor, you should not mind them using this team either. Of course, it is always possible your competitor will stick with its own internal team, which means they will not use the new service and will instead continue fighting you with less than their own full complement of time, talent, and management attention. That's when you gain outsourcer's advantage.

The best companies in high tech know this and are already aggressively pursuing a context outsourcing strategy. HP, long reputed as one of the best manufacturers in the sector, is now driving as much of its manufacturing to outsourcers as it can. At the same time they are aggressively pursuing Web-based business opportunities where their relationships, skills, and heritage can create competitive advantage. The value in their brand, they have rightly concluded, lies in the bits, not in the atoms, and that is where they are assigning their best resources. The same holds true for Cisco, which brags that well over 50 percent of its products ship *without ever being touched by a Cisco employee!* The company creates value across the Internet by shipping design and test information to its supply chain partners and by turning its customer service site into a digital marketplace.

But hang on. Cisco is no longer the darling it once was touted to be. And for all the early adopters of outsourcing, many, perhaps most, companies are still leery of it. If this is such a good idea, why aren't more people doing it?

MISSION-CRITICAL VERSUS SUPPORTING PROCESSES

The key to understanding the pragmatic resistance to outsourcing is to understand core and context in relation to a second distinction, *mission critical* versus *supporting.* The following diagram will help make this clear:

Understanding Outsourcing

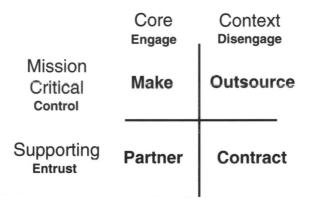

Figure 2.2

In this two-by-two matrix, the columns represent core and context. With core the management imperative is to *engage* resources; with context it is to *disengage.* That much we have already covered. It is the rows that now demand our attention. They separate business activities into those which are mission critical, over which we must maintain *control,* and those which are supporting and which we can therefore afford to *entrust.*

Looked at in this way two of the four categories of business processes are relatively straightforward to manage. If it is core and mission critical, this is something a company will want to do in-house: we call this the *Make* quadrant. Conversely, if it is context and supporting, this is a process companies will definitely want to give over to another company: we call this the *Contract* quadrant. Neither of these two quadrants poses a strategic challenge. The same cannot be said for the other two, however.

Begin with the lower left quadrant, the one we call *Partner*. This represents a business process that is core to the company—it genuinely differentiates its offerings in ways that create competitive advantage—which nonetheless has been entrusted to a partner. How can that be? Why would any company allow itself to be dependent on some other company for something that affects its own stock price?

One answer is because it simply cannot field the requisite capability in-house, at least not to the quality level that is needed to be differentiated. Think about a branding or an advertising campaign: why do the leading consumer packaged goods companies work with outside agencies on something that is so central to their differentiation? Because that is where the bulk of the best creative talent lies. For the same reason, Apple goes to Frog Design or IDEO to get new industrial designs for its iMac products. For the same reason major corporations go to consultancies for help with their strategy. The talented people capable of producing the best work do not want to work for just one client. They are more driven by their loyalty to a craft than to a company, and in truth their clientele is better off for it.

Another locus of widespread partnering is technology-enabled markets that have disaggregated into value chains, with various parts of the total value proposition being provided by various different companies. For value to be transmitted end to end such that the ultimate customer gets the promised rewards, everyone in the chain must partner effectively. Thus hardware manufacturers partner with networking-equipment companies and storage companies to create platforms for systems-software companies, who in turn provide a platform for application software, which is often installed with the help of systems integrators. If the end customer is to get a solution superior to that from a single, vertically integrated vendor, then each of these classes of companies must collaborate with the others to ensure that outcome. In Silicon Valley we often call such a set of companies a "stack," the analogy being to a stack of systems-software services, and bringing everyone together is sometimes called "orchestrating the stack."

Orchestrating independent partners is a tough task, tough enough to make one wonder if maybe we should all go back to vertical integration. The trade-offs between virtual and vertical will be explored in the next chapter. For now it is enough to say that at least certain separations—application software from enabling hardware, for example— have been widely adopted for various reasons and thus partnering is in part built into the structure of modern technology-enabled markets.

MISSION-CRITICAL CONTEXT

The other problematic quadrant in this model is in the upper right, where a process is context, meaning the investor is looking to the company to disengage resources, but is also mission critical, which means the company must maintain control. The combination at first glance seems impossible: how can one disengage and still maintain control? You can't, common sense argues, and thus it is that *mission-critical context* becomes the primary source of context buildup and its consequence of holding scarce resources hostage to nondifferentiating processes.

It is precisely at this juncture that we must learn to redefine *outsourcing*. Traditionally, the word has been indistinguishable from *contracting*. That means, in effect, there has been no conscious distinction between the upper-right and lower-right quadrants. Is it any wonder, then, that outcomes in the upper right have been so unhappy? To go forward we must redefine *outsourcing* as *a business relationship in which the customer disengages from a process but still maintains active control over its outcomes*.

The fundamental mechanism that enables such outsourcing is *control system technology*. At one level this consists of monitoring systems that keep both the outsourcer and the customer apprised of fluctuations in the process. This enables quick response to unanticipated conditions. At another level it consists of dynamically modifiable service-level agreements—dashboards, if you will—that let customers dial up or dial down a level of service in response to changing business conditions. And at still another level it consists of real-time reporting and analysis systems that give customers visibility into the consequences of the actions they have chartered the outsourcer to perform—to get early indication of an inventory buildup in outsourced manufacturing, for example, or a customer dissatisfaction issue emerging in an outsourced customer contact center.

In its first wave of adoption outsourcing did not focus on this technology. Instead it focused on systems to generate the quality, reliability, and scalability that outsourcing economics demand. As it turned out, these attributes are necessary but not sufficient to enable the outsourcing of mission-critical processes. Thus to date the majority of success in contract services has come from the lower-right quadrant, and the bulk of the horror stories from the upper-right.

To date the early winners with outsourcing are the ones who brought their own control systems with them. In the age of EDI, this meant companies like General Motors and Wal-Mart who had sufficient market clout with their suppliers that they could more or less dictate the terms of engagement. In today's world, it has meant Dell and Cisco, who relied more on technology to create the control and visibility.

Cisco is a particularly interesting case. At the outset, it did not intend to outsource manufacturing. Instead, its strategy was to differentiate on the ability to build to order. In pursuing this strategy, however, the company suffered quality-control problems because the complexity of the orders was causing the wrong configurations to get shipped. To put an end to this, Cisco implemented a control system that tested every shippable product for compliance with the customer order, only releasing the shipping documentation if full compliance was achieved. Needless to say, when first implemented, this system created huge bottlenecks, but over time the company worked out the kinks, and the market response was extremely positive. That in turn led to a massive uptick in orders, and it was then, and only then, that the need to outsource became paramount.

As the company prepared to bring contract manufacturers on-line, its first thought was to somehow transfer its own manufacturing systems to the outsourcer to ensure success. But then someone realized it was the quality-control system that was the key. As long as Cisco could enforce compliance at the outsourcer the way it did in-house, it did not matter what systems were used to create the product, only those that determined whether it would ship. So Cisco worked with the outsourcing manufacturers to install its control system in their plants, downloading its customer orders for matching, and keeping to itself the data and key learning so that they could not be shared with competitors also working with the outsourcer.

The end result exactly complies with our definition of outsourcing: Cisco disengaged from a set of manufacturing processes, but it maintained control over their outcomes. To be sure, when the Internet bubble popped, Cisco was caught with $2.2 billion in written-off inventory, but that was due to Cisco's management choices, not to a failure in the outsourcing relationship or the control systems. Indeed to this day Cisco management will argue that, given the extraordinary conditions it was operating under, that write-off was actually a good outcome: under prior models, they believe, it would have been double or more.

REENGINEERING REDUX?

There is still at least one more objection to consider before passing on from our discussion of outsourcing. And that is, didn't we try this once before? Isn't this just another name for reengineering? And has anyone forgotten already what a colossal flop that was? What makes this any different?

To begin with, there is a key distinction to make: outsourcing is about *disengaging the company from context;* reengineering is about *taking a new approach to core.* The former is much less ambitious than the latter (and thus potentially much more likely to come about). Here's why.

Companies do not set out to overcommit resources to context tasks. It happens for the most part during hypergrowth markets, periods of accelerated market development during which demand far exceeds supply, the company and its competitors are all growing like weeds, and the prime directive is *Just ship!* During this period, the company takes in more revenue that it can spend, so resources are plentiful. Moreover, it is under huge time pressure to capture market share. As a result, whenever any glitch shows up, or could show up, management's knee-jerk response is simply to throw additional resources at the problem. That's when we hire in all these troops that we are now trying to spin out.

Then the market transitions from hypergrowth to a more sedate Main Street phase, supply once again returns to its normal state of exceeding demand, competition increases, prices decline, margins decline, and cost-cutting sets in. This is the period when we look to downsizing to reset the balance of resources in the company. It is a perfect time to invoke the core-versus-context exercise. Moreover, at this time the context resources are not so thoroughly entrenched as to be hard to dislodge. It ought to be a relatively straightforward project.

So why are we not more successful in so doing? The truth is, outsourcing, like reengineering, goes against the grain of organizational politics. At the end of the tornado the organization is in a self-congratulatory mood. It wants to hand out rewards all around, and one set of rewards is, in effect, empires. The more people in your empire, the higher your reward. Reducing head count reduces the "reward account." Moreover, the need to reduce head count is not quite yet upon us—we can still get away with several years of coasting—so why fight the tough battles now?

Unfortunately, by the time we do decide to fight them, they have gotten a lot tougher. Now the organizations are entrenched. That is, people in positions of power now owe lots of favors to lots of people, in both core and context functions, and they find it difficult to betray those relationships. As a result, when the need to cut comes, rather than call out context versus core, the company opts for across-the-board cuts instead. This form of cost-cutting is deeply damaging, for it trades a permanent loss in core resources, plus zero progress in disengaging itself from the context resources that are holding it back, all for just a temporary improvement in the bottom line. Which means it is going to do this again. And again. And again. Until it gets permanently dismantled, to be acquired at a fraction of its once-proud valuation.

The path out of this maze does *not* require reengineering core tasks. It does require a thoughtful review of what is core versus what is context, what directly contributes to the company's competitive advantage in the marketplace versus all other work. This effort must not be allowed to degenerate into an exercise in self-justification. All the context work is likely to be justified—well, most of it, at any rate—so the question is not *should* it be done but rather *by whom* should it be done.

Nor is this an exercise in reengineering or simplifying context tasks. That too would absorb too much time, talent, and management attention. The goal instead is to get the entire task suite off your plate and onto some service provider's instead. You are buying your way out of jail. At the outset, you will probably think you are paying too much from an immediate cost-comparison point of view. Think of this expense instead as bail money. You're getting out. Once out, then you can start worrying about costs, and over time, you can engineer a market competition to get them down to where you want them.

The litmus test for evaluating a true outsourcing offer as opposed to a reengineering project is called the *monkey test*. Consider any particular set of context responsibilities as *the monkey*. The question is, at the end of the day, *who has the monkey on their back?* The fundamental value of any outsourcing offer is to move the monkey from your back to theirs. If the monkey stays on yours, you have not won back any of the key scarce resources of time, talent, and management attention. That's a bad deal. But conversely, if you can truly free yourself from the monkey, then regardless of whether there is an immediate cost reduction to take to the bottom line, you have won the key battle of recapturing scarce resources to refocus on core activity.

The key to successful "monkey management" is to construct effective service-level agreements. This is a much easier task in the world of context than in the world of core. When you outsource a core process, you put yourself in harm's way. Now your interests are at odds with the outsourcer's, for you are seeking *differentiation* while they are seeking *standardization*. No service-level agreement can bridge this gulf. This is the realm of partnering, not outsourcing. But when you outsource context, then standardization creates a common ground for you and your provider, and service-level agreements—provided they are subject to dynamic modification as business conditions change—work well.

The management challenge to ensure going forward is that whatever improvements are made, they are done at the expense of the plentiful resources, not the scarce ones. Whenever you seek to parse context from core, and to reallocate resources to improve the core/context ratio, begin by asking the teams in place to dig deep into the following question: *If you and your team were freed from what you are doing now, what could you do to create additional shareholder value?* Focus them on the notion that shareholder value is a metric of competitive advantage, and let them speculate on how they could change the world. Stay with the process until a good-sized laundry list has been developed of truly interesting options that are motivating to the group. Then, and only then, ask them to dig deep into the companion question: *What work do you and your team do today that you would be willing to surrender, provided you were assured it would be handled correctly?*

The result of deep work around these two questions is that the team builds a map of the core/context boundary within the corporation. To be sure, there is still much terra incognita on this map, but large chunks of context appear pretty readily, as do intriguing opportunities for creating new core. Now comes the real challenge, which involves destabilizing the current organization as scarce resources are reallocated from core to context.

In this exercise, the following pair of diagrams can help focus the exercise:

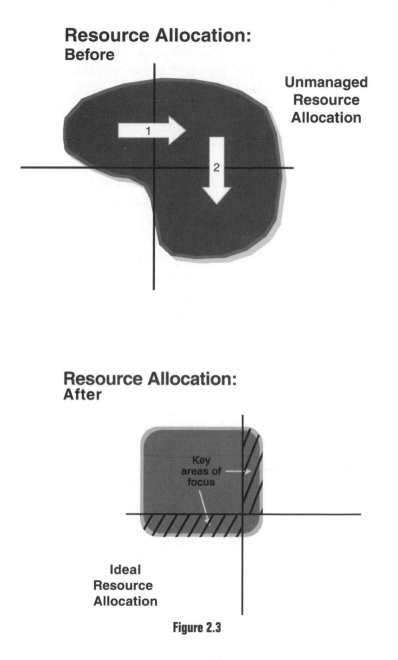

Resource Allocation:
Before

**Unmanaged
Resource
Allocation**

Resource Allocation:
After

Key
areas of
focus

**Ideal
Resource
Allocation**

Figure 2.3

In figure 2.3, arrow 1 shows how over time resources that are assigned to the upper-left Make quadrant drift to the right, as core becomes context under the pressure of competitive responses to differentiation initiatives. Arrow 2 shows how subsequently this buildup of mission-critical context work generates supporting context work in an effort by the company to reduce costs and increase productivity. Over time the resource allocation profile becomes painfully skewed to the right.

The second part of figure 2.3 shows the ideal resource allocation profile. In this model the bulk of the resources are continually reallocated to the upper left. At the same time, however, there is significant investment in relationship management both with partners and outsourcers. In the case of partnering, this is largely a matter of quality and focus: far too many "strategic" partnerships are delegated to legions of junior teams who can do little to overcome the natural repulsion that keeps any two organizations apart. What the leveraged model requires instead is persistent, sophisticated executive attention, with a modest staff in support. At the end of the day partnering happens between the principals engaged in the actual effort, be it in the field selling or in the factory comaking; what is wanted is air cover to ensure that their work gets the proper support from their respective organizations.

In the outsourcing quadrant, the executive focus is not on the *relationships*, but rather on the *systems* needed to ensure control and visibility across company boundaries. Goals and objectives must be translated into observable metrics that can be captured, monitored, and communicated automatically through Internet-enabled computer systems. Analytics must continually be upgraded for faster and better pattern detection and, where feasible, to spawn automatic recovery procedures if processes drift out of control specifications. Remember, these processes may be context, but they are mission critical; just because the corporation is no longer executing the work does not mean it can take its eye off ensuring the quality, reliability, and scalability of the work processes and output.

SEEKING A LEVER THAT CAN MOVE THE WORLD

I hope by now I have made a persuasive case that outsourcing context—particularly, mission-critical context—is a fundamental element of managing for shareholder value. Given the pressures on time, talent, and management attention to create high returns on invested capital, not outsourcing context tasks is, I believe, a fatal mistake. Thus the great challenge of this new millennium is not reinventing our core business processes—that, I believe, management teams are both willing and able to do—but rather clearing the decks for these management teams to get on with it. In other words, the winning teams in this new age will be those that *manage context in order to make room for core*.

Outsourcing context represents a dramatic change from the status quo and thereby inherits the problem of inertia. To be sure, inertia can be a positive as well as a negative force. That is, going forward, once this process gets under way, competitive dynamics are going to play more and more in its favor, and we will find it attracting increasing support and eventually creating its own momentum. It is getting it going in the first place that is the challenge.

This is the problem that Archimedes understood so well. He said, "Give me a lever long enough, and a fulcrum to place it against, and I can move the world." To this end, we need to place a powerful force in our hands, a lever that can overcome the inertia of political alliances that holds the old system in place. That lever, in my view, is stock price. And the fulcrum upon which it is placed is the *stock option*.

Stock price works as a lever because investors are on our side. They want to put their money to work on core tasks that create competitive advantage. They know that for their investment dollars to grow, they must be deployed at the point of attack. If they think instead their capital is going to fund context, they will withdraw it and put it somewhere else, thereby causing the company's stock price to go down. By contrast, where they see a well-focused strategy and an organization aligned to execute it, and not a lot of other stuff getting in the way, then they want to put more money to work there, driving stock price up. That is why outsourcing, at the outset, does not have to be cost-cutting to be successful. Just the fact that you are doing it can raise your stock price because it communicates to investors you are putting your time, your talent, and your management attention to work on core issues.

Because stock price is the lever with which we are going to drive change, we are going to have a lot more to say about it in the next chapter. To close this chapter, it is simply important to see that stock options—making management into shareholders—is the best way of getting the entire organization on the same page. If we all commit to manage for shareholder value, and if we are all significantly compensated as shareholders to reinforce that commitment, then in our own self-interest we will work through the core-versus-context issue successfully and guide our corporate boat back into the market's mainstream.

II

MANAGING FOR SHAREHOLDER VALUE

In my travels and client work I get a chance to meet hundreds of senior executives and discuss their business issues and strategies, and I cannot recall one of them who did not expressly intend to manage for shareholder value. Not only are senior executives compensated heavily on stock price appreciation, they take it as a personal challenge, or if not, they are soon called to do so by the investment community. So the question these executives have about managing for shareholder value is not why, *it is* how.

The first section of this book has argued that the answer is to commit to the following priorities:

1. *Focus on improving competitive advantage through simultaneously increasing GAP via enhancing differentiation and CAP via ensuring the differentiation is sustainable.*

2. *Identify all such GAP- and CAP-increasing processes as* core, *and consign them to the strategies of* Make *and* Partner.

3. *Identify all noncore processes as* context, *and consign them to the strategies of* Outsource *and* Contract, *the key distinction being that in the former your company maintains active control over and visibility into the process outcomes.*

Executing to this agenda, ironically, requires an inversion from normal practice. That is, normally one thinks of core as being the domain of top executives, with context belonging to middle management, but in fact it should be just the opposite. Middle managers are much closer to the competitive realities of the marketplace. They are well tuned in to core. Their biggest problem is that they cannot get sufficient resources to capitalize on the opportunities they have uncovered. Why not? Because those resources are tied up in context.

Moreover, it turns out that freeing resources from context is not something that middle management is well positioned to do. Often, for example, it requires a refusal to support some other manager's process. If I am a middle manager, this is dangerous ground to tread, as that manager may be expected to respond in kind, thereby putting my processes at risk. And so we each support each other's processes, be they core or context, in a mutual alliance to "get things done."

Only top executive action can break this web of alliances. If the top team declares a set of processes either core or context, and if it uses its resource allocation power to enforce core/context boundary management, then mid-

dle managers can and will adjust to the new set of priorities. No one particularly likes these changes—they are almost inevitably destabilizing and disconcerting in the short term—but they must be done if the organization as a whole is to have its scarce resources allocated to improving competitive advantage. Nor is this work that can be done once every several years so we can get back to core. Core becomes context every day, and thus this is a never-ending act of service to the corporation.

So the first rule of managing for shareholder value is to delegate context problems up and core problems down. Don't preempt the core work for yourself, even though it is the most fun. The greatest act of service in a management hierarchy is to create freedom for the resources you manage so that they can create new competitive advantage for the firm.

That said, creating and sustaining core is itself more challenging than managers might think. This is not for lack of demand—it is a rare market in which customers say that vendors have completely satisfied their needs and there is no opportunity going forward to further differentiate. Nor is it for lack of imagination—it is a rare company in which an hour or two of brainstorming cannot generate a rich list of new opportunities to pursue. Rather the challenge instead is that we fall prey to commonplace management mechanisms that actually defocus us from core. That is to say, we actually pursue the wrong goals and objectives, even as we think they are the right ones.

The essence of the problem is that we manage our companies, for the most part, through the lens of the profit and loss statement, or P&L. While that provides an extremely useful view, it also has built-in astigmatisms that distort reality and lead managers to make wrong choices. When *compensation programs are tied to P&L results, as they typically are, management can find itself fighting furiously to drag the company to the wrong place in order to claim the promised rewards. In this way we have learned to earn our bonuses even as we tank our stock options.*

Now just so we don't pick on any one group unfairly, we'll take a look at challenges facing each of the major line functions in a Fortune 500 company—from sales, marketing, and professional services to research and development, operations, finance, and investor relations—and then we'll look at the executive team as a whole as it faces fundamental issues with its P&L statement. In every case the goal is simply to point out how easy it is to think you are doing the right thing when in fact your actions are detracting from, not adding to, shareholder value.

3

LINE MANAGEMENT FOR SHAREHOLDER VALUE

In each section of this chapter we will take up a separate component of typical functional organization for a high-tech firm and view it through the lens of managing for shareholder value. The intent is not to render irrelevant other points of view but rather to balance them with this one. That said, however, in technology-enabled markets shareholder value holds huge sway, so it behooves management not to ignore its demands.

MANAGING SALES FOR SHAREHOLDER VALUE

From an investor's perspective, a sale has value in two dimensions. In the immediate present, it represents the realization of a revenue commitment that fulfills the company's representation of its current competitive-advantage potential. At the same time, a certain type of sale can also help construct an even stronger competitive advantage in the future. This happens when the new customer is added to others in the same market segment to create a majority of customers dedicated to a single vendor—in other words, when the sale contributes to market segment leadership. Such sales represent *good* revenue because they move the shareholder agenda forward.

Even among good revenues, there are gradations of shareholder value. In a high-growth marketplace, only revenues representing significant new commitments from new customers truly reflect increases in marketplace power, so these are the true indicators of changes in shareholder value. As a result, high-tech-sector investment analysts grill management regarding how many new accounts were gained in the quarter and how big a commitment each customer made. In the enterprise software domain, for example, they will always ask how much of the quarter came from license revenue (representing a strong new commitment) versus service revenue (revenue from maintenance contracts that represents a low commitment from existing customers) and how many deals were in excess of $1 million (strong commitments) as opposed to, say, under $100,000.

Implicit in all this quizzing is the notion that there is such a thing as *neutral* revenue and, as we shall see in a moment, even *bad* revenue, which can put the shareholder engine in reverse. It is a rare salesperson who is willing to entertain such a thought, and indeed the management team as a whole is hardly likely to welcome it: *Good God, man, do you know how hard revenue of any kind is to come by? Come down from that ivory tower, boy.* But from an investor's point of view—and thus from a managing-for-shareholder-value point of view—both concepts unfortunately make sense.

Neutral revenue is income from outside the primary domain of market competition, typically the result of opportunistic sales. It adds to working capital, but it does not represent any gain in marketplace power, so it represents a realization of GAP but does not add to—or subtract from—CAP. Now, we need to be clear that no company could ever make its forecast commitments for revenue without quite a lot of neutral revenue. It is baked into the numbers deeply, and it should be pursued aggressively. That said, neutral revenue is not a substitute for good revenue, and a diet containing no good revenue will eventually create a firm that has no CAP. This, indeed, is the state of virtually all small, privately owned businesses, who go in and out of business every four years or so because, while they have no trouble generating GAP, they have no strategy for and make no progress toward CAP.

Neutral revenue may also come from outside operations—say,

from selling an investment, for example, or making money on currency exchanges, or capturing gains from a tracking stock. In addition, from time to time changes in accounting rules may create changes in the P&L that reallocate revenues or expenses. The SEC's handling of pooled-interest transactions is an example of this. In all these cases, however, the revenues in question have nothing to contribute to the CAP question of future competitive advantage. So, whether their impacts are positive or negative, Wall Street tries to "look through them" to the basic dynamics of the enterprise. Its primary interest is to track transactions that create leading indicators of change in the balance of power in the marketplace.

Bad revenue is something else altogether. It is income from outside the domain of market competition that has been earned at the expense of scarce resources, and it puts the shareholder engine in reverse. That is, it creates the illusion of GAP by consuming capital to create an artificial and unsustainable competitive advantage, and in so doing it actually *subtracts* from CAP.

Typically, bad revenue results from a taking a big deal well outside your normal market space. Such deals are bad for two reasons. First, they require a continued future diversion of precious resources simply to continue to serve this customer. If the company is not making a market commitment in this direction, then all subsequent work here is at best neutral to its market power position. To use the terms of the prior chapter, this revenue amounts to context, not core. Second, these deals reflect a lost opportunity to put those same precious resources to work in the critical competitive space. A better-focused company would have used this chance to make progress where it counts, where a sale today would help create multiple sales tomorrow. A better company, in other words, keeps its scarce resources focused on core. By taking this deal the company has shifted scarce resources from core to context and has thus actually jeopardized its shareholder value.

Bad-revenue deals are rarely criticized in the quarter in which they are earned. Indeed the stock market typically is not able to ferret out all the neutral and bad revenue in any quarter's performance. As a result, in the short to medium term, management teams can normally claim credit for all their revenue as forward-looking, CAP-enhancing revenue—that is, revenues that indicate increasing market share.

Here, however, is where it's important not to kid yourself. Simply understand that once bad revenues have been counted as good, once they have been aggregated into the forward-looking category, they establish a market-share growth-rate expectation for revenues within that category that becomes harder and harder to live up to. Next quarter, to keep up with the rate you portrayed last quarter, the company not only has to sell more of its good business faster, it also has to sell additional good business beyond that to hide the bad business in the old numbers. And, of course, having some portion of current capital resources deflected to supporting the old bad business does not help. One does not have to look very far down this track to see that it is a losing game. Sooner or later the company must miss big, and when it does, correction comes with a vengeance.

So what is a sales manager to do? Three practices stand out:

1. Find a way to compensate generation of good revenue over neutral revenue, thereby encouraging your people to make the extra effort to focus on the markets where your company can gain a leadership position.

2. Do not imply that neutral revenue is undesired. No company can make its revenue commitments without a large complement of opportunistic sales. And winning a sale on a playing field that is not tilted in your favor is no mean feat. So hats off to that accomplishment.

3. Do not approve bad-revenue deals. The way to block them is to deny access to the scarce resources needed to close them. If the deal closes anyway, then it is neutral revenue, and all is well.

The tough choice falls between taking bad revenue or missing a quarter. But the answer here is actually straightforward. You now have no chance of not missing a quarter—the only question is, which quarter are you going to miss? If you take this deal, you put yourself even further behind the eight ball in future quarters. A classic expression of this problem was the case of Informix in the late 1990s. Quarter after quarter they pulled out the numbers through diving catches in the end zone. When they finally missed, however, they missed by over $100 million, and the restatements of revenues that ensued over the following year revealed just how grisly bad revenue can be.

The challenge, of course, is the notion that the current quarter is an anomaly, that next quarter momentum may swing back our way, but to signal weakness now would actually make that outcome less likely, so put on a brave face and march forward. This is actually the best practice for the first instance of weakness. It is questionable practice at the second, and it becomes increasingly foolhardy going forward from there. Best practice is some version of a three strikes rule.

MANAGING MARKETING FOR SHAREHOLDER VALUE

The single most important strategic role of marketing is to help the company maximize its good revenue by targeting markets where it can gain a sustainable competitive advantage. In so doing, it typically reviews a large set of possible targets and then winnows them through a set of selection criteria. One of these is market size, where the assumption is normally, the larger, the better. Not so.

True, a large untapped market is always terrifically attractive, especially when no other company has a head start in going after it. That in essence is one of the core mantras of venture investing. But these opportunities are few and far between unless you are spawning a truly disruptive innovation. Consider instead the much more typical choice between the following:

- *Market A:* A large market served by a broad array of vendors that has significant opportunities developing within it. The market as a whole has been tapped but the new spaces opening up are untapped.

- *Market B:* A neglected niche market ineffectually served by market leaders. The market as a whole has never really been tapped, in large part because it would take a significant investment to do so, and the returns are not worth it to an established player.

Which of these opportunities is more attractive? Market A is preferred if you are already one of the vendors that serves it, you have reason to believe you can get to the new opportunities ahead of the others, and the current market leader (if it is not you) cannot muscle in and take away your momentum. But Market B is preferable if you do not have a preexisting position of strength. Remember, the goal is to pick markets based on the size of their *untapped potential*, not their total size, and to factor in the probability of your company gaining dominant market share—essentially what is required to sustain competitive advantage.

By these criteria, narrow vertical markets often bring higher rewards than broad mass markets. In general, they are attractive to investors because they lend themselves to creating strong GAP and CAP positions. Vendors who specialize in a single market can create highly differentiated offers for the targeted segment. This gives them a high GAP, which results in increased segment share. As the vendor's share of segment increases, complementary vendors in the segment begin to operate more intimately with them, creating higher barriers for a competitor and higher switching costs should the partner defect to the competitor. Over time the risk of the company losing its competitive advantage decreases substantially. All this results in a longer CAP.

It is almost always in a company's interests, therefore, to limit its targeted markets to spaces that it has the power and reach to dominate. A strong position in a small market is a much better investment than a weak position in a large market. Of course, if that small market is also growing rapidly, the position becomes even more valuable. By contrast, however, overreaching into marginal market positions that cannot be held over time wastes investment dollars, diminishes competitive advantage, and creates stock price weakness.

Why, then, don't companies pursue vertical markets more aggressively? Why are they more likely to pursue weak positions in large markets at the expense of strong positions in smaller markets? Their answer is that their investors demand greater absolute returns than can come from any particular vertical market. That is, as companies become larger, investors expect increasing growth in both the top and bottom lines, and management teams begin to view target market size as increasingly important because they are looking to achieve growth over increasingly larger numbers. In this light, even dominant positions in small markets do not generate the numbers they are hoping for, so management shifts its focus to larger markets where gaining even a small amount of market share, perhaps only a few percent, can generate the expected revenue gains and thus meet their investors' expectations and sustain their stock price. This is a mistake.

Whenever your goal is to get a small share of a large market, you are at the outset conceding that other companies already have a larger share. The market, in other words, has already formed GAP and CAP structures around its existing participants. These structures inhibit any competitor's entry. So you can count on it costing you plenty just to get into the market.

Nonetheless, at the outset you can expect some initial success because every market has a set of dissatisfied customers who are looking for a new face. Once you get that foothold, however, the power hierarchy in the market works even more strongly to prevent your gaining additional market share. Markets are extremely conservative about changes in their pecking order and spontaneously self-organize to expel late entrants. After an initial jump in revenues reflecting the novelty of your arrival, future sales will be harder and harder to come by. Worse, because you have no power in this market, your offers will be on the losing end of GAP, not the winning end. You will have to discount more and more to gain the sales you do win. This creates a negative impact on your returns line, as more and more capital chases less and less profitable deals, with the net effect of lowering your stock price, not raising it.

A classic illustration of this dynamic is a company's first entry into an international market. Armed with a great offer, and running out of headroom in their home market, they launch an effort to penetrate some far less well served country, confident in their ability to do so because they have already won at least one customer in the new geography. But from the outset trouble looms. It takes much longer to set up the distribution channel than anticipated, and almost immediately a mismatch between the local team's and the home office's expectations of support surfaces. Going forward, the home office will increasingly be convinced they have hired the wrong country managers, and the in-country team will increasingly be convinced that the home office is clueless.

Name this tune "Dysfunction Junction" and know that it has topped the charts year in and year out decade after decade. But what few realize is that this is not a sales mistake, nor a hiring mistake, but rather a marketing mistake, which in turn has been driven by a mistake in executive direction. And that mistake is the notion that investors value revenues per se. It just isn't true.

What investors value are competitive-advantage positions that foreshadow a growing stream of high-margin revenues over an extended time. They care, in other words, about future revenue potential that has high *forecastability* and *low risk*. When marketing pursues marginal positions in large established markets, taking on low forecastability and high risk, it is working against, not for, the investors' agenda. Instead it should be focusing the team on becoming the biggest fish in the largest possible pond it can dominate.

This creates a marketing imperative to monitor *fish-to-pond ratios*, something that Jack Welch made a cornerstone of the management philosophy at General Electric when he said GE will be number one or number two in every one of its markets or it won't play. Once you determine what percentage of your revenue you intend to derive from a given market, then you must determine if you'll be number one or number two in that market. If not, then you must either commit the investment resources to change your competitive-advantage GAP until you can gain such market share, or according to Welch, you must exit the market. If you do not, you will be competing against some other company that has the market leadership advantages that you do not, and your results are bound to disappoint investors.

Now let's be clear about something here. Regardless of how single-mindedly you pursue this strategy, there will always be a large portion of revenue that in fact comes from opportunistic sales into untargeted markets where you are anything but the dominant market-share leader. It is not the advice of this chapter, nor of Mr. Welch, to turn these sales down. Rather, understand that they do not create a firm foundation for stock price appreciation. You will never make your revenue projections without them, but neither can you entrust your future to them. Instead, you must continually build that future by systematically extending market leadership positions where you can create advantaged GAPs that can lead over time to long CAPs.

MANAGING PROFESSIONAL SERVICES ORGANIZATIONS FOR SHAREHOLDER VALUE

The professional services organization (PSO) I am discussing here represents the consulting arm within a large corporation whose product offerings require some level of systems integration. In technology-enabled markets, this group tends to undergo an identity crisis as it looks enviously at the success of both the large independent consulting firms, such as Accenture or EDS, and the example of IBM, where its Global Services group effectively spearheads the entire corporation's engagement with enterprise customers. Our PSO feels its capabilities are every bit as good as any of theirs, and it chafes against the restriction of having to drag its own company's offers into every deal. If the company would just let it compete freely, it could make a much better contribution to shareholder value.

Anyone who has ever had to bring a younger sibling along with them when they went out with their friends knows how this organization feels. But the fundamental premise, that if freed it could make a greater contribution to shareholder value, is flawed. Captive professional services organizations exist to increase the GAP and CAP of the company's core offers. True, they are also expected to generate revenue, and true, this revenue does count on the bottom line, but that is not their primary value-creating function. It is, instead, to contribute to the greater good.

The challenge facing this organization's management is to charter it correctly, to make absolutely clear what is core and what is context. For independent consulting firms, revenue is core; for all but a few professional services organizations, on the other hand, *revenue is context!* To be sure, if revenue is not earned, that is bad, because this organization should more than pay for itself. But earning more and more revenue will not raise stock price. Instead, the PSO's core contributions will lie in the following areas:

- Helping to sell and then implement projects that advance the company's state of the art, featuring products that are fresh from R and D. Such projects get much needed visibility for the company's innovative offers and help start new product categories.

- Doing the gritty, unglamorous work behind the scenes that has to get done to make any system work right, the very work that the independent consulting firms want no part of. By signing up for these tasks, the organization ensures the customer gets a successful result and becomes a superior reference for the company.

- Developing domain expertise in one or more vertical markets to help differentiate the company's offerings in market-domination exercises. Such expertise enables the company to modify its offers in compelling ways that secure deep and abiding loyalty from grateful customers.

- Capturing the essential systems integration knowledge needed to implement large, complex offerings, and then packaging that knowledge and handing it over to third-party partners. This broadens the company's reach to incorporate indirect sales and support, the cost of which is off the balance sheet.

- Offering its services to long-established customers to take on a challenge that no one else will help them with. Not only does this, too, help secure long-term loyalty and commitment, but it can also lead to the discovery of new market opportunities.

In short, professional services organizations create the most shareholder value when they subordinate their own P&Ls to the greater good. This should not be taken as a license for them to be unprofitable. Skilled human resources are simply too scarce to be deployed at a loss. It should, however, be taken as a call to make every project count toward the company's core, toward increasing the GAP and the CAP of the company's offers in its primary target markets.

MANAGING R&D FOR SHAREHOLDER VALUE

When I entered business back in the 1970s, large corporations were the bastion of research and development, and centers like Xerox PARC, Bell Labs, HP Labs, and IBM Labs were perceived as the crown jewels of their respective corporations, sources of innovation that would keep their competitive advantage alive for generations to come. Interestingly, if we fast-forward thirty years, that is not what has transpired. Instead, innovation has in large part emerged from venture-backed start-ups directly exposed to the Darwinian forces of a highly competitive marketplace. Many of these companies die from such exposure, but those that survive and reach critical mass become highly attractive as IPO candidates or acquisitions. And even if they go public as independent firms, in the longer term they are likely to merge into larger and larger entities, and so the function of creating R and D for large corporations is in fact fulfilled, albeit in a roundabout way. It turns out, in effect, that in the long run Darwin may be a better inventor than Edison.

The only casualty is the corporate R and D labs, which, like professional services organizations, look with envy at the unfettered lives led by their outside counterparts and grumble about the lack of imagination and appreciation from within. And indeed they have much to grumble about.

If you think it is hard to get a disruptive innovation to market from an unknown start-up, you ought to try it from a corporate lab. As Clayton M. Christensen described in *The Innovator's Dilemma*, established corporations have highly evolved immune systems that tag and reject disruptive technologies regardless of their origin. A start-up takes this for granted. A corporate lab might be forgiven for thinking the rest of the company is on its side. Add to this that the start-up can offer stock options to attract the hot new talent, and that they get a marketing budget and a sales force that has nothing else to sell but the next new thing, and you see why breakthrough R and D is much more likely to come from a decentralized, venture-funded system.

Okay, so given all the above, what should R and D management do? One key here is to actively align the corporate lab with the producing divisions of the company. At companies like Nokia and Agilent, for example, corporate R and D is largely funded by the divisions themselves, ensuring that development is targeting technologies that have immediate relevance to coming product competitions. Moreover, managers who do work in these labs often go with the projects when they are transitioned into the divisions, to better ensure continuity and successful grafting into established or emerging product lines.

A central lab creates unique advantage by organizing around technology themes instead of specific product lines, thereby facilitating cross-fertilization that can lead to breakthroughs. The themes need to be closely connected to the corporate mission but must transcend the next few years' objectives. The crucial test is whether the bulk of the projects under way tackle the genuinely tough problems that the industry faces going forward.

All this stands in marked contrast to what one might call the "country club" lab, typically justified as a showcase, where projects are allowed to stray, and scientists feel increasingly entitled to pursue their own interests without economic constraints. Nobody sets out to create labs of this type. Instead the focus is on creating enough freedom that scientists can think outside the box and not be tied to the next generation of current product line thinking. And in modest amounts, investment of this type is worthwhile. But when modest amounts become immodest, the organization morphs into a painfully self-indulgent exercise, and top management needs to wade in and whack it back.

Overall, from an investor's point of view, the return on corporate labs depends upon breaking through Christensen's innovator's dilemma, bringing novel and disruptive innovations to market even when they cannibalize the corporation's current generation of offers. This challenge will be the entire focus of Part V of this book, and we will leave it until then.

MANAGING OPERATIONS FOR SHAREHOLDER VALUE

For the purposes of this discussion, consider *operations* in its largest sense as essentially any business process that involves a fundamentally repetitive set of tasks and typically a large number of people. Thus a manufacturing line, a purchasing or personnel department, a customer support or telesales center, a shipping-and-receiving or warehousing function, or a facilities-maintenance and security group could all qualify. Understood in this sense, when it comes to managing for shareholder value, COOs (chief operating officers) should think of themselves as chief outsourcing officers, the primary owners of the core-versus-context challenge.

That is not how COOs tend to think of themselves today. Instead, they are likely to see themselves as chief overseers of in-house business processes, chartered to make them more efficient and more effective. And to the degree that those processes should stay in-house, that is absolutely correct. But if companies are ever going to implement the strategy of outsourcing context to embrace core, then the effort must be led by the team and the executive who can best testify as to which is which. And that is the operations team. Anyone else in the company may think he knows, and certainly everyone will have an opinion about what ought to be either core or context, but only the people who actually do the work can make the determination with any authority. The issue is, will they?

In the old economy, managers of any operation asked to down-size or dismantle itself could be expected to react defensively, taking the charter as an implied criticism of their ability to perform to an appropriate standard. So asking for their support was a little bit like asking the doomed man to help tighten the knot on the hangman's noose. But in the new economy that is not at all the case. The winners in the new economy will be those who can craft the most imaginative solutions to managing context and then put in place pragmatic outsourcing relationships that really work.

Determining which tasks can in fact be outsourced, identifying the outsourcer that can handle them, setting up a relationship of trust anchored in a thoughtful and precise service-level agreement, installing systems that create visibility and provide customer control, supervising the transition to the new workflow including working through the inevitable glitches and complaints, and then managing the ongoing relationship toward the twin goals of improved service levels and reduced costs—all this is not the sort of thing that a "failed" management team can, or should, be asked to do. It is, in effect, the implementation of a whole new business paradigm. The venture capital community, for its part, believes enough in this vision that it is funding scores of start-ups to play the outsourcer role wherever it can envision one is likely to form. But at the end of the day it will be the operational management of the customer company who will make or break this effort.

What I want to make clear here is that successful outsourcing of context tasks represents the most dramatic way in which operations management can raise shareholder value. To be sure, they can also improve stock price by squeezing a bit more productivity out of their in-house teams, increasing margins and earnings per share, and garnering a stock market attaboy for so doing. In other words, it is not that the current efforts are misdirected or lacking value. It is simply that such returns are peanuts compared to the impact operations can have wherever they are able to clear the decks of a great chunk of context work.

Perhaps the greatest challenge of all and the action that will have the greatest impact is for an operations management team to lead a spin-out of one or another of their in-house groups, taking what was historically a cost center and converting it into an independent and profitable entity. This is a huge task and should not be undertaken without a commitment from the host company to guarantee a multiyear contract for the new entity's services to support the transition. After all, the group has never had to run itself as a company before and lacks most of the functions needed to do so.

Many of these, it turns out, can themselves be outsourced in turn, but sales and marketing, to pick just two, certainly cannot. It takes real leadership, therefore, to inject entrepreneurial self-sufficiency into a group that was never recruited with such a vision in mind. But there is no question that, for those groups that can step up to this challenge, the future holds enormous promise, not only to control one's own destiny but to earn the equity rewards of entrepreneurship as well.

To close on a more practical note, any outsourcing of context work is a step in the right direction. Indeed, simply helping sketch out the boundary line between core and context will help the corporation better target its resources. The only truly value-destroying behavior in the face of a challenge to create better returns on invested capital is simply to march forward heads down along the same old paths.

MANAGING FINANCE FOR SHAREHOLDER VALUE

If there is one organization that might feel it is already directly aligned with managing for shareholder value, it would be the finance department. As keepers of the P&L, leaders of the budgeting effort, producers of the monthly variance reports, and publishers of the quarterly report, they often see themselves as the financial conscience of the company and the shareholders' ally.

In actual fact, however, a P&L orientation is not always in the shareholders' best interests. To be sure, in mature markets it normally is. That's because P&L statements accurately reflect earnings performance on short-to-medium-term operations, the appropriate focus in a mature market. Such markets are said to be in their cash cow phase, and thus monitoring "milk flow" is the appropriate focus. Conversely, however, in growth sectors where sustainable competitive advantage is largely a function of staking out early positions in developing markets, a pure P&L approach to strategy and planning is horribly misguided. It would be like monitoring the milk flow on a baby heifer. A proper focus instead would be on the metrics of the heifer's growth and future prospects, not on its present yield.

Success or failure in achieving a sustainable competitive-advantage position in a hypergrowth market does not show up on the P&L until well after the battle for marketplace dominance is under way, with its outcomes potentially already determined. Not understanding this principle results in *P&L myopia*, a widespread affliction not only among finance departments but whole management teams that leads to loss of shareholder value. Here's how it works.

First the good news: *P&L statements can and do detect current deterioration in GAP*. Receding GAPs show up either in loss of sales outright or diminishing gross margins as the company increases its discounts to make up for its lack of GAP or both. In any case, the P&L alerts the management team to the problem, and actions are taken. This is how and why established companies perform successfully when challenged to make continuous improvements to existing paradigms. CAP is rarely the issue; GAP almost always is. Is GAP slipping? Prop it up and get back out there for the next round of sales competitions.

Now for the bad news: *P&L statements cannot and do not detect deterioration in CAP*. Here's why. Recall that a GAP/CAP chart is the projection of a financial future. At the left side of the chart that projection is grounded in the previous quarter's financial performance. The numbers there are solid. Going forward into the next few quarters, the numbers are projections, but there is enough history and momentum in the system to make them fairly reliable. But going forward from there—anything, say, beyond the next twelve to twenty-four months—the numbers themselves become fused into trend lines based not on data but on extrapolation.

We have now entered a domain where ideas and models of competitive advantage, not extrapolated spreadsheets, generate the most reliable forecasts of future outcomes. Here is where a strategic understanding of CAP must take over, supplanting reliance on any numerical tool. Unfortunately, numbers-oriented management teams miss this transition. Their vision effectively ceases at the edge of what we call the P&L window.

The domain of numbers functions as a P&L window. It gives

Numbers versus Ideas

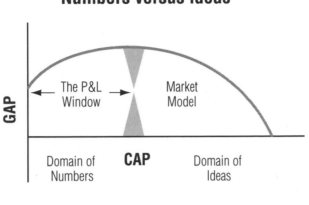

Figure 3.1

visibility into the next two to six quarters, depending on the volatility of the market. Beyond that window, raw numbers offer little or no guidance. Instead one has to model the marketplace, the power of each of the players in it, and the vectors they are on, and then determine who looks to be in the best position to win and why. This is the realm of CAP analysis.

In an established market CAP changes slowly, and largely in predictable directions, with the established players increasing their power positions at the expense of the marginal players. So once CAP is strategically understood, the knowledge becomes taken for granted—effectively, priced into the market—and attention inevitably refocuses on the quarterly numbers, the latest changes in GAP. Thus over time management teams and investment analysts in mature sectors become increasingly numerical in their approach to the market, even on long-term projections. But this approach misses the mark when confronted with the kind of recurrent disruptive change that characterizes high tech or any market that is under a technology-based attack.

In such circumstances, what should the finance team do? The first question it needs to ask itself is, what is moving the company's stock price? Let us assume it has enjoyed a stable P/E for some time so that historically the size of its own earnings has been the prime mover of its stock price. But now let us say that the marketplace has been disrupted by an innovation that threatens to undermine the established power structure by introducing a new category of competition. In such an event, the company's stock price has come under an external negative influence that no amount of earnings can dispel. Shareholders sell off its shares not because of anything it has done but because of a vision someone else has created. A pall has been cast over the company's future, and as the company's designated communications channel to Wall Street, the finance team has to dispel it.

The key learning from the high-tech sector is, no form of arithmetic solves this problem. Instead, it is a matter of storytelling. Hostile forces have sold some portion of the marketplace on a vision of the future that cuts them in and you out. Since this dastardly deed will happen in the future, they argue, of course your earnings will be fine for a few more years, but anyone with half a brain can see you are toast in the long term. To break free from this spell you need to weave one of your own. You need to *state your own vision*, and depending on how well you do it, you will get some of your own back from the market. Market vision is the primary basis of the disrupter's stock price—with little history and only modest financial performance to date, what else do they have?—and its credibility can be questioned. Unfortunately, however, the damage has already been done, meaning that even if this company falters, if the category of disruption is still in play, the question of your company's viability is still on the table. In such circumstances, you must get your story told, and told properly.

Once your company states a credible vision and the competitors have stated their contradictory vision, then the market shifts into the second stage of competition, one that is determined by which company wins the most market share. Here we reenter the domain of the P&L, but not with a focus on earnings. Instead it is on revenues, specifically revenues that reflect gains in market share in the contested markets. That is what drives changes in stock price because market share is a great predictor of CAP. In this contest, the faster the market as a whole is growing, the more rapidly the market share ratios will develop, and thus the more important it is to invest in immediate and massive acceleration in revenues. Such investment is bound to wreak havoc with near-term earnings, and investors may punish you for such effects, but that cannot be helped, and if you are successful, the effects will be temporary. Losing the market-share battle creates a far worse outcome, one in which your strategic path forward has been blocked, and you must either seek a new path or be permanently marginalized.

So when it comes to managing for shareholder value, the key learning for finance departments is that stock price is not always a simple a matter of earnings per share. To be sure, the promise of *future earnings* is always the issue with investors, but in emerging markets, especially technology-enabled markets that have a history of spinning up fast and of having a winner-take-all outcome, *current earnings* should readily be sacrificed to achieve the sustainable competitive advantage of market-share leadership. And if your company is to receive its optimal valuation from investors, in addition to earnings in established markets and revenue growth in emerging markets, it should also be credited with additional competitive advantage coming from its vision and strategy for future markets.

MANAGING INVESTOR RELATIONS FOR SHAREHOLDER VALUE

Recall that most investors have but one goal, to sell your stock at a time when your future prospects are more attractive than when they bought your stock. They look, therefore, for companies who are on such a trajectory.

In this light, demonstrating your ability to gain dominant share in a single fast-growing market creates perhaps the clearest unit of investment possible. As any number of start-ups going public can testify, such an effort is easily positioned and readily communicated, and these companies garner some of the highest P/E multiples on Wall Street. Their success, however, breeds a new set of challenges. The continued need to grow—forced by the desire of the current investors to see even more improvement in future prospects—leads these same companies to expand their operations to field multiple categories of offerings in service to multiple marketplaces. As a result of these efforts, competitive-advantage positions become blurred. That is, GAP and CAP are always specific to a particular category within a single market. Change either the category or the market, and GAP or CAP can change dramatically. So how should investors understand and value the GAP and CAP of a diversified company?

Actually, the first question is, should they assign any value to diversification at all? Most investors, it turns out, do not. They are not interested in individual stocks as instruments of diversification because they see that goal is far better accomplished by mutual funds, index funds, or similar aggregating instruments. Instead they are looking to individual stock investments to provide returns in excess of the funds and indexes, and here the pure-play stocks have a big advantage over the diversified ones.

Specifically, in the high-tech sector investors often use pure plays to invest in hypergrowth markets, ideally focusing their holdings on an emerging market leader and riding its success up and up and up, a strategy described in some detail in *The Gorilla Game*. By contrast, a mature corporation comprising a portfolio of varied operations is invariably held back from such dramatic appreciation because not everything in the portfolio can be in hypergrowth at the same time.

To counter this effect and garner appreciation for their own stock, the management of large established companies must create a case for synergy among their various operations. Moreover, the case has to be real because in every future quarter the company's performance is going to be measured against it. In prior eras, a prime source of such synergy was vertical integration. In a new economy where investors are becoming more insistent on capital being invested in core, however, this strategy is becoming increasingly obsolete. Today investor-attracting synergies are more likely to be found in shared technology and intellectual property, shared distribution and support infrastructure, and shared market and customer knowledge. Regardless of where synergy comes from, however, the real question is, how does it affect the GAP and CAP of the company's various offerings in its various markets?

To speak to this question authoritatively, the company would ideally present its operating results category by category and market by market, for GAP and CAP are market-specific by nature. In so doing the company could guide investors and analysts in constructing a market capitalization model for each area and comparing its results to others in the same category. By summing the results across all its lines of business, it could then present a model upon which one could evaluate the appropriateness of the current market valuation of the company. That is what investors and analysts would want. But it is not at all a common practice in the *Fortune* 500. Why not?

Traditionally *Fortune* 500 companies have withheld the kind of details needed to break out cleanly a corporation's offers for comparative purposes, primarily for two reasons. First, they do not want to reveal any more of their warts to investors than they have to. And second, they want to give as little information as possible to competitors about the strengths and weaknesses of their individual operations. In service to both these ends, traditional shareholder-reporting practice has sought to cloak the corporation's internal operations wherever possible, providing financial results in as aggregated a form as investors and analysts are willing to tolerate.

This practice, to the degree it is accommodated, drives investment analysts toward an increasingly abstract form of financial comparison. That is, following the principle of pricing relative to comparables, they identify a set of grossly similar stocks (finding ones that are precisely similar is what cloaking makes impossible), then calculate and average the price/earnings ratios for them, then use that ratio as a benchmark for valuing the cloaked company. Under this mechanism they put increasing scrutiny on the company's financials, especially its handling of earnings, because granting any increase in earnings is the equivalent of granting an increase in stock price. Since accounting practices give significant leeway to how revenues and expenses are recognized, this leads to a complicated game of hide-and-seek, with the quarterly report becoming the occasion for an increasingly specialized set of questions.

In mature markets this practice, although not particularly useful, does no apparent harm. But in markets undergoing rapid change—markets where future prospects are determined more by CAP than GAP, in the domain of ideas rather than in the domain of numbers—the entire system falls of its own weight. Threatened disruptions call into question both the GAP and CAP of traditional market leaders, and they in turn need to quell investor anxiety directly. Unfortunately, however, the very facts that would allow them to do so are the ones they have systematically been withholding from their reports.

Look at it from the investor's point of view. Instead of responding with specific operational breakouts, your company announces instead that it has launched important innovations of its own, not to worry. But from your cloaked reporting, all investors can see is that overall revenues are still growing at single-digit rates. By contrast the true disrupters are displaying extraordinary growth rates, in part benefiting from the law of small numbers. From this vantage, investors tend to infer that either you are missing the mark with your innovative offers, or else they are but a paltry amount of your total effort, or else some undisclosed problem is seriously dragging your highflier down. Your reporting practices, of course, make it impossible for them to determine which of these conditions actually obtains. After some thought, however, investors decide they don't much care after all which one it is: they just want out.

One emerging response to this challenge has been to create *tracking stocks* for operations that have investment attributes significantly at variance with the traditional lines of business, thereby opening up a particular business operation for direct reporting and direct investment. General Motors took this line with its Hughes Aircraft and EDS operations. Microsoft from time to time has discussed doing the same with various of its Internet properties. During the dotcom bubble, companies like the Internet Capital Group specialized in assembling entire portfolios into what amounted to a loosely held set of tracking stocks.

As a practice, tracking stocks are at best still a work in progress. Many corporations find over time that this structure tends to bring to an end the kind of internal cooperation needed to achieve synergy benefits. Moreover, there is some confusion about the interaction between the valuation of the tracking stock and the valuation of the shares of the parent company that owns the preponderance of that stock. But there should be no confusion about one thing, and this is the warm reception granted to decloaking the corporation. So regardless of whether literally creating a tracking stock is a good idea or not, there is nothing to stop the investor relations department from creating comparable effects—creating virtual tracking stocks, if you will—by reporting on operations less discreetly and more discretely.

MANAGING FOR SHAREHOLDER VALUE IN TOUGH TIMES

I want to close this chapter with a bizarre notion: how does one manage for shareholder value when one's stock price is going down, and worse still, is probably not done yet? At first blush, one would say, this is simply the consequence of not managing for shareholder value. Let's just chuck the current lot and find some folks who are up to snuff! But in fact all businesses are cyclical, and value investing has demonstrated repeatedly that most stocks revert to the mean, so it can't always be attributed to incompetence when they go down. The real thing investors need to watch for then is, what is management doing about it?

Again, in mature markets where GAP is the determinant issue, the best practices are well understood, largely around the disciplines of belt-tightening, housecleaning, and refocusing, often through divestiture. The specific challenge I want to address here is something different. It is, in essence, the challenge of the fault line itself. How does an established enterprise manage for shareholder value when disruptive innovators have attacked its traditional strongholds and gained a beachhead?

Here you must begin by facing a sad fact. That solid CAP that you used to enjoy, the one that has been the mainstay of your stock price for lo these many years, is no longer solid. Worse, it may be if you are going to compete going forward, it will take major rein-vestment in an area of business you have been treating for some time as a cash cow. This is bound to produce highly unattractive financial results, and investors are bound to punish your stock accordingly. So both CAP and GAP are in for a bad time. It is not that you have done the wrong thing, it is that the world has changed, and what had higher value before has lower value now.

Essentially, investors are applying a new and unfamiliar dis-count for risk. They have seen the "next big thing," the source of the industry's *future* earnings streams, and they are concerned about your ability to get on with the new program. If you choose to underinvest in what is admittedly an unproven category, they worry that you are leaving your home markets open to occupation by new entrants, thereby exposing the company's current market positions to future undermining. That is why the company's stock price takes a hit.

Even now a P&L-oriented management team may respond with bewilderment. That's because, despite increasing anecdotal evidence of competitive risk, the threat has yet to find its way onto the P&L, has yet to manifest itself inside the P&L window, and sadly is not likely to do so until it is too late. Thus it was that Nov-ell's stock price in the 1990s was hammered due to the threat of Microsoft NT displacing Netware, even though the company had over 60 percent market share at the time and was generating record earnings. Imagine management's dismay.

To compound the problem, all along this way to perdition a P&L focus continues to encourage management to stay out of the new market altogether. Looked at through the domain of numbers, the new market simply looks like a bad investment—market risk is high, short-to-medium-term revenue opportunities are modest at best, margins will be negative for the forecastable future, and dis-ruptions to operations will not only be challenging in themselves but will threaten margins in other parts of the business. Why would anyone want to enter a bad business in order to cannibalize an existing good business? Through the P&L lens, management simply cannot see upside gain, only downside pain, and thus strides confidently into the jaws of a calamity.

The failure in reasoning here is an inherited assumption from mature markets—namely, that any large market is essentially immortal. That is, there will always be an automobile market, a steel market, a beverages market, a cigarette market, an insurance market. In this context, continuous innovation will result in increased value creation indefinitely—always has, always will.

This simply is not true of markets suffering from technology-enabled disruption. As the title of this book asserts, they *live on the fault line*. That is, their fundamental underpinnings can be completely overthrown with remarkably little notice. When I joined business in 1978, for example, the word processor of choice was an IBM Selectric typewriter, the one that had the on-keyboard white-out key, and was that a boon! The Selectric cost $1,000 and was the flagship product in the typewriter industry, and the consumables aftermarket was every bit as lucrative, if not more. Today, there is no typewriter market. It isn't weak. It isn't aging. It is *nonexistent!*

What were the other big office-automation expenditures back then? Telex machines, dedicated word processors (remember when *word processing* was a place, not a product?), calculators, and cash registers. These were huge revenue-generating categories. Today they too simply do not exist. Moreover, in recent years the window for a given technology's life expectancy has been getting shorter, not longer. The answering-machine market did not come into existence until the 1980s and today it is virtually extinct, succumbing to ubiquitous voice-mail services. That's less than twenty years beginning to end. Local area networks did not come into prominence until the late 1980s and now they are succumbing to intranets—fifteen years beginning to end. Internet browsers did not come into existence until the 1990s and now are succumbing to an expanding operating system—less than ten years beginning to end. We're not talking about new models replacing old models—we're talking about the wholesale eradication of market categories.

In this context, management thinking needs to jettison the assumption of market immortality. This does not mean there are no more long-lived markets. Hewlett-Packard's printer franchise looks very long-term indeed—no one at present can foresee a disruptive displacement technology. PCs look long-term as well, provided one is willing to take some liberties with the definition of a PC. The Internet looks to be very, very long-term at this date, granted that it is still very young and is largely being viewed through rose-tinted glasses. The key point here is not that technology-based markets cannot be long-lived, only that they are not *necessarily* long-lived.

As soon as you accept this premise, mature market management takes on a new dimension. It is no longer simply an exercise in effective P&L management. It now becomes that, *plus* an exercise in technology-paradigm life-cycle management, which requires that management expand its arsenal of tools to incorporate an additional set of metrics.

This is precisely where the rest of this book is headed. In the next section we are going to reexamine and hopefully expand our understanding of competitive advantage so that the familiar ways of being successful are seen in a larger context of alternatives, some of which will be unfamiliar, many of which will be key to building a successful response to technology-enabled disruption.

III
COMPETITIVE ADVANTAGE

Market capitalization represents the investment community's evaluation of a company's chances of improving its prospects. This, in turn, is a function of its perceived competitive advantage, so market cap, in a very real sense, is a grade on your company's competitive advantage strategy, *factored by investor confidence in whether you can successfully execute that strategy. The most straightforward way to raise stock price, then, is to communicate a revised strategy that has greater prospects than the one investors believe you are currently pursuing and follow that up with financial results that demonstrate you are executing on this new vector successfully. This is what an investor means by* core.

So how are you going to generate competitive advantage? What will your company do that will differentiate your offers in a sustainable way? Rather than try to answer these questions off-the-cuff, we are going to review a model that has an ambitious objective—namely, to represent a universe of possible options from which you can choose—all on a four-by-four grid. The intent of this model is to help management teams winnow their aspirations down from pursuing all sixteen options in parallel to finally choosing one as their prime focus. If that exercise is successful, management not only gains consensus on core but identifies fifteen potential sources of context. It is a major win all around.

In essence the Competitive Advantage Grid represents the intersection of a model describing four types of competitive advantage *with a model describing four* sources of company differentiation. *The resulting grid gives rise to sixteen distinct and sustainable competitive-advantage strategies, each one exemplified by multiple* Fortune 500 *companies. This grid is primarily used as a framework to help management teams clarify first to themselves and second to their various constituents just where they intend to invest to create sustainable competitive advantage.*

Like any prescriptive model, the grid has two identities. In its restrictive mode, it seeks to cut through the clutter and persiflage that surrounds many discussions of competitive advantage and in this sense is intentionally reductive in nature. If your strategy does not fit in one of the squares, it implies, then maybe it isn't much of a strategy at all. We call such fighting words a provocation. *And management can respond either by adopting a chastened posture and obediently seeking out a square, or throwing the challenge back in the model's face and explaining precisely why its nongrid approach is better than anything shown. In this latter scenario the grid represents a point of departure for creativity, and my only request is that you e-mail the thought process so I can make the next release of the model better.*

In its expansive mode, the Competitive Advantage Grid is a dynamic model, implying a past and a future, a kind of chessboard in which companies may be expected to move from square to square, with the strategies of competitors helping to shape the landscape of available choices. Used in this context, it helps set new directions and frame change-management agendas as it makes clear both what territory the company is abandoning and what it intends to occupy. And as a dynamic model, as the saying goes, it afflicts the comfortable and comforts the afflicted; for the one constant in a changing world is that if you do succeed in occupying a square that fits you perfectly, odds are you won't get to do it for long.

With that happy thought in mind, let us turn to the model.

4

THE COMPETITIVE ADVANTAGE HIERARCHY

The four columns of the Competitive Advantage Grid represent the four types of competitive advantage described in the Competitive Advantage Hierarchy. The model portrays competitive advantage as an inverted hierarchy in which each lower layer provides a stronger basis for power in the marketplace than the one above it:

Types of Competitive Advantage

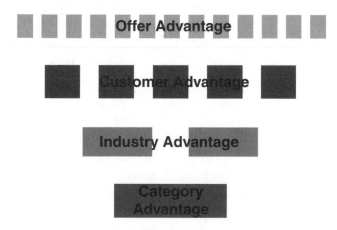

Figure 4.1

Let's walk through each layer to see what kind of marketplace power it can mobilize.

OFFER ADVANTAGE

Offer advantage represents differentiation embodied in the offer itself. It is the most fundamental of all advantages, and most organizations devote most of their resources here. The output of this dedication is readily captured by a model like the Four P's of marketing: *product, price, place,* and *promotion.*

In commodity markets where buying power is concentrated in the customer, offer advantage is about the only advantage that a vendor can really count on, and often it is *price,* and price alone, that carries the sale. This is about as low as one can go in the power game, although we shall see that even here there are strategies that can end up pleasing investors.

In markets where a range of acceptable prices are arrayed against a range of desired benefits, offer advantage becomes the basis for product-line management. This is the domain of price/performance marketing. In its simplest form, it is a retailer offering within a given category *good, better,* and *best* selections. *Product,* in other words, is asserting its differentiation and claiming a price reward for so doing. As complexity increases, customization of the product to meet differing needs or uses adds further weight to this claim. Moreover, the greater the complexity and customization, typically the greater the sustainability of the advantage gained, as custom solutions create switching costs for customers and barriers to entry for competitors. In technical markets, in particular, product-based offer advantage can easily represent the bulk of a company's competitive advantage.

Offer advantage can also be a function, however, of the buying experience. *Place* represents a factor of convenience for the customer, which in turn allows the seller to charge for either providing the place (a store) or going to the customer's place (an outbound sales force). Having an established sales channel or a privileged location in a store increases offer advantage by improving the buyer's experience with your product. In particular, with considered purchases, sales channels that buyers can trust are able to advise them about pros and cons of various choices, reducing their risk, saving them time, and increasing their comfort that they are making the right choice. With consumer purchases that are not considered—say, the brand of salt you bring home from the grocery store—place is a function of shelf space (did you have to stoop?) as well as amount of space one product gets versus its competition (all those blue cylinders!).

The buying experience is also heavily influenced by the fourth P, *promotion*. In considered purchases, the biggest influence on buyer decision-making is word-of-mouth references. In particular, pragmatic buyers are loath to make any significant purchasing commitment without first hearing from other buyers like themselves about their experience with the same decision. This leads savvy vendors to spend marketing dollars on public relations efforts to call out and amplify the voices of satisfied customers and to educate independent third parties about the virtues of the offering compared to alternatives.

In consumer purchases, by contrast, buying decisions are based more on interactions between the product's brand image and the values and aspirations in the consumer's psyche. Modern advertising has exploited this intersection to such a degree that savvy consumers have developed a set of sophisticated defense mechanisms that seek to decode what the ad is trying to do even before it does it. That said, however, identity-based appeals still work, particularly around products like clothing and automobiles that symbolize identity choices. Elsewhere, where all the consumer wants is a reliable, predictable result, reassurance branding, based on an image of corporate trustworthiness, fills the bill. In all cases, promotion is not just informing but actually seeking to improve and enhance the buying experience.

Such is the domain of offer advantage. It is the sine qua non of commerce. If you have no offer advantage, you'd better be able to force the customer to buy your product, else you are out of business. But offer advantage migrates from vendor to vendor over the product category's life cycle. This year Ford has the best sport utility vehicle, next year it is Chrysler, then Toyota. So from a shareholder's point of view, it is a necessary but not a sufficient condition for strong valuations.

Specifically, offer advantage creates GAP, impacting short-term returns, but does not create CAP, that is, sustainability of those returns. If you are only as good as your most recent offer, miss once and you are back at the end of the line. This creates a high-flier scenario with the potential for a steep drop-off, the worst kind of effect from a long-term investor's point of view (although it is a speculator's delight). Even companies with long-established track records for innovation are not safe. And that is what leads us—and management—to look toward the next level down in the hierarchy.

CUSTOMER ADVANTAGE

Customer advantage is demonstrated when prospective buyers purchase a company's offer even when they perceive another offer as more attractive. They justify this decision as an investment in their ongoing relationship with the company. This is *customer loyalty* at work and it takes its roots from multiple elements.

In business relationships with high switching costs, such as with computer vendors or factory equipment providers, customer loyalty is rooted in the practicalities of maintaining compatibility with installed systems and maintaining continuity with shared understanding of problems and solutions. For most complex systems most customers are loyal to their incumbent vendors for the life of the technology paradigm, simply because that is the most practical thing to do.

To gain customer advantage leverage from such loyalty vendors need to spread it over a group of companies in the same segment of the economy. If the top three or four companies in a given segment have all standardized on the same equipment from the same set of vendors, that sets a de facto standard for that industry, which unleashes a series of attractive outcomes for the vendors. First, as yet uncommitted companies will be unlikely to go against the accepted standard, so it will be harder and harder for competitors to compete. Second, partners and allies who flesh out the solution set with complementary products and services will seek to reinforce the de facto standard as it simplifies the number of options they need to support. Sales forces in these companies will start to send prospects to the standard-setters as a way of getting in good with them. And seeing all this, the sales forces of competitors will simply migrate away from the segment, seeing the deck stacked against them.

All this represents sustainable competitive advantage, the power of successful niche marketing when it comes to business buyers making considered purchases. But note how a minor variation in this scenario creates a very different outcome. Suppose instead of persisting in a niche to win the top three or four companies, a vendor moves on to another segment, wins one or two companies there, and then moves on to a third or fourth. In every case, a second vendor is allowed to come in and reach parity in segment penetration. This neutralizes the impact of both companies and ensures that neither, nor any other company, will ever win the niche. As a result, customer advantage is squandered, and companies must continue to slug it out on offer advantage only. This sort of performance drives shareholders nuts as it reduces the market caps of every company involved.

On the consumer market front, the most powerful form of customer loyalty comes from inertia around *brand preference*. Consider the average consumer—you yourself would be fine—entering the average department store, grocery, pharmacy, or hardware store. There in front of you are some ten thousand products or more, and even if you are an avid shopper, you have a finite amount of time to get in, out, and on with life. To be sure, you will want to linger over several categories of product—your personal favorites—but you also have a whole list of other stuff you are supposed to buy.

This is where brand preference shows its value. You already know what brand of each of these other products you are supposed to buy. You have negotiated this choice with your spouse or significant other. As a result, you can blaze through the bulk of your purchases with the decisions premade. This is *consumption* at work. It is the only way to handle markets of abundance. And so it is that persistent brand value is a major component of shareholder value. Because the company with the brand gets the default purchase decision, and because every year of brand commitment creates more inertia in favor of sustaining that commitment in the following year, brand loyalty is a great contributor to a long CAP.

Brand loyalty is separate from *brand strength*. The latter is the power the brand exerts upon the buyer to justify a premium price. Brand strength is thus a great contributor to GAP, particularly for purveyors of luxury goods like upscale pens, designer clothing, or high-end automobiles. Again, the actual offer these companies are making, when it is compared feature for feature with lower-cost competitors, does not win the price/performance battle. But that does not matter: the customer *wants* the top brand and overrides the other inputs to make the purchase decision.

Needless to say, if you can sell the same product for more money than your competitor, you have an excellent opportunity to create attractive shareholder returns. And if on top of that you can also field the best offer, then you have a chance to roll up the market all to yourself. Such is the power of customer advantage. By combining brand strength for GAP with brand loyalty for CAP, companies generate attractive returns *over the span of the customers they have in their camp.*

In terms of managing for shareholder value, therefore, customer advantage represents a significant step up from pure offer advantage. It requires marketing savvy to select the best targets and market discipline to execute through to a sustainable position. Companies able to meet these requirements enjoy much greater control over their destinies than their peers, especially in down markets when customers have most of the negotiating power.

That said, however, there is another form of advantage that can trump customer advantage in that it can generate equal or greater impact *over the span of the entire available market*, touching not only all the customers in the market, but partners and even competitors as well. And that is *industry advantage.*

INDUSTRY ADVANTAGE

Industry advantage is the power companies accrue when they so dominate their own offer category they can dictate terms to suppliers, partners, distributors, and even customers. In the high-tech sector this is the domain of a handful of companies whose attributes are described in *The Gorilla Game:* companies like Microsoft, Intel, Cisco, SAP, Oracle, Siebel, and the like.

All these companies share a common advantage. They have *proprietary control over an open architecture that underlies an entire sector of the high-tech landscape and has high switching costs*. If you want to build a mass-market PC, you have to go to Microsoft to get the operating system and the office automation suite, and while you can go to AMD for your chip, Intel is the market leader by far and thus the safe buy. If you want to build standard enterprise software, you had better build it on top of Oracle, and if you are architecting a standard enterprise network, it better be built on top of Cisco.

This is true even though every one of these companies has competitors fielding products which on a pure price/performance basis are likely to be superior. That is, the challengers are throwing offer advantage up against industry advantage and losing. Sometimes, of course, the leader actually does have the best product, but always it will claim it does, and it will use its market share as evidence. This is clearly disingenuous, but there is no percentage in either the customer or the partners in the value chain calling foul. Pecking orders are inherent in virtually all social systems, and kowtowing to the alpha leader is part of the game.

Dominant market shares in categories with high switching costs create the most impenetrable barriers to substitution. Companies that enjoy them, therefore, enjoy long, stable CAPs. At the same time, because they are in every practical sense the only game in town, they have a built-in GAP advantage, particularly when it comes to the whole product. That is, even if these companies themselves do not provide everything the customer needs to be successful, they make a market for their partners to fill in the gaps, and thus the overall offer is superior to the competition in the customer's eyes. This is why pragmatic customers agree that nobody ever got fired for buying IBM—or Microsoft or Cisco or Intel.

Industry power outside of high tech comes from a variety of sources, but they all come down to one thing: the company with the power is the *market maker* not only for itself but for a whole host of other companies in the marketplace. Wal-Mart is a market maker for consumer packaged goods companies like Colgate-Palmolive: that is why Colgate-Palmolive's SAP customized implementation has been driven largely by changes to meet Wal-Mart's demands. Similarly, the Big Three automakers are market makers for a raft of first-, second-, and third-tier suppliers and call the tune for their dance. As does Boeing in aerospace. As do Goldman Sachs and Morgan Stanley in investment banking. As does Disney in media and entertainment.

In all these cases getting on the wrong side of the company in power can lead to devastating consequences for the offending company. That in turn leads most companies to go out of their way to accommodate the market maker. With such leverage market-dominating companies can redistribute the workload along the value chain, sending the low-margin or low-leverage work to other companies and keeping the most profitable pieces for themselves. Intel and Microsoft have demonstrated this in the PC industry dramatically, while Wal-Mart's ability to orchestrate vendor-managed inventory and the Big Three automakers' ability to impose Electronic Date Interchange systems onto their suppliers are other examples of enforced collaborations that shift workload away from the market dominator.

To see this force at work it helps to model what Michael Porter and others have taught us to call the *value chain*. In a typical high-tech sector, the value chain looks something like the following:

Industries Self-Organize Into Value Chains

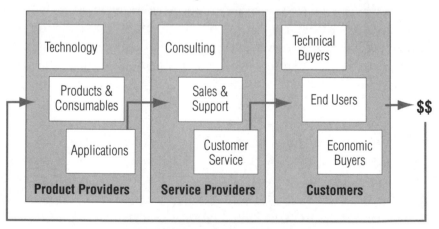

Industry power = value chain power

Figure 4.2

Although value chains develop from left to right, the easiest way to grasp their dynamics is to read them from right to left. Start at the very right: that's the money. Money represents the successful conversion of vendor-promised value into actual customer-realized value. This is the goal of the *economic buyers* who fund the end purchase that in turn funds the rest of the value chain. In so doing they are counting on the *end users* using that purchase to realize the value gain, be it from lower costs, better productivity, or increased competitive advantage. And these users in turn rely on the *technical buyers* to help select the correct system and get it installed.

Further back in the value chain the product providers and service providers collaborate to create the whole product. Reading from left to right, differentiating *technology* is embedded into *prod ucts* (and downstream, into *consumables*) which are assembled into *applications* that create business value. These applications are introduced into customer companies through the labor of *consulting*, the work of a *sales and support* team, and the follow-up of a *customer service* team. When all these elements of the chain successfully line up with each other and with the customer constituents, then, and only then, is value transmitted end to end, resulting in positive economic returns, which encourages the customer to reinvest in the solution, thereby starting a cycle of positive returns that makes a market.

In most value chains power migrates left and right along the chain depending on where the technology is in its life cycle, and at no time does any one company get a persistent hammerlock on the other members of the chain. We'll be tracing those dynamics in Part IV, which covers the technology adoption life cycle. But from time to time events unfold in a way that does lead to the emergence of a gorilla. Inevitably the Justice Department takes issue with this sort of power, and to be sure, it is subject to abuse. Nonetheless, it is important to see that it evolves naturally wherever power positions cross over a tipping point and become market-defining. In high tech this happens faster and more radically than in other industries, hence it has been a major target for antitrust forces. But at the end of the day much of this advantage is legal, and all of it is attractive to investors looking for high GAPs and long CAPs.

Which leads us to a final question. When such power monopolies emerge, can any force overthrow them other than regulatory intervention? Yes, one market-based force can: *category advantage.*

CATEGORY ADVANTAGE

Markets self-organize into categories once offers attract enough customers to "make a market," that is, to bring into existence a value chain of suppliers. At this point, there is enough interest and enough money changing hands for both customers and vendors to take the opportunity seriously, each baking commitments to that effect into next year's operating plans. These commitments lead suppliers to compete with one another for top-dog status in their specific niche in the chain. At the same time, there is also a higher-level competition to determine which roles in the chain get to call the shots. If a company cannot only rise to power in its niche role, but also establish that role as the power broker for the whole chain, then it can increase its competitive advantage both dramatically and rapidly. And that is the essence of category power.

Category power, in its most dramatic manifestation, is the ability of a company to "surf the wave" of a category's adoption life cycle, to ride it from obscurity to prominence. Companies on this wave inherit the GAP and CAP of the new category. Indeed, they become the vehicle by which investors put money into that category. As the category passes through the technology adoption life cycle, and in particular when it reaches the hypergrowth tornado stage, both GAP and CAP increase dramatically in a very short time. This creates the most dramatic appreciations in stock price ever seen and throws into the limelight management teams whose skills are not remarkably different from those of their peers, but whose timing and luck is.

In this hypergrowth phase, where the disruptive effects are most intense, new categories create what Clay Christensen has called the "innovator's dilemma," a paradoxical form of paralysis in which the incumbent market leaders are self-prevented from competing in the new market category. We'll have a lot more to say about this phenomenon later on in the book, but for right now, let us examine it from the point of view of impact on shareholder value.

Put yourself in the place of the incumbent management team. You are not dumb. You see the new category emerging and you are perfectly aware of the threat that it poses. Why then do you not invest aggressively in it?

The answer, in simplest terms, is that to do so would *violate your covenant with your existing investors.* They want to see the best return on their invested capital. A dollar spent toward reinforcing your existing position in the current marketplace creates such a return. It reinforces both your GAP and your CAP within that category. A dollar spent on the disruptive category creates no near-term returns and may in fact help undercut your established position. That is, to the degree the new category is perceived to have become endorsed, it hastens the demise of the old category, hastening the demise of your established GAP and CAP. To be sure, there is some promise of new GAP and CAP around the new category, but you are trading in a "sure thing" for a lottery ticket, and thus your discount for risk will escalate dramatically.

Now some investors may want to play both sides of this opportunity, but if they do, most would like to invest in separate companies to do so. It is the very scarce investor who actually supports management, when confronted with two roads diverging in a yellow wood, to actually take both. They want you instead to stay on your established route. And this may not be bad strategy, for the new paradigm may not cross the chasm, in which case staying on course was the winning play. So it is that the innovator's dilemma, which is often criticized as a failure in management leadership or imagination, is actually a form of managing for shareholder value.

That said, there are ways that established companies can have their cake and eat it too, and it is the goal of this book to demonstrate them.

SUMMING UP

Once the hypergrowth wave has crested and the category has become established, then category power has exerted its primary impact on valuation change. Going forward, industry power will once again be the dominant form of competitive advantage, followed by customer power, and then offer power. This is the basic logic of the Competitive Advantage Hierarchy.

It argues for the following generic strategy principles:

1. If you can catch a new category-formation wave, by all means do: this is the fastest path to valuation appreciation and it protects you against being rendered obsolete.

2. In category maturation, if you can achieve industry power, it is the most valuable form of competitive advantage to secure, and you should do whatever it takes to get it.

3. If in the process some other company gains industry advantage, then reframe your market focus to go for customer power, using niche-market boundaries to create defensible barriers against the stronger competitor.

4. In either case, once you have an advantaged position in an established market, if that market comes under attack by a disruptive innovation, do whatever you can to disrupt the disruption. That is your best chance to sustain shareholder value.

5. If you cannot disrupt the disruption, then accept that you will have to face unhappy investors regardless of what path you take forward.

6. Throughout all of the machinations described above, remember that customers can only buy offers at the end of the day, and so maintain an investment in offer power throughout. Just don't rely on it exclusively.

All of these principles address what kind of advantage one should seek and why. None address how a company could actually gain that advantage. To that end, we need to turn to the next chapter and its discussion of *value disciplines*.

5

THE FOUR VALUE DISCIPLINES

The Competitive Advantage Hierarchy supplies the four columns of the Competitive Advantage Grid. The four rows of the model are supplied by the four value disciplines. This may come as a bit of a shock to promoters and practitioners of the value discipline model, as it is generally agreed that there are only three. I hope these constituencies will bear with me for the remainder of this chapter, understanding that I bear the model no ill will and intend it no harm. I just think a fourth discipline is in the wings that deserves equal time onstage.

The strategic idea behind value disciplines is that companies create competitive advantage through differentiation and achieve that differentiation by disproportionately investing in a particular discipline to a point that a more balanced strategy cannot match. Take the pizza business. Domino's pizza disproportionately invests in delivery capability so that it can make a "fastest to your door" customer experience that differentiates it from its competitors. Little Caesar, by contrast, disproportionately invests in cost management so that it can make an economical "two for $9.99" offer. In neither case are these companies competing on pizza quality, or what value discipline experts would call *product leadership*. Instead, Domino's is competing on *customer intimacy* and Little Caesar on *operational excellence*. In their advertising, Round Table tries to stake out the product leadership position ("the last honest pizza" emphasizing fresh ingredients), but operating as a focus group of one, I would give the nod to Frankie, Johnny, and Luigi Too, at least in Silicon Valley.

In any event, operational excellence, customer intimacy, and product leadership are the three classic value disciplines. The need for a fourth comes to us when a company like Chuck E. Cheese emerges. This is a pizza restaurant where animatronic entertainment is its claim to fame: it is differentiating, in other words, outside the space of normal pizza industry variables. We call such a strategy *disruptive innovation*. It attacks a known flow of dollars along a known value chain by substituting something from outside instead of within the category. In so doing it seeks to hijack the economics of the segment from the established value chain participants.

This last discipline is critical to understanding the impact of technology on established industries. It takes very little time, when looking at upstarts like Internet retail, digital photography, or voice-over-IP, to see that the challengers have little to no operational excellence, customer intimacy, or product leadership, assuming one is comparing features and functions available in the market today. So how to explain the ability of these intruders to capture investment capital and customer enthusiasm? How indeed? In fact, most established companies simply throw up their hands and complain of the irrationality of the world or say they have been "outmarketed" somehow. This in turn creates the breeding ground for Christensen's innovator's dilemma, because how can one respond to something that begs any response?

Once one understands disruptive innovation as a fourth value discipline, however, one can train one's sights on it and build an appropriate competitive response. As we will see in Part IV, this strategy has a gaping weakness, namely the challenge of crossing the chasm, during which incumbents have numerous opportunities to disrupt the formation of the new value chain or, better yet, co-opt it for their own purposes. At the same time, once formalized, disruptive innovation can also be launched from within an incumbent position, as HP ink-jet printers did within the HP LaserJet franchise, which can be hugely powerful. The challenges here, however, can be every bit as great, and this will make for the material covered in Part V.

For now, let us gain a deeper sense of how each value-discipline strategy plays out in a technology-enabled marketplace.

OPERATIONAL EXCELLENCE

Operational excellence seeks to differentiate from others in category through superior execution as measured by productivity and ultimately by price. It is most successful when the offering can be commoditized, thereby neutralizing the power of product leadership, and when it is context rather than core, thereby neutralizing the power of customer intimacy. Outsourcing of virtually any type, therefore, is a natural ground for differentiating through operational excellence. Mass production represents another venue for the same, as does megastore retailing of commodity items.

The key to operational excellence is a focus on *process*. Using disciplines like value chain reengineering, management meticulously identifies the minimum set of attributes required by the customer and then ruthlessly expunges any step in production that does not directly contribute to one or another of these attributes. Even within steps, it seeks to root out any subactivity that does not explicitly add value. It then looks closely at sources and uses of funds, seeking to get the funds paid in earlier, and seeking to eliminate or defer outlays of funds as long as possible. Thus just-in-time inventory management, advanced supply-chain planning, and vendor-managed inventory are all attempts to make uses of funds for inventory more productive.

One of the corollaries of a focus on process is a focus on *timing*. Operationally excellent organizations attend to rhythm first, speed second. Once rhythm is achieved, then cycle times can be ratcheted up systematically to optimal levels. The critical metric is volume of quality output consistently over time as opposed to intense spurts of effort with diving catches in the end zone.

Process focus works best in situations that are repetitive where output quality can be measured objectively and statistical quality-control techniques applied. In addition to mass manufacturing, this also includes service operations such as claims processing or consumer banking transactions, crowd control at theme parks, or forms processing by governmental organizations. It is more challenging to apply the discipline to project-oriented businesses where a high degree of customization is built into the work and where quality measures are more subjective. That said, however, the imaginative application of operational excellence, or for that matter any value discipline, outside its normal boundaries often results in exceptional differentiation.

Success in operational excellence is measured by reducing the number of misses rather than increasing the number of hits. This aligns it with handling the context work for customers and not with helping them with their core. The ultimate accolade of *six sigma* simply means that defects represent a minute fraction of the throughput, and *zero defect tolerance* is simply a mechanism for stimulating the continued process refinement necessary to reach a six-sigma outcome.

Inherent in this approach is the notion of navigating by data. Specifically, output attributes are correlated with process parameters to locate and reengineer sources of defect. Throughout this effort everyone is made to understand it is the system, not the individual, that is being criticized and improved. Individual acts of heroic service are not only not required, they are undesirable, for they mask flaws in the underlying system and thus delay arrival at the six-sigma destination.

As we shall see in the final section of the book, operational excellence is the value discipline most aligned with *control* cultures, and it is often found with such cultures in finance organizations, as well as manufacturing, logistics, data centers, and anywhere else in the enterprise where a high volume of repetitive tasks makes up the bulk of the workflow. When it is elevated from its natural departmental seats to be the overriding source of corporate differentiation, that calls for all the other elements in the enterprise who are not naturally drawn to the value discipline to imaginatively redefine their operations through its lens.

What would it mean, for example, to have operationally excellent R and D? It might turn out that you can in fact reform R and D through a process focus, reducing scrap and rework through a series of stage-gate reviews, for example. Or it may be that R and D is intractable in this respect, that it is inherently haphazard, in which case it might be core work that should be subcontracted to a partner. What would it mean to have an operationally excellent sales force? Again, some organizations impose process discipline through adoption of sales force automation software or other aids to systematic pipeline management. When they succeed, this is highly differentiating as the default preference of sales organizations is much more individualistic, much less predictable.

Overall, the goal of operational excellence is to minimize variability and maximize predictability, and it is most distinctive as a strategy where these goals are hardest to achieve.

CUSTOMER INTIMACY

Companies elevating customer intimacy as their primary strategy seek to differentiate from others within their category through superior matching of customer expectation with offer fulfillment, thereby justifying a pricing premium based on greater perceived and received value. When the offer is core to a business customer, this means fielding superior domain expertise in a consultative sales and service relationship leading to tailored offers that solve the customer's problem end to end. When the offer is context to a business customer, the premium comes from taking the entire monkey off the customer's back so that the customer simply does not have to worry about it. In consumer marketing, there is a similar parallel. When the offer is core to the customer—say, a key piece of their identity theme—then personal service and tailoring are key. When it is context, then automated personalization based on prior history can create the same hassle-reducing outcome that business customers appreciate.

The focus throughout is on the *customer experience,* both of the offer and the transaction, including both presales and postsales service. Indeed, advocates of this approach claim that all offers are really experiences in hiding, that people do not want to buy a drill so much as they want to buy holes, not mouthwash but fresher breath, not hip clothing but acceptance as being hip. Customer intimacy works best when the offer is relatively commoditized, reducing the impact of product leadership, and where discretionary funds are available to pay the premium, thereby warranting the differentiation from pure price-driven operational excellence. In all cases the key is superior knowledge of the customer's domain and personal expectations and values, combined with the ability to customize the offer to capitalize on this knowledge.

One of the corollaries of this strategy is a focus on *response time* calibrated by the interval between the customer's becoming aware of a need or an opportunity and the vendor's being able to present the offering that matches. The more context the offer, the shorter the interval the customer will tolerate, which is why so many abandoned shopping carts litter the Internet retail highway. Customers are willing to grant significantly more time when the offer is core, but they also set the bar higher for making the match. To meet these demands at scale companies must embrace a strategy of *mass customization*, in which they can premake the offer and stage it for final configuration and customization at the point of purchase. This is in itself a form of operational excellence, focused on earning a premium as opposed to increasing a discount.

Customer intimacy works best when the buyer and the user are one and the same, as they are in most consumer purchases. In business buying of technology-enabled offers, by contrast, the strategy demands a two-pronged approach to direct sales, one thrust toward the technical community, the other toward the line-of-business executives whose workflow will be altered. Managing these two efforts concurrently, often when the two constituencies are at odds with each other and jealous of your involvement with the other, is a real challenge. The other major challenge is that domain expertise is scarce, customer-sensitive representatives even scarcer, and both are hard to scale. As a result this strategy tends to work best in niche markets where the need to scale is curtailed by the size and structure of the market itself.

In direct contrast to operational excellence, success in customer intimacy is measured by the number of hits, not the number of misses, and additionally by the depth of impact of each hit. The result of these hits is a buildup of relationship equity in the customer's mind that justifies both paying a premium for your offer and staying loyal to you voluntarily when a competing vendor offers a better deal. Because this equity is intangible, it is hard to reduce customer impact to numerical data, and the more common currency of information is the representative anecdote, be it a voice mail, letter, or videotaped testimonial. Again, in direct contrast to operational excellence, here acts of service heroism are cherished as exemplifying the go-to-any-lengths nature of the commitment to the customer.

Customer intimacy strategies work best in *collaboration* cultures where the customer's problem or need becomes the focusing element of the collaborative effort. Indeed these cultures excel in involving the customer in all phases of their business, from planning and design through to disposal at end of life. Marketing and customer service are the natural home for such efforts. When customer intimacy is extended to engineering and product development, it is typically only after the underlying technology has become fully assimilated and future value is more likely to be created by making surface modifications to the offer. When it is extended into the operational areas of logistics or finance, there is similar need to isolate the customer-touching surface from the underlying transaction flow, such that the former may be customized without the latter becoming disrupted. This is the challenge facing all companies who want to Web-enable their customer relationships without destroying their core efficiency and effectiveness.

Overall the goal of customer intimacy is to optimize offerings in relation to the customer's experience as opposed to optimizing the means of production, the goal of operational excellence, or optimizing the competitive performance of the offer itself, which is the goal of product leadership, to which we shall now turn.

PRODUCT LEADERSHIP

Product leadership strategies seek to differentiate from others within the same category through superior design and engineering leading to superior performance warranting a premium price. This strategy is most effective when the offer is used in mission-critical applications, either core or context, as that is where performance characteristics are most highly valued. In this way it can distance itself from lower-cost commodity-level performance achieved through operational excellence and minimize the significance of a superior buying experience by emphasizing the criticality of actual offer performance. When the offer is not used in a mission-critical application, it is much harder for this strategy to earn the premium price it needs to underwrite its high-cost R and D focus.

The focus of product leadership is on quality as measured by the performance attributes of the offer itself. In technology-enabled offers, these attributes are created primarily during the design and engineering phases of product development, where the focus is on measurably improving the vectors of *better, faster,* and *cheaper.* Better, in turn, often means smaller, lighter, and longer-lasting, as the competitions in cell phones, laptops, and digital cameras make clear.

Because product leadership is inherently competitive and comparative, a focus on time to market—specifically relative to actual or potential competitive product releases—is critical to its success. In performance-driven markets, the company first to market with the next generation of product garners a disproportionate share of the total profits over the life of that product generation. Latecomers must increasingly compete on price, which in turn drives everyone's margins down, but the first-comer who has the market all to itself has a precious few months to win the critical premium margins. As product life-cycle times shrink, more and more pressure is put on first-to-market outcomes such that winning strategy frequently is to abandon a product generation if one is clearly behind and try to leapfrog ahead to the next.

Product leadership strategies are most successful when the buyer is also an engineer and both understands and values the performance attributes achieved. As systems evolve, products inevitably become subordinated to overall system performance issues, and product leadership strategy begins to suffer from this subordination. Thus an established competitor with strong customer intimacy can often overcome an unfavorable comparison at the point product level by asserting superior overall performance at the systems level, diluting the impact of any one product across a whole value chain of products and services. Elsewhere, as more and more competitors match the performance attributes achieved, the offer becomes commoditized, and product leadership must either move on to the next generation or cede the field to operational excellence.

Success in product leadership is based on comparing objectively measurable attributes, the kind of data that engineers like to call "speeds and feeds," all duly recorded on the product data sheet. Framed as such, the first marketing challenge is to beat the competition on the numbers within the given time frame. That said, the next major challenge is to ensure that customers translate these enhancements into application value, turning features into benefits, thereby justifying the price premium sought. Product leadership strategies go astray when they become obsessed with the competitor and overshoot the performance level the market can productively assimilate.

Product leadership works best in *competence* cultures where outperforming the competition is a core focus. It is most commonly found in design and engineering organizations. It also gains strong support in sales organizations when the focus is beating the competitor as opposed to serving the customer. This occurs primarily during the hypergrowth phase of the technology adoption life cycle. Having bragging rights to the best product is a boon during such competitions.

To sum up, while the goals of operational excellence and customer intimacy include a deprioritization of product in favor of other systems—the system of production in the first case, the system of customer relationships in the second—the goal of product leadership is to reassert the priority of product as the primary source of value delivery.

DISRUPTIVE INNOVATION

Whereas the other three value disciplines differentiate from one another within an existing set of market dynamics, each accepting and reinforcing the legitimacy of the other two, disruptive innovation takes a more revolutionary path. It says in effect the best way to proceed is with a wholly different approach, what is often meant by "thinking outside the box." The strategy is amplified when it is enabled by discontinuous technology such as digital photography, cellular telephony, or microprocessors, one that creates effects that are simply not matchable by the existing technology infrastructure. But one can create disruptive innovation without discontinuous technology, as we shall see in the next chapter when we discuss companies like Federal Express and Charles Schwab.

The focus of disruptive innovation is imaginative engineering or "imagineering," the ability to create something out of nothing, something unprecedented. This entails a series of recruiting activities: recruit the seed team, recruit the seed capital, recruit the seed customers, and finally, when it comes time to cross the chasm, recruit the capital required to cross it and the companies needed to seed the value chain on the other side. In every case, what carries the day is a vision of the possibilities communicated so persuasively that people bet on the outcome despite whatever conservative instincts they may have.

As with the other disciplines, time plays a critical factor here as well, in two places. The first is time to market with the first definitive demonstration of the new technology. Here sooner is better, and soonest is best. The second is timing the chasm crossing. Here one must assess the readiness of an emerging value chain to provide the *whole product*, for with disruptive technologies the challenge is not only to make your product or service work but to orchestrate all the other market changes to make the end-to-end solution work as well. At this transition point disruptive innovations are painfully vulnerable, and counterattacks by incumbents normally focus here.

Disruptive innovations are most successful when they can promise what Andy Grove calls a 10X change in a factor critical to some industry's competitive advantage. Seen in this light they appeal to visionary line-of-business executives, particularly those leading an organization that is currently back in the pack, looking for a way to leapfrog to the front. Conversely, these same innovations struggle when they seek adoption from companies that are winning in the current round of competition or when sponsorship is sought not from the line-of-business side but rather the infrastructure managers. So many things can go wrong implementing a disruptive innovation that only the most motivated leaders are willing to take on the challenge.

The first metric of success for disruptive innovation is to enable at least one flagship customer to achieve the 10X competitive advantage. This puts the category on the map for everyone in the marketplace—potential prospects, partners, investors, and competitors. The second metric is to successfully establish a viable niche market such that all customers within the niche acknowledge the need for the new solution, leading to repeatable sales throughout the segment, creating the kind of steady stream of business needed to create and sustain a value chain specializing in fulfilling the solution requirements end to end. As a corollary to this second metric, the sponsor of the disruptive innovation should succeed in installing itself as the de facto standard for its own portion of the overall solution, with the stretch goal of becoming the market-controlling company that orchestrates the value chain and is able thereby to claim additional tribute from the others in the chain.

Disruptive innovation appears most often in *cultivation* cultures where the core focus is on breaking the mold. Typically these are venture-backed companies where everyone involved, employees and investors alike, gain big rewards if the high-risk effort comes off. Typically these companies take on two colorings. For innovations that require deep science, there is a technical founding team, often coming out of academia, which needs a lot of help with the business side of entrepreneurship. Alternatively, for innovations that are rooted in reengineering an ineffective business process, the founding team is often based in customer domain expertise, and it is the technical side that needs help. In either case, venture capital must be prepared not just to fund the fledgling enterprise but to backfill its management needs in the short term, until it gains sufficient traction to recruit a full team, and then help the founders recognize and recruit the top talent required to go forward. All in all this is quite a challenge and a key reason why venture capital does not scale well.

The overall goal of disruptive innovation is to create a new source of competitive advantage, and its primary form of compensation is in rapid appreciation in market capitalization. This is particularly evident when it is focused on creating category advantage. That is, not only does the first company into the category get credit for its

own GAP and CAP, it also inherits the lion's share of the category's
GAP and CAP, at least until some other company can come along and
prove why not. To be sure, in recent years investors have been chastened with respect to attributing future earnings too readily and paying too little attention to determining an appropriate discount for
risk. But when a new category does genuinely emerge, and a single
company does genuinely achieve an early dominant position, then
there is every reason to believe that a genuinely new stream of future
earnings has been created with that company due a disproportionate
share. That is the fundamental basis for venture capital's returns, and
it has stood up over thirty years in the high-tech sector.

SUMMING UP

The following table summarizes the major defining differences
among the four value disciplines:

	Operational Excellence	Customer Intimacy	Product Leadership	Disruptive Innovation
Focus	Process efficiency	Customer experience	Offer quality	Categorical differentiation
Orientation to time	Internal timing (rhythm)	Customer response time	Competitive response time	Time to adoption
Key metric	Number of misses	Number of hits	Product specifications	10X advantage
Culture fit	Control culture	Collaboration culture	Competence culture	Cultivation culture
Organizational leadership from	Operations, Finance	Marketing, Customer support	Sales, Engineering	R and D

All companies need to meet some level of acceptable perform-ance in all four value disciplines as part of minimum market stan-dards. After that, best strategy proposes that companies overachieve in one of the four areas as a means of differentiating themselves from the others in their category. Which discipline to choose is a function of multiple factors, the strongest of which are the state of the technology adoption life cycle at the time and the core compe-tence of the organization making the choice.

In the third and concluding chapter of this section, we are going to examine how the intersection and interaction between the value discipline focus of this chapter and the competitive advan-tage focus of the prior chapter creates a matrix of sixteen different strategies. We are not sure this represents the universe of all possi-ble strategies, but we do think it is a rich enough model to be a proxy for the same. As such we encourage management teams to locate both their past and their future strategies on this grid, along with those of their primary competitors, with the goal of focusing their execution programs accordingly.

With that thought in mind, let us turn now to the Competitive Advantage Grid.

6

THE COMPETITIVE ADVANTAGE GRID

The purpose of the competitive advantage grid is to display an array of targets from which a management team can select its *core focus*. Ideally, this will consist of a single square on the grid calling out the strategy that will drive the greatest increase in shareholder value. Each square carries with it its own risk/reward ratio and not all squares are available in all situations or to all comers. Sometimes, an attractive square is already occupied by a competitor, and management must decide whether to compete directly for that ground or seek another focal point. Strategy development thus intersects market realities, with the grid offering a lens through which to view both strengths and weaknesses, both opportunities and threats.

Specifically the Competitive Advantage Grid is formed by the intersection of the four types of competitive advantage with the four value disciplines for creating differentiation.

Readers will note that seven of the squares have a gray background, signifying that all these strategies are inherently unstable. That is, if any strategy in the category-creation column is successful, as the category becomes established, it will develop its own three-by-three "white grid" going forward. Similarly, if any strategy in the disruptive-innovation row is successful, it too will become institutionalized over time and "join the white grid," subdividing into versions emphasizing operational excellence, customer inti-

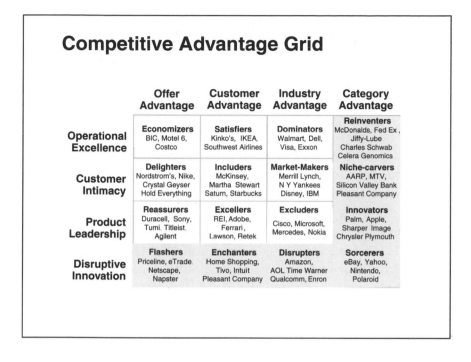

Competitive Advantage Grid

	Offer Advantage	Customer Advantage	Industry Advantage	Category Advantage
Operational Excellence	Economizers BIC, Motel 6, Costco	Satisfiers Kinko's, IKEA, Southwest Airlines	Dominators Walmart, Dell, Visa, Exxon	Reinventers McDonalds, Fed Ex, Jiffy-Lube Charles Schwab Celera Genomics
Customer Intimacy	Delighters Nordstrom's, Nike, Crystal Geyser Hold Everything	Includers McKinsey, Martha Stewart Saturn, Starbucks	Market-Makers Merrill Lynch, N Y Yankees Disney, IBM	Niche-carvers AARP, MTV, Silicon Valley Bank Pleasant Company
Product Leadership	Reassurers Duracell, Sony, Tumi, Titleist, Agilent	Excellers REI, Adobe, Ferrari, Lawson, Retek	Excluders Cisco, Microsoft, Mercedes, Nokia	Innovators Palm, Apple, Sharper Image Chrysler Plymouth
Disruptive Innovation	Flashers Priceline, eTrade, Netscape, Napster	Enchanters Home Shopping, Tivo, Intuit Pleasant Company	Disrupters Amazon, AOL Time Warner Qualcomm, Enron	Sorcerers eBay, Yahoo, Nintendo, Polaroid

macy, or product leadership. All entrants from the gray squares are committed to destabilizing existing value chains occupying the three-by-three grid of white squares. It is critical, therefore, that all companies—both disrupters and defenders—be aware of these options as well as all the others, as they go to build their own competitive advantage strategy.

Turning to the grid as a whole, note that each square is tagged with a name and a set of representative companies. Neither is intended to be exclusive of other possibilities. Both are intended to be representative of the kind of competitive advantage that can be sustained in that square. And all sixteen squares are intended to be distinctively different from each other so that strategy development can proceed as an act focusing within a charted field.

We'll talk more at the end of this chapter about how strategic planning efforts can utilize the grid, but before doing so, we need to take a closer look at its details.

THE OPERATIONAL EXCELLENCE STRATEGIES

All the strategies in this top row of the model focus on using *process innovation* as the critical lever for creating competitive advantage.

1. ECONOMIZERS: *THE LOW-COST PROVIDER*

Companies that use operational excellence to create offer advantage include Bic, the makers of Bic pens and lighters, Motel 6 ("No mint on the pillow, but we'll leave the light on for you."), and Costco, a retail wholesaler. Also in this category are all the generic brands in your local supermarket or local PC store.

The game here is to win on price and still have enough margin left over to pay your investors an acceptable return on capital. The strategy is to construct and deliver to the minimum commodity level and not a whit further and to ruthlessly eliminate any expenditure of resource that is not directly on that path. Waste, in the form of scrap or rework, is the enemy, and process design, followed up with process discipline, is the method for eliminating it.

The good news for investors here is that there is a low discount for risk. That is, the strategy aims at large, preexisting markets where lowest price is always a significant value proposition. The bad news is that the company is subject to attack from all sides, both from ongoing competitors and distressed inventory dumpers, so that earning even bond-level returns is a big challenge.

For most companies, therefore, this is the square they most want to avoid. Ironically, however, it is also the square of last resort, the place we end up when competitors have thwarted one or another of our more ambitious strategies. So it is a rare management team that does not have to play this game at one time or another in its career.

2. SATISFIERS: *SAVE TIME* AND *MONEY*

Companies that use operational excellence to create customer advantage include Kinko's, the "office" for self-employed entrepreneurs working out of a spare bedroom; IKEA, the furniture people who let you assemble it yourself; and Southwest Airlines, the no-frills folks who invented fast, fair check-in. Also in this category are the banks who brought us ATMs and all the government Web sites on which folks pay fines or get permits over the Internet.

The strategy here is to use process expertise to create a better customer experience, all the while reducing rather than increasing one's own costs. Wherever bureaucracy has been allowed to become institutionalized, this strategy has a terrific opportunity because bureaucracy puts the convenience of the position holder ahead of the interests of the customer. Not surprisingly, this strategy often leads to a self-service operation where customers discover, once again, that the people who care most and understand best what they want and need are they themselves.

What is delightful to investors about this strategy is that it garners customer loyalty, and thus better returns, without increased expenditures. What is not so delightful is that competitors are often quick to copy these measures so that, over time, what used to differentiate now becomes market standard, and a new wave of process redesign must be rolled out.

3. DOMINATORS: *SIZE MATTERS*

Companies that use operational excellence to create industry advantage include Wal-Mart, Dell, Visa, and Exxon. All these companies have created superior earnings by squeezing out costs not only from their own operations but from their suppliers' operations as well.

The key to the dominator strategy is to impose a process discipline on the rest of the value chain that it voluntarily embraces and to extract sustainable competitive advantages from so doing. At the core of these advantages is control over the scarce resource in the ecosystem, typically the customer, although in Exxon's case it is a natural resource instead. Leveraging that control, the dominator then rearchitects that value chain for optimal throughput, wringing out process and market inefficiencies, forcing these best practices onto its suppliers, then passing on to the customer a better value, all the while withholding for itself and its shareholders a premium return. This is not a way to make friends. It is, however, a proven way to make money.

What investors love about this strategy is that it creates increasing returns, meaning that as more customers go to the dominator, more competitors drop out or redefine their businesses such that still more customers go to the dominator. A key challenge is that it must continue to grow aggressively, which competitors in new geographies lobby to block, and it must grow for the most part organically rather than by acquisition, since its own processes are its key competitive advantage ingredient. Eventually, the inertia of size creates a crisis, forcing a change in structure, and potentially therefore, a change in strategy.

4. REINVENTORS: A BETTER WAY

Companies that have used operational excellence to create category advantage include McDonald's (fast food), Federal Express (overnight delivery), Jiffy Lube (car servicing while you wait), Charles Schwab (discount brokerage), and Celera Genomics (mass manufacturing of gene sequencing).

In every case, the driving force was a conviction that an established process model was inherently inefficient and could be reengineered not just for cost reduction but to create a whole new type of offering. There is something miraculous in each of these stories as the materials for creating the category were ready for anyone who had the imagination and vision to reassemble them.

What investors love about reinventors is that they can attack large markets with a highly differentiated offering that earns a premium margin because the other players in the market simply cannot organize a competitive response. (It may seem odd to think about McDonald's today as having a differentiated offering, but at the time it was introduced, fast food was a wholly new way of eating, especially attractive to teenagers and parents with kids.) What investors have learned about reinventors over the long term is that, as the category becomes institutionalized, the company must migrate to a strategy "in the white space" or suffer displacement along the lines, for example, of what UPS has done to Federal Express.

THE CUSTOMER INTIMACY STRATEGIES

All the strategies in this row of the model leverage *customer relationship innovation* as the critical enabler of competitive advantage.

1. DELIGHTERS: *WE GET IT*

Companies that use customer intimacy to create offer advantage include Nordstrom, Nike, Crystal Geyser, and Hold Everything. Also included in this category are the host of small business service providers who win our patronage by remembering our names or going the extra mile to make our lives a bit easier.

In the case of the public-company mass-market efforts, value creation begins with a deep analysis of the target customer's experience, be it during the transaction (Nordstrom), during its use (Nike), during its selection (Crystal Geyser), or during the pre-selection decision-making (Hold Everything). The company then spends its best resources on creating a sustainable differentiation at that point, be it from salesperson behavior (Nordstrom), aspirational branding (Nike), reassurance branding (Crystal Geyser), or depth of selection (Hold Everything).

What investors like about this strategy is that the value it generates is not a function of cost, which allows for higher margins *if* the company can dramatically outexecute the others in its category trying the same thing. This is a challenge that only a few companies succeed at. Those that do, however, particularly those that build sustainable brands, are some of the highest value creators in industry.

2. INCLUDERS: *WELCOME TO THE CLUB*

Companies that use customer intimacy to create customer advantage include McKinsey, Martha Stewart, Starbucks, and Saturn (this last company perhaps more for its attempt than actual success). Also included are institutions like Ivy League colleges, private banks, the Mayo Clinic, and clubs of all sorts.

The essence of this strategy is building a bond with the customer that precludes competition and to use that as a platform to initiate opportunities proactively. Thus McKinsey, Martha Stewart, and Starbucks do not compete against other companies except in a macroeconomic sense. Instead their customers treat them as their sole source of whatever they provide, and they welcome them coming in and telling them what they should do, buy, or drink next. That permission comes from their having generated such cachet in their respective fields that they are perceived as an entry portal into a community to which their customers aspire. In effect customer and company each include the other in an exclusive relationship. Saturn is the outlier here: while it made a marvelous run at this, peaking with a pilgrimage to the factory back in the middle 1990s, for a variety of reasons it was unable to sustain the effort and has now fallen back into an Economizer position.

What investors love about cachet is that it has the highest return on assets imaginable. What keeps them up at night is that it is a fragile substance, as any rock star or onetime media darling can testify. Institutionalizing cachet is very close to an oxymoron, and so it is that the mystiques of yesterday, particularly evident in retail brands in clothing, become the discounts of today. And even the most venerated institutions must find ways to renew their substance or else fall from grace.

3. MARKET MAKERS: *CONNECTIONS MATTER*

Companies that use customer intimacy to create industry advantage include Merrill Lynch, the New York Yankees, Disney, and IBM, and more generally, any company that makes the market in their industry or niche and does so by bringing the customer to the table.

The core of this strategy is to leverage customer connections to gain power over the rest of the value chain, becoming in essence the gatekeeper to whom tribute must be paid to get to the party. Connections, therefore, are key. IBM and Merrill Lynch are examples of *trusted adviser connections,* earned over multiple decades of delivering to a strong standard. Disney and the Yankees are examples of *brand connections,* forged in the depths of the personal and collective psyche, again over multiple decades of delivering to a strong standard. Once bonds to the customer are established, leveraging those connections becomes key. Working the rest of the value chain, trading favors, playing rivals off against each other, constructing deals to lock in ongoing rewards—it's an art form that these companies have excelled at.

Investors love industry power in any form, but what they love especially about market makers is that they are so deeply entrenched in the market's structure that they enjoy built-in advantages their competitors simply cannot match. Investors' biggest concern about these companies is that they are so advantaged as to become fat and happy, allowing them to take their customer relationships for granted, eventually causing their position to erode.

4. NICHE CARVERS: *SPECIAL NEEDS*

Companies that have used customer intimacy to create category advantage include the American Association of Retired Persons, MTV, and Silicon Valley Bank. All have created new categories of business by focusing intensely on the special needs of a marginalized customer group and by so doing creating persistent customer loyalty with high barriers to competitive entry.

The key notion here is that society self-organizes into a myriad of microcommunities characterized by idiosyncratic shared interests. Companies who specialize in addressing those interests in a highly differentiated way gain a virtually exclusive relationship with the customers that make up that niche and can expand their businesses by meeting more and more needs going forward.

What investors love about this strategy is that it is high-margin forever because the customer is so loyal to the vendor's in reward for the vendor giving deep loyalty back. They also love that these markets are "discovered in plain sight," meaning there is little market development cost and almost no market risk in going after them. What they are concerned about is the limits on absolute scale, for while niches can create entries into other niches, many companies who win in this strategy later fall prey to overexpansion leading to brand dilution and loss of high-margin status.

THE PRODUCT LEADERSHIP STRATEGIES

All the strategies in this row leverage *performance innovation* to create superior performance characteristics in a product offering.

1. REASSURERS: *THE SAFE BUY*

Companies that use product leadership to create offer advantage include Duracell, Sony, Tumi, Titleist, and Agilent. Every one of these companies has designed one or more industry-leading offerings such that now their brand has come to stand for the safe buy in their respective categories.

The core of this strategy is to invest heavily in R and D to come out with the strongest offer as the product category moves into its first wave of high growth. Catching that first wave and winning the first competition is critical to getting mass exposure as the "right choice." Going forward, these brands are most successful in categories with long life, for that simply extends the period of advantaged returns. Thus HP's ink-jet printers have fared much better than Motorola's cell phones because the former's category is still thriving whereas the latter's fell prey to the technology disruption caused by wireless converting from analog to digital transmission.

Investors are impressed by the scalability of these markets, their sheer size, and the reward they give to products and consumables. They are also impressed by the CAPs of leaders in nondisrupted categories where brand inertia creates ongoing high margins and relatively low ongoing R and D investment. The concern they have is that those margins often get reinvested in speculative R and D investments on next-wave opportunities that do not pan out.

2. EXCELLERS: *THE VERY BEST*

Companies that use product leadership to create customer advantage include Recreation Equipment Incorporated, Adobe, Ferrari, Lawson Software, and Retek. REI makes mountain-climbing gear for teams that take on Mount Everest; Adobe makes software for professional illustrators; Ferrari makes race cars. All have leveraged their investments in leading edge into mass-market positions for consumers who aspire to those goals. By contrast, Lawson Software and Retek are both, by total sales, second-tier enterprise software suppliers, but each has focused on a particular niche—health care and retail, respectively—to become the gorilla in the niche by overdelivering on the needs of their target segment.

The key to this strategy is to go the extra mile in a market where that approach will only pay returns if the vendor gains dominant market share and can defend it against subsequent attack. Large established companies have trouble generating the focus required to launch this strategy and frankly can often get better returns on capital elsewhere, given their broad portfolios. But for companies in the next tier, as well as for companies willing to embrace a smaller total available market, this is a powerful way to differentiate sustainably.

Investors like sustainable market leadership positions of any kind; they are the most common basis for granting a given company a lower discount for risk and thus a higher stock-price multiple. Investors are nervous, however, about running out of headroom, fearful not that the earnings will falter but that growth will as the boundaries of the niche curtail direct expansion, as do competitors in adjacent niches.

3. EXCLUDERS: *GORILLAS AND KINGS*

Companies that use product leadership to create industry advantage include Cisco, Microsoft, Sun, and Nokia. Prior occupants of the sector include the Digital Corporation, Compaq, General Motors, and U.S. Steel.

The minimum entry qualification for this strategy is domination of a hypergrowth market, riding not just a product life cycle but a technology adoption life cycle to market-share leadership in a mass market. That qualifies you to be a *king*. As the list of prior occupants is intended to show, however, kings can be deposed. Thus, even though it seems a step backward in the evolutionary chain, it is actually preferable to be a *gorilla*. Gorillas have the added attribute of owning proprietary technology with high switching costs such that the market requires their ingredient and can get it from no other source. Of the examples cited, Microsoft has the highest degree of such exclusivity and is the most gorilla-like. This allows them to leverage their success within category to a larger success across the entire value chain, extracting tribute from everyone else in the chain. This is directly comparable to the market makers in the customer intimacy strategies and the dominators in the operational excellence strategies except that technology lock-in creates even more permanent dependencies.

Investors simply love gorillas. By contrast they love kings right up until the time they get deposed. That act of disappointment, accompanied by the ritual sacrifice of the CEO, effectively expels the company from the excluder square, and it is critical that management realize this and make a beeline for a more accommodating one. Unfortunately, most teams in this situation are still enamored of their pasts and try to re-create them, something no one else in the market will support.

4. INNOVATORS: *COOL!*

Companies that have used product leadership to create category advantage include Palm Computing, Sharper Image, Apple, and Daimler-Chrysler, as well as most venture-backed firms, many advertising agencies, bands creating new music categories (the last being reggae for my generation, which more than dates me), and movie production houses that succeed in backing—gasp!—original, nonsequel, nonremake films. All these are known for coming up with offerings, product lines, and design changes that lead the pack by a long shot.

The key to this strategy is design innovation accompanied either by deep market insight or great luck. Actually, a substitute for both might be *product taste*, something that the executives who champion these initiatives all have in common. Operationally, these companies give enormous design freedom to "creative" individuals who are assumed to be "crazy," not only by their competitors but by their peers and family members as well.

Traditional investors do not look kindly on this category, but more venturesome investors do. It is a "hits" business, not for the faint of heart. It is hard to incorporate this strategy into a traditional corporate portfolio, both financially and culturally. This is part of the root cause of the innovator's dilemma that we shall be taking on in Part V of this book.

THE DISRUPTIVE INNOVATION STRATEGIES

The fourth and final row of the grid is built around *discontinuous innovation* with a focus on entrepreneurship as a key enabling resource.

1. FLASHERS: *CHECK IT OUT!*

Companies that have used disruptive innovation to create offer advantage include Priceline, E*Trade, Netscape, and Napster. Each created an enormous splash upon launch and garnered widespread adoption in record time. Unfortunately, translating those early gains into a sustainable and profitable business is more than a little challenging. In order to gain market share rapidly, offers have to be "too good to be true," and sooner or later the customer has to be weaned away to more profitable transactions. Unfortunately, however, that typically undercuts the very offer advantage created, and the result is massive customer defection.

The key to this strategy is to get out while the getting is good. That is, there is no sustainable competitive advantage here, so the real question is which square to transition to. For some companies, the Economizer square is a possibility, for others the Enchanters, and for others, unfortunately, the correct outcome is simply to shut down and start over somewhere else.

Investors hate this square, as it tends to be all GAP no CAP—the financial representation, in other words, of a fad. Its inherent flaw is that it takes enormous risks in product and market development and then gains an insufficiently sustainable market position from which to pay back an appropriate return.

2. ENCHANTERS: *CHANGED MY LIFE!*

Companies that have used disruptive innovation to create customer advantage include Home Shopping Network, Intuit with its
Quicken line, TiVo with its TV replay product and service, and
Pleasant Company, which tied its American Girls doll and doll-
house lines to a series of books about girls set in various periods of
history, each book spawning a new market from within its existing
customer base. All these companies have created deep loyalty from
customers who continue to find ways to spend more money with
them.

At the core of this strategy is leveraging a profound insight into
social psychology into a radically innovative offering that really
speaks to its consumers. For Scott Cook, founder of Intuit, the
insight was that PC financial software doesn't compete against
other software packages but against a pen and paper. For Home
Shopping Network it was that some people really like being couch
potatoes. For Pleasant Company it was the realization that toys are
simply fantasies made concrete, and thus one could "vertically
integrate" by going upstream to create the fantasies first.

Investors often do not know what to make of enchanters
because their competitive advantage, and thus their value, is not
really a function of their category so much as of the business idea
working itself out within the category. Over time, to be sure, the
category will catch up to them, typically causing their position to
migrate to satisfiers, which makes them more readily investable
but also reduces their differentiation, and thereby the multiple
they can claim. But if management has been able to convert customer goodwill into brand loyalty, there can be long-term sustainable competitive advantage and thus a healthy market cap.

3. DISRUPTERS: *CHANGE THE RULES*

Companies that have used disruptive innovation to create industry
advantage include Amazon, AOL Time Warner, Qualcomm, and
(prior to its apparent corruption) Enron.

A key act of entrepreneurship here is keeping unwavering faith with a business model that all around you are decrying. That is one quality Jeff Bezos, Steve Case, and Irwin Jacobs all have in common. (The same was true at Enron, although at the end the model became overwhelmed by management chicanery.) What all these cases have in common is the use of a technological discontinuity to enable a heretofore impractical business practice, one that undermines the very foundations of the status quo.

Investors have a love-hate relationship with these companies because they destabilize *category* GAP and CAP even as they generate *company* GAP and CAP. Until the world settles down around the new order and formally admits them as the new leaders, a counterattack is always possible because powerful entrenched interests can often use their connections to protective legislation or the equivalent. That was the fate of the Competitive Local Exchange Carriers in their battle with the incumbents. This leads to the worst of all outcomes—a terribly battered industry in which even the leaders are weak investments.

4. SORCERERS: *CHANGE THE WORLD*

Companies that have used disruptive innovation to create category advantage include eBay, Yahoo, Nintendo, and Polaroid. Each of these companies was able to bring into existence a genuinely new category of business including a complete value chain of players all coming together around their offering. Yahoo and eBay have taken an open-systems approach here, helping to make markets for their partners, and using this market-making capability to enhance their position as industry leaders. By contrast, Nintendo and Polaroid took a closed-system approach, extracting more profit from the system, but making themselves ultimately more vulnerable to displacement.

Public investors are puzzled by sorcerers because they tend to be categories of one, and thus there are no direct comparables against which to benchmark their valuation. Private investors, especially venture capitalists, on the other hand, are overjoyed by these companies as they generate dramatic appreciation in shareholder value far earlier in their company history than other types.

USING THE COMPETITIVE ADVANTAGE GRID

Stepping back from the individual squares and looking at the Competitive Advantage Grid as a whole, we see sixteen different versions of the formula: *Use value discipline X to create competitive advantage type Y.* The question that remains is simply, what combination of X and Y will produce the best results for the operation your team is managing? Or to put it another way, the primary use of the Competitive Advantage Grid is to help management teams address the question, *How do we manage for shareholder value around here?*

When a management team constructs an answer to that question around a single square in the grid, everything that contributes to the type of advantage highlighted in the square is immediately identified as *core*, and reciprocally, everything else becomes identified as *context*. Management's top priority is thus starkly delineated: focus more and more of the company's scarce resources on the target square, migrating resources from all other squares as needed, thereby intensifying its competitive advantage, increasing both GAP and CAP, and creating a rise in stock price as a result.

In the real world this end point of clarity is rarely the starting point. Management teams typically see themselves in multiple squares on this grid and often misinterpret where they actually are. As a point of departure, therefore, it helps to begin the discussion by looking at other companies in the category first and seeing if the team can agree on how those companies should be positioned on the grid. This allows the team to calibrate their understanding of the model in a context that is much less polarized and politicized than when they are talking about themselves.

As the team turns to itself, it is typically easier to work the columns first, then the rows. On the columns, the first question to ask is, are we today the undisputed leader of our industry? If not, is it our expectation that we can attain this position shortly? If not, then who is the leader and what advantages do they have that we must overcome? The key issue here is that, if winning dominant industry advantage is a reasonable expectation, it should become the focal point of strategy, and if not, then we should eliminate this column from further consideration at this time.

The next question to ask is, do we have anything more than offer advantage today? In particular, with respect to customer advantage, is there any segment of customers where, within that segment, we are the gorilla in the niche? If not, are there reasonable targets where with modest effort and focus we could become same? If so, these should be noted. At the same time, the team should ask, are there opportunities to create category advantage, perhaps around a coming technological discontinuity? Again, if so, these should be noted. And the final preliminary "space-clearing" step is to look to the rows and ask, are there one or more rows here that are simply not in alignment with the company's culture, "not us." If so, then tag them, and eliminate them from future consideration.

Once the space is cleared of the "not us," there is room to debate what is us. In single-product companies emerging into viability for the first time, this debate should resolve itself in a single-square strategy. In more mature companies with multiple lines, it is more common to come up with a one-square-per-product-line strategy, and even there, if there is a technological refresh under way, there might be two squares involved, one for legacy, the other for future developments. That said, companies that pursue a multiplicity of squares face a significant challenge to get traction out of shared services, be that shared engineering, manufacturing, sales, professional services, or finance, because each of the grid strategies proposes different priorities for each of these line functions.

To impose a layer of manageability on this problem, top executives should define its default set of priorities by identifying an "ubersquare." This square represents the long-term direction of the firm and becomes a unifying theme for the corporation as a whole. Over time all businesses are encouraged to make their way toward it. If local circumstances demand a different strategy, well and good, but managers taking such directions need to understand that they are not sailing with the wind and the tide. Perhaps most usefully, for those many decisions that could go either way, the uber-strategy should get the nod so that over time more and more wood ends up behind a single arrow.

AN EXTENSION FOR REGULATED INDUSTRIES

In working with the Competitive Advantage Grid in regulated industries, the model should be supplemented with one additional square, with its own column, called *regulatory advantage*, and row, called *resource control*. Taken together they represent the law's view of business as consisting of *contracts* and *property*.

Regulatory advantage is typically achieved through successful lobbying of political bodies. That is why we see large corporate contributions to the campaigns of public officials. When the practice is perceived as abusive, then campaign reform weighs in, but few people are so idealistic as to assume this form of influence can be eradicated. Moreover, lobbying itself is an industry, and a perfectly legal one, and companies who devote considerable amounts of resource here expect a shareholder return in the form of regulatory advantage.

When companies do not win their battles on Capitol Hill, then their real competitive savvy comes into play. A recent example of this is the recent history of the telecommunications sector in the United States. Deregulation mandated that the incumbent vendors open their markets to competitors, in part by creating equal access to their customer base through their networks. Based on this legislation, a huge amount of investment poured into the sector.

The investors behind this movement assumed that the data-oriented Internet protocol would so disrupt the incumbent voice-oriented, circuit-switched protocol that companies deeply entrenched in the latter would be simply obliterated. Clearly their monopoly-formed cultures and heritage would be no match for the aggressive take-no-prisoners attacks from Silicon Valley and elsewhere. This perception in large part accounted for the "Internet changes everything" mantra that drove the investment bubble.

The ultimate irony here is that early in 2002 it is the old guard companies, specifically the local exchange carriers, who are the "last men standing" in the subsequent shakeout. Meanwhile, nimble, agile, well-focused entrants in, say, the DSL (Digital Subscriber Loop) market, companies such as Rhythms, Northpoint, and Covad, are either out of business entirely or desperately on the ropes. Similarly, as of this writing, two darlings of the long-haul market, Global Crossing and Williams, have filed for bankruptcy.

If we look back and ask, how did this happen, the key winning tactic was the ability of the incumbents to slow the deployment of the challengers just enough to cause their investors, who had been providing them huge amounts of capital at very favorable rates, to throw in the towel. They did this in the case of DSL by complying with the letter of the law that required them to cooperate with DSL vendors but in such a minimal way that the market threw up its hands in disgust with the system's overall inability to get service to new customers efficiently or effectively. In other words, they played the regulatory game with much more sophistication than did their competitors.

That game is at the heart of a number of industries besides telecommunications. Pharmaceuticals jumps immediately to mind, for example, along with medical devices and anything else requiring FDA approval. A more subtle playing out of the same forces, however, can be seen in the alcohol distribution industry, where a host of Internet wine sites were blocked by state regulations forbidding interstate shipments of alcohol. While the stated rationale for these blocking maneuvers was that children might order alcohol over the Internet, it was not lost on the legislatures that their tax base might be at risk as well.

In parallel with regulatory advantage being a specific type of competitive advantage, there is a corresponding additional value discipline to consider: *resource control*. This is simply the concept of property in its largest sense. Oil and gas companies, for example, are valued largely based on their proven reserves, resources they control. Technology companies are valued in large part on their portfolio of intellectual property and its ability to create barriers to competitive entry, another form of resource control. Protectionist legislation, both within an economy and between economies, creates similar effects by controlling access to the resource of distribution, as U.S. companies seeking to do business in Japan, for example, had to learn during the 1980s and 1990s.

Resource control is critical to the exceptional valuations of the leading technology companies that, in effect, have a monopoly on a critical ingredient for the functioning of their ecosystem, be it the Oracle database, the Windows operating system, or Intel's 8X86-instruction-set for microprocessors. It is also at the heart of the recent outcry against Napster and other peer-to-peer file sharing systems. Here the counterattack was led by the entertainment industry, which sees in the new technologies a direct and dire threat to its own ability to protect its core properties. And resource control is also at the heart of the pharmaceutical industry's conflict with African nations over the price of AIDS drugs.

We should note in closing that high tech as a sector has a blind spot here. Its libertarian instincts are offended by government in general and protectionist legislation specifically. It decries all such actions as unfair. At the same time, of course, it wants its own intellectual property protected and decries any violations of same as piracy. In short, it is conflicted and naïve when it comes to this topic. Most important, perhaps, that means there is a weakness in the sector's vision, which old-guard companies can exploit when technology-enabled attacks are mounted.

SUMMING UP AND TAKING STOCK

As we bring this discussion of competitive advantage to a close, we are now halfway through our journey through managing for shareholder value. We began by looking at ourselves through the lens of an investor's perspective, seeing our company as a financial instrument, understanding our obligation to increase shareholder value, and translating that into the proxy of increasing our competitive advantage.

In the second section, we termed this focus *core* and used that tag to identify those business practices that had the capacity to differentiate our offerings powerfully and sustainably. Simultaneously, we identified all other business processes as *context* and drilled down deeply into the inevitability of context build-up, the risks thereof, and the types of action management must take to recycle its scarce resources back into core.

One of the keys to this recycling action is to have an extremely clear focus on what you have chosen to make core. In light of this goal, this third section has built up a grid model to help articulate and define a reasonable universe of choices. By targeting a square on this grid, management can frame the core/context challenge in actionable terms and benchmark its differentiation strategy against some of the best-in-class examples cited.

In light of all this, one might argue we are done—were it not for *the fault line*. The fault line represents the "creative destruction" that disruptive innovations and new categories—all those gray squares—wreak on established market positions. In particular we are concerned with technology-enabled disruption and how it is forcing industries to resurvey their competitive advantage land-scape and companies to revisit their positions within it.

In other words, some technology wave comes along and kicks us out of our "perfectly comfortable, thank you very much," square. It is not appreciated.

Indeed, not only is it not appreciated, it is hard to understand. Where are these new forces coming from? What can incumbent players do to defend themselves against them or, better yet, co-opt them to their own ends?

To answer these questions, we need to revisit a fifty-year-old model called the technology adoption life cycle.

IV

LIVING ON THE FAULT LINE

The fault line over which technology-enabled markets are built is the technology adoption life cycle. *Because it models the unfolding of a fundamental revolution in category power, it is directly linked to dramatic, subsequent shifts in industry power, customer power, and offer power. Thus the implications of yet another wave of technology unleashing itself on the marketplace are immense.*

This alone causes investors to revisit and revise their expectations of long-established market leaders, as the executives of Digital, Xerox, Kodak, Lucent, and AT&T can all painfully testify. Under the pressure of a newly evolving category, whatever differentiation was developed by focusing on one or another value discipline in the old category must now be reinvented, assuming it is even applicable. As a result, competitive-advantage positions that once seemed secure are abruptly overthrown, and management teams on the verge of congratulating themselves must now scramble to recover. It is a nausea-inducing experience to say the least.

Here's how it all plays out.

Before a disruptive technology can be assimilated into a mainstream marketplace, it must pass through multiple phases of adoption during which the market behaves in different ways specific to each phase. The end goal of all these mutations is to create and populate a sustainable value chain that can transform the new technology into reliable, deployable offerings, thereby creating a new and permanent market category. We call this goal Main Street, *a state of business maturity in which technology-enabled businesses resemble most other sectors of the economy.*

To reach Main Street, however, technology-enabled markets must pass through three prior phases—what we shall call the early market, *the* bowling alley, *and the* tornado *respectively. There are thus four phases of adoption in all, and each one rewards a very different market development strategy. Indeed, the competitive-advantage strategy that brings success in any one phase causes failure at the subsequent stage. This creates extraordinary confusion and serious management challenges as organizations develop momentum and inertia during any one stage and find they must now transition to the next.*

Depending on when and how your company rose to prominence, you could have gone through your last technology adoption life cycle several years or several decades ago. That will determine to some degree your familiarity with the material covered in this chapter. Its goal is simply to lay out the market dynamics involved so that they can readily be understood by all involved in setting strategy. Then in the remainder of the book we will tackle the organizational challenge of coping with so much variability while trying to maintain a coherent business and a consistent culture.

Before starting on that journey, however, I would just like to remind you all once again that the fault line, this thing that is driving us all crazy even as it brings enormous wealth creation into the economy, is all Moore's fault! Not me, not Geoffrey Moore—Gordon Moore! *To be specific, Moore's law, which observes that the semiconductor industry doubles the price/performance of its products roughly every eighteen months, is at the heart of the continuous eruption of disruptive technologies that has characterized the last twenty years. You can just do so much more new weird stuff nowadays than you ever could before because there is so much more horsepower to do it with. Moreover, as these disruptions build upon previous disruptions, both their frequency and their cumulative impact are increasing, so that we all feel that we are riding up a monstrous wave that shows no sign yet of cresting.*

The Internet is both a culmination of all this disruption and at the same time a starting point for another, even bigger wave. Because it has the power over time to radically shift the locus of wealth creation in virtually every sector of business, it is in effect a fault line running under the entire world economy. The offer it makes is at once exhilarating and terrifying—totally change what you are doing (terror) to achieve an order-of-magnitude greater effectiveness (exhilaration). This is the classic fault-line offer—disruptive innovation enabled by discontinuous technology. It has been studied at length under the heading diffusion of innovation, *and the model that best describes its impact is the technology adoption life cycle.*

7

THE TECHNOLOGY ADOPTION LIFE CYCLE

The technology adoption life cycle models the response of any given population to the offer of a disruptive innovation, one that forces the abandonment of traditional infrastructure and systems for the promise of a heretofore unavailable set of benefits. It represents this response as a bell curve, separating out five subpopulations, as illustrated in the following figure:

The Technology Adoption Life Cycle

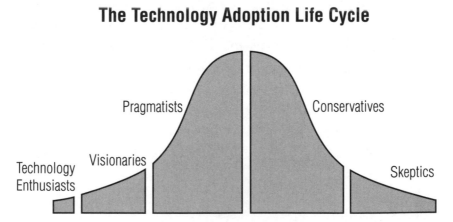

Figure 7.1

The bell curve represents the total population of people exposed to a new technology offer. The various segments of the curve represent the percentage of people predicted to adopt one or another of the five different strategies for determining when and why to switch allegiance from the old to the new. The five strategies unfold sequentially as follows:

1. The *technology enthusiast* strategy is to adopt the new technology upon its first appearance, in large part just to explore its properties to determine if it is "cool." The actual benefits provided may not even be of interest to this constituency, but the mechanism by which they are provided is of great interest. If the enthusiasts are entertained by the mechanism, they often adopt the product just to be able to show it off.

2. The *visionary strategy* is to adopt the new technology as a means for capturing a dramatic advantage over competitors who do not adopt it. The goal here is to be the first to deploy an advantaged system and to use that head start to leapfrog the competition, establishing a position so far out in front that the sector realigns around its new leader. Visionaries are mavericks who want to break away from the herd and differentiate themselves dramatically.

3. The *pragmatist* strategy is directly opposed to the visionary. It wants to stay with the herd, adopting the new technology if and only if everyone else does as well. The goal here is to use the wisdom of the marketplace to sort out what's valuable and then to be a fast follower once the new direction has clearly emerged. Pragmatists consult each other frequently about who's adopting what in an effort to stay current but do not commit to any major change without seeing successful implementations elsewhere first.

4. The *conservative* strategy is to stick with the old technology for as long as possible (a) because it works, (b) because it is familiar, and (c) because it is paid for. By putting off the transition to the new platform, conservatives conserve cash and avoid hitting the learning curve, making themselves more productive in

the short run. Long term, when they do switch, the system is more completely debugged, and that works to their advantage as well. The downside of the strategy is that they grow increasingly out of touch for the period they don't adopt and can, if they wait too long, get isolated on old technology that simply will not map to the new world.

5. Finally, the *skeptic* strategy is to debunk the entire technology as a false start and refuse to adopt it at all. This is a winning response to all those technologies that never gain mainstream market acceptance. For those that do, however, it creates extreme versions of the isolation problems conservatives face.

Each of these strategies has validity, and a single individual is perfectly capable of choosing different strategies for different offers. But for any given technology, the market will develop in a characteristic pattern due to the aggregate effects of a population distributing its choices in the proportions outlined by the bell curve. The resulting market development model looks like this:

Technology-Enabled Market Development

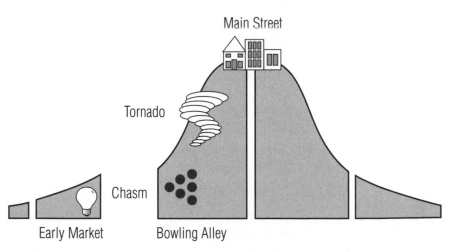

Figure 7.2

The model segments the evolution of a technology-based market as follows:

- The first phase, or *early market*, is a time when early adopters (technology enthusiasts and visionaries) take up the innovation while the pragmatic majority holds back. The market development goal at this stage is to gain a few prestigious flagship customers who help publicize the technology and celebrate its potential benefits.

- The early market is followed by a *chasm*, a period of no adoption, when the early adopters have already made their choices, but the pragmatist majority is still holding back. The barrier to further progress is that pragmatists are looking to other pragmatists to be references, but no one wants to go first. The market development goal at this stage is to target an initial beachhead segment of pragmatists who can lead the second wave of adoption.

- In the development of most technology-enabled markets, specific niches of pragmatic customers adopt the new technology before the general pragmatist population. We call this period the *bowling alley* because the market development goal is to use the first group of adopters as references to help win over the next group, and the next, and so on. Typically the "head bowling pin" is a niche of pragmatists who have a major business problem that cannot be solved with current technology but that does respond to a solution built around the new innovation. Once this first group starts to move, it takes much less of a motive to overcome the inertia of the next group.

- As pragmatist adoption builds in niches, one of two futures emerges. In one, adoption continues to remain localized to niche markets, creating a pattern we call "bowling alley forever." In this pattern, each niche's solution is relatively complex and differentiated from every other niche's. As a result, no mass market emerges, and the market development goal is simply to expand existing niches and create new ones as the opportunity arises.

In the other pattern, a "killer app" emerges—a single application of the innovative technology that provides a compelling benefit that can be standardized across multiple niches. The killer app transforms niche adoption into mass adoption, creating an enormous uptick in demand for the new technology across a wide range of sectors. We call this period the *tornado* because the onrush of mass demand is so swift it creates a vortex that sucks the supply out of the market and puts the category into hypergrowth for a number of years. The market development goal here is to win as much market share as possible during a period when the entire market is choosing its supplier for the new class of technology-enabled offering.

• Once the supply side of the market finally catches up with the backlog of demand, the tornado phase subsides, and the market reaches a state we call *Main Street*. The new technology has been broadly deployed and, with the support of conservatives, now settles down to a (hopefully) long engagement as the incumbent technology. The market development goal here is to continuously improve the value of the offering, decreasing its base costs and recouping margins by increasing the number of value-adding extensions that can supplement it. The ultimate extension in many cases is to convert the offering from a product sale to a services subscription, allowing the customer to gain the benefit of the product without having to take on the responsibility for maintaining it.

It is important to note that the end of the technology adoption life cycle does not represent the end of the technology's productive market life. The category of offering can be sustained indefinitely on Main Street, coming to an end only when the next disruptive innovation renders the prior technology obsolete. Indeed, despite all the emphasis on shortening life cycles, Main Street markets normally last for decades after complete absorption of the enabling technology—witness the car, the telephone, the television, the personal computer, and the cell phone. Importantly, however, the marketplace pecking order set by market share that emerges during the bowling alley and tornado phases tends to persist for the life of Main Street. That is, while Main Street represents the final and lasting distribution of competitive advantage, its boundaries get set prior to arrival. Thus success in every prior stage in the life cycle is key to building sustainable Main Street market success.

WHERE WE ARE HEADED

In the remaining chapters of this section we are going to work through the dynamics of each of these stages, focusing on three elements, as follows:

- *What is the market trying to accomplish independent of the desires of any individual participant within it?* The framework for this discussion will be the value-chain model and how, at each stage of the market, different relationships are privileged and come to the fore. The goal here is to describe the forces at work in the market and to set the context for what any individual company can hope to accomplish at each phase.

- *What kinds of competitive advantage are useful at each stage?* The framework here will be the Competitive Advantage Grid model and how, at each stage of the market, different forms of competitive advantage are privileged. The goal here is to align company ambition with market intention and to focus company management on the right critical success factors for each phase.

- *What impact does success at each stage have on stock price?* The framework here will be the GAP/CAP valuation model and how, at each stage of the market, GAP and CAP can be expected to mutate. The goal here is to align management with shareholders, displacing the P&L statement with stock valuation as the key metric for company performance for all the market phases leading up to Main Street, where the two will finally rejoin each other to interoperate to the same end.

At the end of this review, we will have a comprehensive framework for understanding how to manage for shareholder value at each stage in the development of a technology-enabled market. The goal is to have no ambiguity on this front. That will then leave us with the extraordinary challenge of transforming our organizations to execute this agenda, a task we will leave to the remainder of the book.

8

STAGE ONE ADOPTION: THE EARLY MARKET

VALUE-CHAIN STRATEGY

The early market begins with the ambitions of two constituencies who live at opposite ends of the value chain.

Early-Market Value Chain

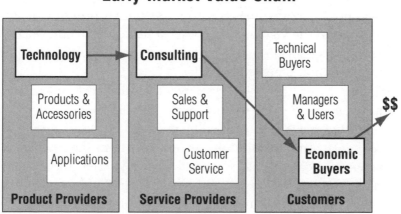

Figure 8.1

On the left is the *technology provider*, the supplier of the disruptive innovation, with ambitions of constructing an entirely new marketplace based on a new platform. On the right are one or more visionary executives, in the role of *economic buyer*, who also have ambitions of their own. They want to rearchitect the marketplaces they participate in to install their company as the new market leader—and they want to do it fast. They see in the new technology an opportunity to disrupt the established order and insert themselves into the lead.

Between these two poles, however, no existing value chain presently links their ambitions. Indeed, the existing value chain is appalled by them. There is, however, one institution in the market that can bridge the gulf between the two, can transform the technology provider's magic into the economic buyer's dream, and that is the *consulting firm*. Rather than try to incubate a value chain in the marketplace, this consultancy will instead create a temporary value chain to serve a single project's specific needs. That is, they will pull together the products, the applications, the sales and support, the customer service, and in extreme cases even substitute their own people for the customer's technical buyer (and even for the customer's end users), all to make the value chain work *in a single instance for a single customer.*

Needless to say, this is expensive. But if it pays off, if the sponsoring company really does leapfrog its competition in a new market order, then the visionary becomes a hero, and whatever money was spent was pocket change by comparison to the appreciation in the customer company's stock price.

So much for the primary players in the early-market value chain. Every other constituency exists in some marginalized role. Thus products are not yet really productized, and applications exist primarily in presentations as opposed to in the real world. In the services sector, sales, support, and customer service are all organizations that are just ramping up. Technical buyers in corporations are leery of taking responsibility for anything this immature, and managers and end users in general think it is way too early to be reengineering their functions. Note that these constituencies are not deleted from the diagram—they are very much present during an early-market project—but they are treated more as obstacles than as allies.

What makes the early-market value chain distinctive is that the consulting-services function is playing many, many roles. To do so, it must operate inefficiently in that it must take responsibility for tasks with which it has no previous experience and for which it has no currently trained resource. People who can rise to this challenge are scarce, and thus the organization must bill out its services at rates that substantially exceed those of standard contract labor. Moreover, since there is as yet no market for the new technology, once the project is done, there is not likely to be another like it in the pipeline, and thus the resources and their learning will be dispersed. Again, this drives up the costs of the project, as they cannot be amortized across other efforts. Thus scarcity creates inefficiency, which in turn further exacerbates scarcity.

The end result is that neither the value chain nor the market persist past the end of the project (hence the absence of an arrow showing how money recycles to create additional business). In the early market, that is, customer sales are so few and far between that each must effectively be treated as a onetime event. Service providers can make money under this model, although it is a challenge to do so; product providers simply cannot. Although the customer is not price sensitive and thus does not require a discount to close the sale, there simply is not enough repeatable business to make the economics of a product-focused business model work out.

COMPETITIVE-ADVANTAGE STRATEGY

In a market with no persistent value chain, what kind of competitive advantage can a sponsor of disruptive innovation hope to leverage or achieve? The answer is *category advantage*.

What all the companies in this column share is a common commitment to create a new market category and to dominate it.

- *Reinventors* are exploiting legacy inefficiencies in existing value chains that have become so institutionalized that the

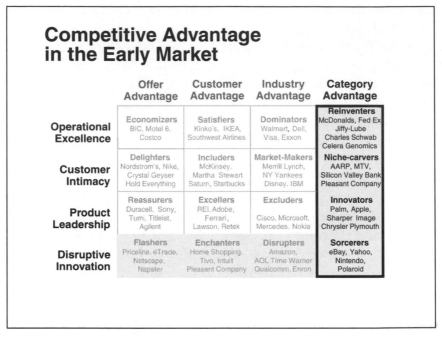

Competitive Advantage in the Early Market

	Offer Advantage	Customer Advantage	Industry Advantage	Category Advantage
Operational Excellence	Economizers BIC, Motel 6, Costco	Satisfiers Kinko's, IKEA, Southwest Airlines	Dominators Walmart, Dell, Visa, Exxon	**Reinventers** McDonalds, Fed Ex Jiffy-Lube Charles Schwab Celera Genomics
Customer Intimacy	Delighters Nordstrom's, Nike, Crystal Geyser Hold Everything	Includers McKinsey, Martha Stewart Saturn, Starbucks	Market-Makers Merrill Lynch, NY Yankees Disney. IBM	**Niche-carvers** AARP, MTV, Silicon Valley Bank Pleasant Company
Product Leadership	Reassurers Duracell, Sony, Tumi, Titleist, Agilent	Excellers REI, Adobe, Ferrari, Lawson, Retek	Excluders Cisco, Microsoft, Mercedes, Nokia	**Innovators** Palm, Apple, Sharper Image Chrysler Plymouth
Disruptive Innovation	Flashers Priceline, eTrade, Netscape, Napster	Enchanters Home Shopping, Tivo, Intuit Pleasant Company	Disrupters Amazon, AOL Time Warner Qualcomm, Enron	**Sorcerers** eBay, Yahoo, Nintendo, Polaroid

Figure 8.2

incumbent leaders simply cannot divest themselves of them. To give but one example, the U.S. Postal Service is so locked into a fabric of social and economic alliances it simply does not have the freedom to conduct logistical experiments of the sort that enabled Federal Express, and more recently UPS, to carve out the most lucrative segment of the category for themselves.

- *Niche-carvers* are exploiting a different kind of legacy inertia, the inability of established leaders that have optimized for scale to profitably devote deep attention to niche markets. All niche markets have idiosyncratic needs that make them receptive to niche-specific offers, which, in turn, create deep customer loyalty, allowing niche carvers to charge premium margins and eventually to market even commodity offers to this community at a modest premium. The key is that initial point of attack, where the market winner goes the extra mile, is the mile that the incumbent both cannot afford and is not inclined to go.

- *Innovators* exploit yet a third form of legacy inertia, this one in product design, where a given paradigm becomes so ingrained in people's minds they cannot think outside the box. Thus Palm Computers, for example, came to market with perhaps the *tenth* attempt by a vendor to create a handheld device that was useful and attractive to consumers, succeeding in large part not because it put in the most features, but because it took the most out. Apple's Macintosh was famously derived from Xerox's Star Workstation but was repositioned as "for the rest of us." Innovators, in short, solve existing problems with known solutions, making their breakthroughs in elegance of design rather than in core concept.

- In this they stand in contrast to *sorcerers,* who really do invent new universes and then populate them with customers. This is the closest thing to economic magic on the planet, exploiting the legacy of species by creating a new mutation. eBay's Internet auction marketplace is the most remarkable of these creations to come out of the dotcom era, but it was preceded by personal computers, local area networks, cellular telephony, e-mail, and Web sites.

All these various companies are exploiting category advantage in part because at this point in the technology adoption life cycle it is the only advantage available to exploit. There is as yet no industry, hence no industry advantage. Nor is there any known set of customers, so scratch customer advantage as well. On the other hand, there is definitely offer advantage, but it exists largely in the imagination, since there is no value chain to support delivering these offers. It's as if someone had written a great play, but the world had no actors, no directors, no set designers, and no theaters. How can one proceed?

The essence of early-market strategy in industrial markets is to win one or more major deals with highly visible customers and to use these to create visibility for the new category of offer and the company touting it. In consumer markets there is a comparable result from winning celebrity endorsement, particularly if it is genuine so that the celebrity voluntarily evangelizes the offer (but this strategy has problems later in the life cycle, as we shall see subsequently.) The sponsoring vendor must then leverage this win to:

1. Communicate a vision of the future, focusing on the end state, blithely ignoring that the product as shipped performs a mere fraction of what is promised. The goal is to establish the category, not the product. In the early 1990s, Apple did this brilliantly for the personal digital assistant with a video called *Knowledge Navigator,* which came out a full year before they had product. Unfortunately, they then shipped the Newton, which was so far off the mark they lost all ground gained.

2. Show proof that at least one customer has achieved something truly magnificent. This customer serves as a flagship account, and vendors must do whatever it takes to enable the executive sponsor's vision. Needless to say, established companies with marketing guidelines have enormous challenges seeing their way clear to making this commitment, hence the advantage of being a start-up in the early market.

3. Create a sense of urgency that the wave is breaking. This is, to put it as gently as possible, a considerable exaggeration. But it is absolutely critical to the marketing of early-stage offerings. Hence the term *evangelist* to describe those who are best in this effort. Guy Kawasaki is the world's best-known evangelist for his work with the Macintosh, and his first book, *The Macintosh Way,* is a manual for early-market marketing.

4. Secure publicity. Categories at their outset are artifacts of the communications media, ideas that circulate in the culture. The early market is in a very real sense a media event. This is no time to be shy.

To sum up, for technology providers competitive advantage comes solely from positioning for a future market and not from gaining value-chain or market-segment advantage in an immediately exploitable market. There is a key implication here for corporate strategy—at this point in the life cycle one should not invest to build either value-chain or market-segment advantage. Thus, the technology-providing organization should not at this point be ramping up sales, marketing, customer service, manufacturing, procurement, logistics, human resources, information systems, or even financial projections. The only supply-side institution that should be making such plans is the professional services organization, which, because it is not tied to any particular new technology, can amortize its investment across a portfolio of "all the new stuff." For everyone else on the supply side, however, early-market buildup of infrastructure is bad strategy.

STOCK PRICE IMPLICATIONS

Technology-oriented investors take great interest in early-market developments, hoping to get in on the "next big thing" before the bulk of investors catch on to it. At the same time, however, they are wary of falling prey to a lot of hype that never turns into sustainable competitive advantage. Their dilemma is reflected in the following diagram:

Impact of Early-Market Success on Stock Price

Figure 8.3

The chart calls attention to both the positive and the negative implications of what has been accomplished—namely, that a few customers have made a major commitment to the new technology. On the positive side, this can be taken as proof that there is a true GAP. This is a big step up from theoretical GAP, and it calls into being the *shadow* of a GAP/CAP chart.

On the negative side, however, there is no proof of any CAP, no evidence of a sustainable marketplace as yet. That is why we have a shadow of a chart. Because there is no persistent value chain in view, it is not clear yet exactly how much ground has been captured. Hence the question marks: is this, or is this not, the next big thing?

Nonetheless, if the company sponsoring the innovation is a venture capital–backed start-up, the impact of early-market success is significant. Consider that its first round of funding was based on the current market value of a wing, a prayer, and the founding team's personal reputations. To get a second round at a higher valuation, it needed to garner at least one flagship customer. Now it has. Depending on how high the flag got raised and how broadly it unfurled, second-round valuations might see a step up from ten to one hundred percent. Where has this new value come from? It has nothing to do with the actual revenues or earnings, although the bigger the deal, the better. Instead it has everything to do with the usefulness of the new customer in communicating the value proposition of the company and demonstrating first-mover advantage. That is what captures the imagination and enthusiasm of the second-round investor. So winning a flagship deal in the early market is a very big deal for start-ups.

For large public companies, however, the issue is more problematic. Here total corporate revenues and earnings play such a dominant role in valuation that the communication of early-market wins, which typically do not show up in the numbers, must be managed carefully to extract shareholder value. The key audience to influence is the investment analyst community, so this communication must typically be channeled through the investor relations department. Unfortunately, that department tends over time to become "financially focused," falling prey to P&L myopia, because that is the orientation to which investment analysts default in their interrogations. To break free from this, the CEO has to be the communicator of the win, positioning it not as a financial event but rather as a market-making one, and holding up that single customer win as an icon for potential future streams of earnings.

If this approach is successful, a public company's stock will move gently upward on a halo effect. In general, however, history has shown that public companies tend to underplay early-market wins in their investor relations. This creates a relatively blank canvas upon which start-ups can paint. And once these analysts have gotten engaged with the idea of the next market, that begins to affect their valuation ideas about the established market. In short, it is simply unwise for the investor relations team at established companies to neglect early-market events, both within their company and in the marketplace around them.

To wrap up this account of market development strategy for the early market, the core focus is on winning a few flagship customers to demonstrate to the marketplace and to investors that the company has first-mover advantage in catching a new wave of technology. These communications are targeted to the visionaries and other forward-thinking members of the market. Pragmatists in the same marketplace overhear these communications, not without interest. This may be the next thing they adopt—but not yet. Moving the first set of those pragmatists into the adoption window is the next market development challenge.

9

STAGE TWO ADOPTION: CROSSING THE CHASM INTO THE BOWLING ALLEY

For technologies to gain persistent marketplace acceptance, they must cross the chasm and take up a position on the other side. Now we are in the realm of the pragmatists. To get pragmatists to move at all, companies must rethink their marketing objective from the early market. There the goal was to win a customer, and then another, and another. To cross the chasm, however, you have to *win a herd.* Here's why:

- Pragmatists only feel comfortable moving in herds. That's why they ask for references and use word of mouth as their primary source of advice on technology purchase decisions. Selling individual pragmatists on acting ahead of the herd is possible but painful, and the cost of sales more than eats up the margin in the sale itself.

- Pragmatists evaluate the entire value chain, not just the specific product offer, when buying into a new technology. Value chains form around herds, not individual customers. There has to be enough repeatable business in the pipeline to reward an investment in specializing in the new technology. Sporadic deals, regardless of how big they are, do not create persistent value chains.

The visible metric for crossing the chasm, therefore, is to *make a market* and *create a value chain* where no market and no value chain existed before. This is a difficult undertaking. To increase its chances for success, and to decrease the time it takes to achieve, it is best to focus the effort on creating a niche market first before trying to create a mass market. It is simply prudent to minimize the number of variables at risk.

Think of a niche market as a self-contained system of commerce with its own local set of specialized needs and wants. Isolated from the mainstream market, which does not serve these special needs, it can function as a *value-chain incubator* for emerging technology-enabled markets. That is, its isolation protects the fragile new chain from direct competitive attacks from the incumbent value chain. The customer community, in effect, nurtures the fledgling enterprise because it hopes to gain great benefit from it.

VALUE-CHAIN STRATEGY

To visualize the changes in moving from the early market to the bowling alley, let us return to our value-chain diagram, this time focusing on a new set of market makers:

Bowling Alley Value Chain

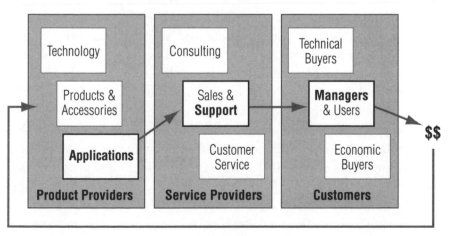

Figure 9.1

At the right-hand end of the chain, the *managers* in the customer domain represent the preassembled herd, an aggregation of relatively homogeneous demand. These are department managers in charge of a broken, mission-critical process, all huddled in a mass, desperate for a solution to their common problem. At the other end, an *application provider* in the product domain offers that same solution, albeit based on unproven technology. If the problem is severe enough, the risk/reward ratio is such that at least some department managers will take the plunge. The application provider will bring its solution to market through a sales and support organization where it is the *support function* that really counts. That is because at the outset of a market the remaining value-chain partners are just getting recruited and cannot be relied upon to assemble the whole product correctly on their own. Later on these same partners will compete to take over the support function—and the enlightened application provider will let them, as it will greatly expand its market and its reach—but for now it is all just too new. So the application provider's support team must take the lead in working through all the glitches until a working whole product is in place, even when the problem is with someone else's part of the offering and not their own.

Note that the money-recycling arrow has now been restored to the diagram. This is the whole point of the niche-market strategy. We are now creating for the first time a self-funding persistent market where the economic gains of the customer lead to increasing and ongoing investment in the products and services that bring them about. Even if no other market ever adopts this technology, it will still be economically viable to maintain this niche. To be sure, the returns will not be all that the investors hoped for, but they will not be a total bust either. That is because niche markets have persistent competitive advantages that allow them to sustain themselves even when the marketplace in general fails to adopt the new technology. Moreover, if the value chain extends its reach into additional niches, then it can add market growth to its already attractive price margins to produce highly attractive returns indeed.

The major beneficiaries of this strategy are the application providers. It is they who harness the new wave of technology to the specific needs of the target segment, and they who rally the rest of the value chain to support this effort. Because the application provider is the company that really does "make the market," it gains a dominant market-specific competitive advantage during this market gestation period. This advantage will persist indefinitely, even after the technology adoption life cycle goes forward, since once any market falls into a particular pecking order, it is loath to change.

Everyone else in the value chain—the core technology providers, the hardware and software product companies, the business consultants and the systems integrators, the customer service staff, and even the client's own technical staff—all happily take a backseat. That's because they will all be operating primarily as cost-effective generalists, making relatively minor modifications to their way of doing business, whereas the application vendor, interacting intimately with the problem-owning department managers, must operate as a value-creating specialist and invest significantly to be able to do so effectively.

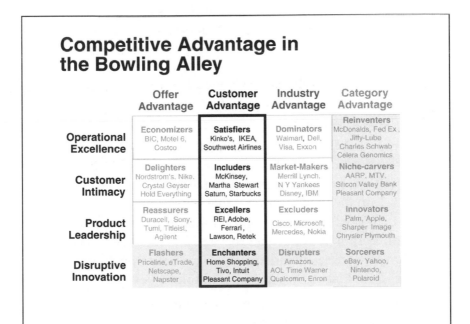

Figure 9.2

COMPETITIVE-ADVANTAGE STRATEGY

Because the essence of bowling alley strategy is to exploit the incubation properties of niche markets, the fundamental competitive advantage strategy for this stage of the life cycle is *customer advantage.*

What all the companies is this column share is success in privileging a class of customers who would otherwise be marginalized in the marketplace and who in return reward these companies with exceptional loyalty.

- Thus *satisifiers*, through exceptional operational excellence, empower a set of customers who cannot afford the market-standard service, typically by leveraging these customers' willingness to substitute self-service. As these customers congregate, they tend to develop a clubby rapport, which savvy marketers exploit to reinforce a sense of community and loyalty.

- *Includers* take this rapport-building to a higher level, typically targeting the other end of the market, where individuals with discretionary funds will pay a premium to be treated in a premium way, even if it is just to a *venti latte.* Again, clubbiness develops around the service elements of the offer, leading to loyalty. Interestingly, Saturn's inability to hold its position in this quadrant may be because its target market was more of a *satisfier* constituency.

- Whereas satisfiers and includers tend to provide standard offerings with exceptional service, *excellers* build their loyalty through exceptional offers, products that are well beyond the norm. Initially they serve only those customers truly committed to exceptional outcomes, be it climbing Everest or retouching its photograph, but later on they attract customers who admire and aspire to be included in this category, participating in a sense of exclusivity in the club that reinforces loyalty over time.

- Finally, *enchanters* are companies who are so committed to their target customer they create whole new value chains to serve them, whether they be young girls hungry for fully realized worlds of imagination or busy beavers needing to time-shift their TV watching. This is an expensive, and thus high-risk, strategy, but when it pays off, it does so in spades.

Customer advantage strategies can be used at any time in a market's development, but they take on a specific coloration in the context of crossing the chasm. Technology-enabled offers require sophisticated, coordinated value chains to be viable. The existing chains are focused on other categories and are not free to support a new one without special inducement. In industrial markets, that inducement is the opening up of a new niche market that will pay a substantial premium for specialized goods and services enough to fund a newly emerging value chain through its early stages. In consumer markets, there are no such customers, and the value-chain partners for distribution services simply cannot afford to take up the slack. Thus consumer markets normally form only on the back of a killer app, a force that drives the creation of a new mass market, the subject of the next chapter, which looks at competitive advantage inside the tornado. They are almost never suitable as a beachhead for crossing the chasm. For crossing the chasm, an industrial market with a deeply troubling problem is the ideal target.

Given that target, the keys to successful market development are:

1. Focus on fixing a *broken, mission-critical process*, something the customer is desperate to accomplish such that there is no chance they will not entertain a sales call from a vendor making this promise. Getting the customer to arrive is the key to attracting the rest of the value chain.

2. Orchestrate the value chain to deliver on fixing the process. All the other vendors in the chain have other customers to serve, so they will not naturally be able to focus on the target niche. The purveyor of the disruptive innovation, on the other hand, is highly motivated to create and sustain this focus, not only for its own company but for every other company that must be involved.

3. Develop deep domain expertise in the customer's problem. Vendor credibility here is rooted in being the first to break the back of a challenging and persistent problem. This does not come easy, regardless of how good the technology is, hence the

need to engage intimately with the specifics of the challenge, not only to guide your own engineers but to help orchestrate the other companies in their roles.

4. Shepherd each deal through to fulfillment until the tipping point is reached. After some number of customers in the same segment succeed with essentially the same offer, word goes out, demand escalates rapidly, and the other vendors in the value chain need no further supervision. But until this happens, this fire you are trying to start is not well and truly lit and must be carefully supervised.

The ability to harness the technology wave to solve the critical problem of one or more specific niche markets creates category-based competitive advantage at this stage, with the bulk of the rewards going to the application providers. Because they reap the bulk of the rewards, it is relatively easy for them to understand and adopt niche marketing, especially if the alternative is to spend another year in the chasm. It is much more problematic, however, for a platform product or transaction services company to embrace it. Their business plans are normally predicated on either broad horizontal adoption across a multitude of business segments or a broad cross-section of consumers. They are not well positioned to go after niche markets. Vertical industry domain expertise holds little value for them, and voluntarily subordinating themselves to an application vendor just to gain entry into one little niche seems like a huge price to pay. Moreover, even if the tactic proves successful, the resulting order stream will be relatively modest and, worse, may inappropriately cause the rest of the market to misperceive the company as a niche player. For all these very good reasons, platform products and transaction services vendors tend to shy away from taking the niche approach to crossing the chasm. And yet it is still a mistake. Here's why.

As we shall see shortly, platform products are optimized for tornado markets, and transaction services offers are optimized for Main Street markets. Those are the phases of the life cycle in which they will shine. So their strategy should be to accelerate technology adoption to get to "their" phase as quickly as possible. Time spent in the chasm for either strategy represents a huge opportunity cost, giving their competitors a chance to catch up to first-mover advantage while making no progress for themselves at all. This makes exiting the chasm as quickly as possible their top strategic imperative—hence their need to perform the admittedly unnatural act of niche marketing. To be sure, it is a little bit like asking a caterpillar who has a stated goal to be a butterfly to first spin itself into a cocoon and melt—the intermediate step is so disconnected from the end result that it is hard to warrant taking it. But there is now sufficient history to show that not taking the step is fatal—as demonstrated by the market-development failures of ISDN networking, object-oriented databases, IBM's OS/2 operating system, pen-based PCs, infrared connectivity protocols, and artificial intelligence.

STOCK PRICE IMPLICATIONS

To help management teams support niche marketing, which always seems to be an overly focused market development effort given the size of their company or their ambition, it helps to show them the impact bowling alley success can have on stock price. The following figure illustrates the GAP/CAP implications of winning a niche market:

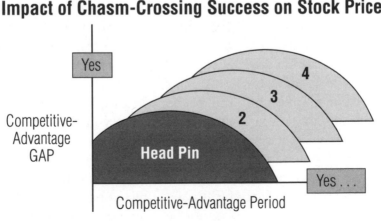

Impact of Chasm-Crossing Success on Stock Price

Figure 9.3

The size of the darkly shaded curve represents the valuation gained from winning market leadership in the first niche or head-pin. It is a function of the amount of market share gained coming from sales of the new category in that niche. At the Chasm Group we use a three-tiered ranking system, as follows:

30 percent share of new sales and you can call yourself: **a leader**

50 percent share of new sales and you can call yourself: **the leader**

70 percent share of new sales and you can call yourself: **the dominator**

For the bowling alley strategy to work properly, companies must become "the dominator" in the first niche they attack and then achieve "the leader" status in the next one or two. After that, any of the three rankings contributes to the overall market-share momentum in the sector. The rationale for these rules is that at the outset the pragmatist herd must hear a clear consensus forming around a single solution set, else they will dither in their purchase decisions and the market-capture effort will lose momentum.

So let us suppose in the headpin niche you gain dominator status, and you have some additional niches under development: what is all that worth to investors? First, as the dominator of the first niche, it means you have a high GAP, else others would have taken a larger percentage of the new sales. Second, it means you have secured a long CAP *for that niche* because now that the value chain has formed around your standards, there are huge barriers to entry for competitors and barriers to exit for customers and partners. So, unlike the early market, where you created *potential* shareholder value, now you have created *actual* shareholder value—hence the darker shading of the first curve.

For the first time, therefore, Wall Street can estimate with confidence the present value of future earnings at least within this one niche. For a start-up company in the application software sector, that estimate can be enough to merit a public offering. That is, a dominator position can be expected to generate high-quality earnings for a long period, and if these are your company's first earnings, they open up a promising future.

But if you are already a public company with a substantial earnings flow in place, then the impact on your P&L from adding the new niche may be negligible. Without a vision for how local niche dominance can be leveraged into additional niches, only modest shareholder value can be gained. You simply must go further with the story to gain the uptick in stock price. That is why we labeled the CAP axis "Yes . . ." To overcome lingering investment concern about future market size, it is critical to communicate the larger vision, educating the investor via the bowling alley metaphor, showing how the company will grow forward into a second, third, and fourth niche, each time securing a strong leadership position with high GAP and long CAP.

Finally, if you are a platform product or transaction services company, you may worry that your investors will become confused by too much emphasis on what is in essence a niche-market success. In such cases management is often tempted to downplay their market-making achievement. This is a big mistake. Crossing the chasm is a major accomplishment, and you must take credit for it. The goal is to announce mainstream market acceptance for your new offering, citing all the buzz that has formed around you in the targeted niche market, and "creatively" interpreting that as a harbinger of a mass adoption just around the corner. If you do not do this yourself, you leave the door open for some other competitor to come out of some other niche to claim this achievement for itself.

To wrap up our discussion of managing for shareholder value in the bowling alley, the core focus at this stage is on value-chain creation and market-segment domination, both leading to persistent competitive advantage, particularly for application providers. For all others at this stage, crossing the chasm is a critical transition vehicle to future competitive-advantage positions. The most powerful of these are created inside the tornado.

10

STAGE THREE ADOPTION: INSIDE THE TORNADO

A tornado occurs whenever pragmatists across a variety of market sectors all decide simultaneously that it is time to adopt a new paradigm—in other words, when the pragmatist herd stampedes. This creates a dramatic spike in demand, vastly exceeding the currently available supply, calling entire categories of vendors to reconfigure their offerings to meet the needs of a new value chain.

VALUE-CHAIN STRATEGY

The overriding market force that is shaping the tornado value chain is the desire of everyone in the market, beginning with the customer but quickly passing through to all the vendors, to drive the transition to a new paradigm as quickly as possible. That calls to the fore the three constituencies that are highlighted in figure 10.1.

Each of these constituencies is well positioned to benefit from standardization for rapid deployment.

- In the product sphere, it is *products*, not technology and not applications, that get the privileged position. The problem with technology is that it is too malleable to be mass-produced and thus does not lend itself to rapid proliferation of common, standard infrastructure. The problem with applications is that they must be customized to sector-specific processes, and so again they do not deploy as rapidly as desired. By contrast, products, and specifically those that serve as platforms for a broad range of applications, are the ideal engine for paradigm proliferation.

Tornado Value Chains

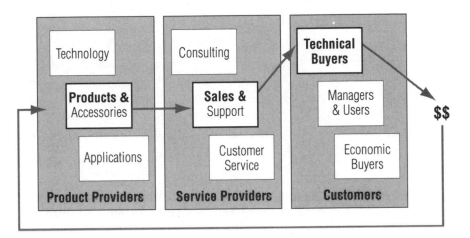

Figure 10.1

Now, to be sure, there must be at least one application that warrants the purchase of the platform in the first place, but in a tornado that application must be essentially the same for every sector. Such an application is called the killer app, and it becomes the focus for horizontal expansion across multiple sectors of the economy. *Accounting* was the killer app for mainframes, *manufacturing automation* for minicomputers, *word processing* for PCs, *computer-aided design* for workstations, and *electronic mail* for local area networks. But in every case, it was the platform product providers, not the killer app vendors, who were ultimately the big tornado winners because as other applications came on-line, they created still more demand for their platforms.

• In the services sphere, it is the sales and support function, with the emphasis on *sales*, that carries the day. The drawback with consulting is that its projects are too complex, take too long, and require resources that are too scarce to ever permit a tornado to go forward. The drawback with customer service is that it is too focused on serving existing customers at a time when the overwhelming emphasis has to be on acquiring new customers.

Generating sales in the tornado is not a problem of winning over the customer so much as it is of beating the competition. It is critical, therefore, to field the most competitive sales force you can at this time. Because so much wealth is changing hands, and because the long-term consequences of market share are so great, tornado sales tactics are brutal, and sales aggressiveness is the core discipline. This is the time when nice guys do finish last.

On the support side, the key issue is to get new customers up and running on a minimal system as quickly as possible and then move on to the next new customer. The more cookie-cutter the process, the faster it replicates, the more new customers you can absorb. The push is for operational excellence, not customer intimacy. This is not a normal support profile, so once again focusing the team on the right value discipline is a critical executive responsibility.

- On the customer side of the value chain, it is the *technical buyer*, not the end-user departments and not the economic buyer, who becomes the key focus. The problem with end users is that they inevitably seek customization to meet their department-specific needs. Not only is such complexity contrary to the vendor's wishes, it also works against the host institution's imperative to roll out the new infrastructure to everyone in the company as quickly as possible. Such rapid deployment requires a one-size-fits-all approach for the initial rollout, something that the technical buyer understands far better than the end user. It is also not the time to court senior executives in their role as economic buyers. Once the tornado is under way, they sense the need to get over to the new infrastructure and delegate the task, including the selection process, to their technical staff.

When technical buyers become the target customer, their compelling reasons to buy drive sales outcomes. High on their list is conformance to common standards, followed by market leadership status, which is initially signaled by partnerships with other market leaders and later on confirmed by market share. The technical buyers' biggest challenge is systems integration, and this is where the support function can contribute to faster rollouts by building standard interfaces to the most prevalent legacy systems.

The tornado, in essence, is one big land grab—a fierce struggle to capture as many new customers as possible during the pragmatist stampede to the new paradigm. Increasing shareholder value revolves entirely around maximizing market share, and to that end *industry advantage* becomes the critical form of competitive advantage to seek.

COMPETITIVE-ADVANTAGE STRATEGY

Because the tornado represents a once-in-a-life-cycle chance to grab dominating market share during a free-for-all, the focus of shareholders and managers alike should be on industry advantage:

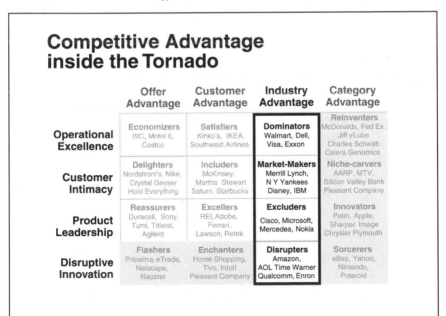

Competitive Advantage inside the Tornado

	Offer Advantage	Customer Advantage	Industry Advantage	Category Advantage
Operational Excellence	Economizers BIC, Motel 6, Costco	Satisfiers Kinko's, IKEA, Southwest Airlines	**Dominators** Walmart, Dell, Visa, Exxon	Reinventers McDonalds, Fed Ex, Jiffy Lube Charles Schwab Celera Genomics
Customer Intimacy	Delighters Nordstrom's, Nike, Crystal Geyser Hold Everything	Includers McKinsey, Martha Stewart Saturn, Starbucks	**Market-Makers** Merrill Lynch, N Y Yankees Disney, IBM	Niche-carvers AARP, MTV, Silicon Valley Bank Pleasant Company
Product Leadership	Reassurers Duracell, Sony, Tumi, Titleist, Agilent	Excellers REI, Adobe, Ferrari, Lawson, Retek	**Excluders** Cisco, Microsoft, Mercedes, Nokia	Innovators Palm, Apple, Sharper Image Chrysler Plymouth
Disruptive Innovation	Flashers Priceline, eTrade, Netscape, Napster	Enchanters Home Shopping, Tivo, Intuit Pleasant Company	**Disrupters** Amazon, AOL Time Warner Qualcomm, Enron	Sorcerers eBay, Yahoo, Nintendo, Polaroid

Figure 10.2

What all the companies in this column share is power over not only their direct competitors but also their suppliers and even their customers, all due to market share positions that are, in the short term at least, unassailable.

- *Dominators* use operational excellence to achieve scale and then use that scale to create industry advantage over suppliers and distributors. They then pass on to the customer enough of that advantage to gain their support. This in turn gives them the leverage they need to extract even more advantage upstream, some of which they are again careful to pass on. Over time, in effect, they become de facto market makers by virtue of commanding a significant percentage of the total transaction volume in the market.

- By contrast, *market makers* invest deeply in customer intimacy to develop trusted adviser relationships with premium customers and then leverage that position to gain power over the rest of the value chain. At the high end of the market, where complexity rules out scale, they exploit sophisticated understanding to gain their advantage. In mass markets, they substitute brand relationships for literal knowledge of the customer to establish a loyalty-engendering rapport. In both cases, their goal is to monopolize the customer such that suppliers have no choice but to access the market through their portal.

- *Excluders* represent the classic high-tech form of industry advantage based on product leadership. A single company's product line becomes so dominant that its competitors, at least for the current technology life cycle, cannot compete directly. Once again this creates the virtual monopoly condition that allows companies in this column to extract concessions from the rest of the supply chain.

- Finally, *disrupters* attack established industry advantage by displacing the existing value chain with a rival one, thereby calling into question the value and sustainability of the old guard. As noted before, the inherent instability in this strategy can only be removed when the operations become institutionalized sufficiently to move into one or another of the unshaded squares in the grid. But even during their probation the disruptors attract speculative investors to their camp and cause investors in the old guard to begin to hedge their bets.

The essence of tornado strategy is simply to capture the maximum number of customers in the minimum time and to subordinate all other efforts. Specifically this creates the following priorities:

1. Focus on rapid deployment and improvement of the "killer app," the driving force behind the pragmatist migration. For the PC this was word processing, for the PDA it was calendar and phone book. Being the best here drives customer choice. Do not get distracted by the extras at this stage.

2. Focus on beating the competition, not serving the customer. This is a hard rule for customer-oriented management, but the point is that pragmatic customers, at the end of the day, prefer to do business with whatever company becomes the de facto standard. No matter how nice you are, if that isn't you, then they will defect.

3. Win *some* market-share battle. Only one company gets to be the gorilla or the king. If that is clearly not going to be you, then you must target a niche market where it can be you. Once the tornado has passed the market leader seeks to continue its growth by "cleaning house," and if your company does not have a defensible customer base, you are right under the broom.

4. Win *value chain support*. This is an extension of winning a market-share battle. Value chain partners support market leaders because they set the market-making standards. Everyone else they exploit or ignore.

To sum up, the power of market-share leadership is rooted in the pragmatist preference to make the safe buy by going with the market leader. That is, rather than rely on their own judgment, pragmatists prefer to rely on the group's. Once that judgment has been made clear, once one vendor has emerged as the favorite, then pragmatists naturally gravitate to that choice, which of course further increases that company's market share, intensifying its gravitational attraction.

This cycle of positive feedback not only spontaneously generates market leaders but, once they are generated, works to keep them in place. That is, the value-chain advantage a market leader gains over its direct competitors is that it has become the default choice for any other company in the chain to round out its offers. Thus the company gains sales that it never initiated and gets invited into deals its competitors never see. Such sales not only add to revenues but to margins, since the absence of competition removes much of the pressure to discount price. In short, winning the market-share prize is a very sweet deal, which, if it is not working for you, is working against you. Hence the need to focus all guns on market share.

STOCK PRICE IMPLICATIONS

When it comes to investor returns, the tornado is the greatest wealth-creation force on the planet. It plays out to two endgames depending on whether the market develops around proprietary technology or an open-systems standard. In markets that develop under the influence of a proprietary technology, the roles of leader, challenger, and follower take on the following pattern:

- **Gorilla.** The market-share leader in a tornado with proprietary architectural control, this company creates massive shareholder value by gaining value-chain-domination power and forcing the rest of the market to serve its ends. Microsoft, Intel, and Cisco are all gorillas.

- **Chimp.** A direct challenger to the gorilla, this company also has proprietary technology, but it has lost the competition to establish the market's de facto standard. Once the market becomes aware of this outcome, it throws more and more of its business to the gorilla, effectively expelling the chimp from the standard value chain. Chimps have no recourse except to retreat into niche markets where they can make themselves over into "local gorillas," focusing on specialized applications where their nonstandard technology is acceptable because of the exceptional added value they supply. Apple's Macintosh, Digital's Alpha chip, and Bay Network's Wellfleet routers are all chimps.

- **Monkey.** A follower of the gorilla, this company licenses the gorilla's architecture to offer a low-cost substitute for its products that is compatible with the de facto standard. Price-sensitive customers in the market are happy to support monkeys *as a class*. They do not, however, support any particular monkey as a company, and as a result monkeys can never gain lasting market share. As soon as a cheaper, better offer comes along, the market immediately shifts its allegiance to it. Attempting to buy market share, therefore, is always a losing strategy. The correct strategy instead is to opportunistically take advantage of holes in the gorilla's product line and to move on as soon as they are filled. Hitachi with its mainframes (cloning IBM's standards) and AMD with its K-series microprocessors (cloning Intel's) are both monkeys.

Now let's see how investors value these different roles for relative competitive advantage.

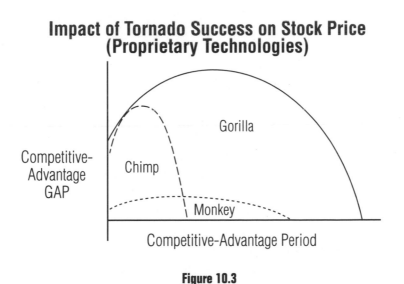

Impact of Tornado Success on Stock Price (Proprietary Technologies)

Figure 10.3

Note first the huge market cap of the gorilla. As we have already discussed, it gains a high GAP because it has a monopoly on a critical piece of new technology without which the tornado market cannot function. Moreover, since there is no substitute for its component, the company also has a long CAP, essentially equivalent to the CAP of the whole market category. It is no accident that at the time of this writing, Microsoft and Cisco have the two highest market caps in the world.

Turning to the chimp, note too that it has a high GAP. That is because it too has proprietary technology for which there is no substitute. Unfortunately, however, this technology is not the de facto standard, and thus its CAP is severely limited. It can expand into niche markets where the gorilla chooses not to compete, but it has no chance in a head-to-head battle.

A monkey's prospects are just the opposite. It has a long CAP but can generate no significant GAP. That is, because its offers are compatible with the de facto standard, it can benefit from the category's persistence. However, since its presence is not required, its CAP is not as long as the gorilla's. Moreover, since it has no unique offer, it cannot generate any GAP to speak of except through price discounts. In short, monkeys do not make for good long-term investments.

In contrast to the above, when tornado markets evolve in the absence of proprietary architectural control, the competitive dynamics within the hierarchy play out very differently. Such markets are frequently termed "open-systems markets," and to understand their dynamics executives need a second set of terms, as follows:

- **King.** The market leader in an open-systems tornado, this company has outexecuted its competition early on and is now enjoying the increasing-returns effects of market-share leadership. But unlike gorillas, kings have no proprietary technology to keep customers from exiting or competitors from entering their market. As a result, they can always be replaced, and thus the valuations of kings are significantly lower than those of gorillas. In the PC market, IBM was the original king, then Compaq, and now Dell.

- **Prince.** The market challenger in an open-systems tornado, this company's long-term prospects are dramatically different from the chimps'. That's because a prince can substitute for a king, whereas a chimp cannot substitute for a gorilla. Open-systems markets embrace princes as a mechanism to keep kings responsive to the rest of the chain's needs. In the PC market, Compaq began as a prince, as did Dell. HP has always been and still is a prince.

- **Serf.** A market follower in an open-systems tornado, this company has even less power than a monkey, since princes already serve as price competition for kings. As a result, it must discount even further to get its products purchased. As a class, serfs are significant because they can drag prices down to a point where even the king's business becomes unprofitable. In the PC market, the no-name "white box" PCs that are assembled by hundreds of resellers represent the serfs—and about one-third of the total market.

The following diagram reflects valuations in an open-systems competition:

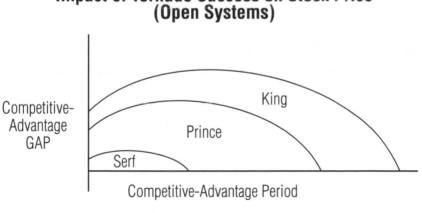

Impact of Tornado Success on Stock Price (Open Systems)

Figure 10.4

Here the king and the prince are on more equal footing, with the serf trailing. In this type of market, brand and distribution are the critical success factors. Serfs typically have neither, hence their minuscule market caps. Princes, by contrast, can challenge market-leading kings on either front. In the PC market, in particular, exploiting new channels of distribution has led to several changes in the hierarchy, first when Compaq used its retail skills to unseat IBM, and then when Dell used its direct-selling skills to unseat Compaq. On the GAP axis, because all players must conform to a common standard, they end up competing on price to some degree, which reduces the maximum attainable GAP for any company, even the king. This has long-term consequences for every company in the market.

It is important to remember, however, that while a tornado market is in full swing, everybody gains simply by virtue of tornado demand far exceeding tornado supply. That is, the tornado creates an extended period of shortages that allow all companies to charge premium prices during this phase. Thus all stocks in the category tend to gain in valuation initially, and only after the competition sorts itself out, and the market implications of the various roles are understood, do stock prices adjust to meet these charts.

To wrap up our discussion of the tornado, the core focus is on grabbing as much market share as one can during this period of exceptional opportunity. Relatively early on in the process, these land grabs resolve themselves into one or the other of the two patterns we have just discussed, and companies end up in one of the six roles just reviewed. Once this has happened, the best strategy is to accept the role the market assigns you and execute as efficiently as possible from within that position for the duration of the tornado. Any fighting to change roles will only confuse the market and slow its adoption of your offerings. Your goal instead should be to build the biggest possible installed base as a prelude for a prolonged stint on Main Street.

11

STAGE FOUR ADOPTION: ON MAIN STREET

Main Street begins as the market-share frenzy of the tornado subsides. The overwhelming bulk of the pragmatists in the market have by now chosen their vendor, made their initial purchases, and rolled out the first phase of a multiphase deployment. Only a fraction of the total forecastable sales in the segment have actually been made, but from here on the market-share boundaries are relatively fixed. This has significant implications for the value chain.

VALUE-CHAIN STRATEGY

The fourth and final mutation in the value chain is shown in figure 11.1. This one will endure for the life of the paradigm. In effect, it is the value chain we have been setting up all along.

The key change underlying this entire value chain is that the technology adoption life cycle has evolved from the pragmatist to the conservative agenda, and every constituency in the value chain is affected by this change. Let's start with the customer.

In mature—or maturing—markets, both the economic buyer and the technical buyer recede in importance. The economic buyer is no longer looking for competitive advantage or to support a manager in fixing a broken business process; now the issue is simply staying within budget, and that can be delegated. And the tech-

Main Street Value Chain

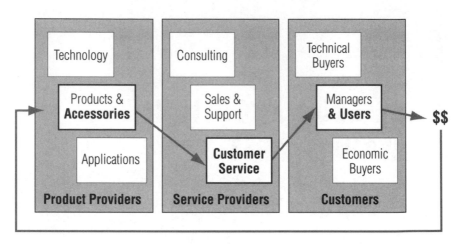

Figure 11.1

nical buyer is no longer concerned about how to either manage or postpone the introduction of a disruptive technology; now the concern is simply to stay compliant with established standards, and that too can be delegated. Even within the user community, department managers are now taking the new system for granted, assuming that it must be doing pretty much what it was bought to do (a naïve but all too frequent point of view). Thus it is only *end users,* the people who actually interact with the system frequently, who (a) know anything about how it really works and (b) have a stake in sponsoring improvements to it.

If these end users do not voice their desires, then the offering becomes a complete commodity, with the purchasing department driving a *supplier relationship* going forward. If they do voice their desires, however, and gain their managers' approval, then end users can drive a *vendor relationship,* a condition that allows a company to earn margins above commodity levels. We are long past the time for customers to embrace you in a *strategic partner relationship,* something that is confined to earlier phases in the life cycle.

To earn preferred margins from end-user sponsorship, focus shifts to those aspects of the value chain that end users can directly experience. On the product side, this suppresses the importance of technology, platform products, and even the core of the application. All these are still important, but they are more directly experienced by the technical buyer rather than the end user. By contrast, any product element that is consumable, as well as any change to the surface of the application, is highly user visible. Here, minor enhancements for a modest increase in price can generate dramatic changes in gross profit margin, the way, for example, the cup holder has done in the automotive industry.

Lucrative as the accessories and consumables business is on Main Street, however, an even bigger opportunity lies in what we call the *product-service shift*, the basis of all outsourcing. That is, what customers used to value and buy as a product becomes reconceived as a service offering—shifting the burden of system maintenance from the customer back to the vendor. This is reflected in such marketplace adjustments as the shifts from answering machine to voice mail, from videotapes to pay-per-view, or from barbells to health clubs.

The primary organization tasked with masterminding this shift is *customer service*. This creates a real challenge because that organization was not constructed nor were its personnel recruited with the thought that it would eventually become a lead contributor to the P&L and market valuation of the company. Nonetheless, if that is where the best returns now lie, companies must reengineer themselves to take advantage of them—as IBM and GE have done so well—or risk losing their markets to a rival who does.

COMPETITIVE-ADVANTAGE STRATEGY

As Main Street focuses more and more on serving existing customers, competitive advantage devolves more and more to offer advantage (as shown in figure 11.2).

What all these companies focus on is gaining greater "share of wallet" from selling more into their established customer bases:

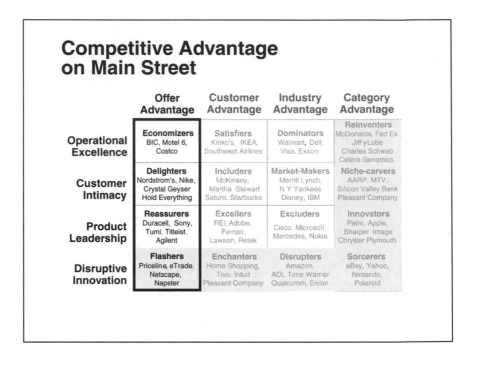

Figure 11.2

- *Economizers* upsell not on margin but rather on volume, as companies like Costco do when their customers buy sixty-four packs of toilet paper or the like. These purchases effectively preempt any other channel from competing for the business for a considerable time to come. Or economizers use low price to gain a discretionary purchase that would otherwise be outside the scope of their customer, as Motel 6 and Bic demonstrate. In either case, they continue to experiment with price elasticity to gain maximum returns on their economies of scale.

- *Delighters,* by contrast, are upsellers from birth. They take relatively commoditized offers—water might be a good example—and find ways to get people to pay a premium for it. For some, this is the miracle of branding at work, where consumers attach identity themes to their everyday purchases and then pay a premium to communicate who they are. In other cases, boutique stores overdeliver on a narrow niche of products to create selection advantage such that the aficionado who wants to be upsold ignores other channels to come to their shop.

- *Reassurers* sustain attractive gross margins long after their competitors have had to resort to discounting by establishing themselves as the *safe buy.* These are usually context purchases, not core, and the consumer is willing to pay a premium not to have to worry about them. In technology-enabled markets, in particular, conservative customers will pay a significant premium to keep their technophobias at bay, and elsewhere consumers gravitate to the established brand just to simplify their buying decisions (and keep them compatible with those of their spouse).

- *Flashers* try to disrupt this party by using novelty to capture the attention of some established vendor's bored and taken-for-granted customer base. They typically enjoy a huge burst in sales as their ploy catches the imagination of the market and then, more often than not, a symmetrically swift drop-off once it no longer charms. The key for flashers is to institutionalize their offer before this drop-off occurs, an uncommon but not impossible outcome.

Inherent in all these approaches is a product or service deployment strategy called *mass customization.* Mass customization separates any offering into a *surface* and a *substructure.* The surface is what the end user experiences. Changes are made here to enhance that experience. This is the *customization* portion of the offer. By contrast, the substructure is the necessary delivery vehicle for the entire performance, but it is not directly experienced by the end user. The goal here is to provide maximum reliability at the lowest possible cost, and the preferred tactic is to reduce variability and increase standardization to achieve high volume. This is the *mass* portion of the offer.

This leads to the following strategic priorities:

1. Focus on the end users. They experience the surface of the offer, and thus they are the source of margin-enhancing purchase preferences. One of the most exciting elements of Internet-enabled commerce is that industrial vendors can now, often for the first time, establish contact with end users and market directly to them, often to the consternation of the purchasing department.

2. Focus on the end-user experience. By the time it reaches Main Street, the actual utility of the offer is pretty much taken for granted. Now it is the secondary differentiators that take over, the nice-to-haves. This has the effect of moving the locus of R and D from the engineering to the marketing department.

3. Drive down costs, both in production and fulfillment. In product, this is where the leverage of separating surface from substructure pays off. In fulfillment, the goal is to eliminate intermediaries over time, both in sales and service, to position oneself as convenient as, say, an ATM machine.

4. Defer customization until late in the value delivery process. This is key to reducing inventory carrying costs and ensuring you do not end up with a carload of the pink ones when the blue ones are on back order. This typically leads to a need to redesign the value chain, creating new opportunities for service providers to create customization value at the point of customer contact.

The implications of this restructuring of the market are far-reaching, and not just for service providers. Consumables have the same potential to deliver customized value. Consider, for example, the razor–to razor blade transition in Gillette's history, or Kodak's move from cameras to film, or HP's transition from ink-jet printers to ink-jet cartridges. In every case, once Main Street is reached, it is the consumable at the surface, and not the underlying engine at the core, that becomes the basis of differentiation and the locus of high profit margins.

STOCK PRICE IMPLICATIONS

The returns from Main Street business models are based on the assumption that the market is not under a technology-enabled attack and can be forecast to last indefinitely in its present state. Within that context, investor returns are created by selling modestly profitable offerings repeatedly with a low cost of sales. This is possible only when you are selling to an *existing loyal customer.* The mortal enemy of the Main Street model is churn—a continual enrollment of new customers at high cost of sales accompanied by a continual loss of existing customers, the most profitable to retain.

Companies that minimize churn and maximize gains from existing customers generate one of two types of valuation depending on whether they follow a commodity or a value-added strategy:

Impact of Main Street Success on Stock Price

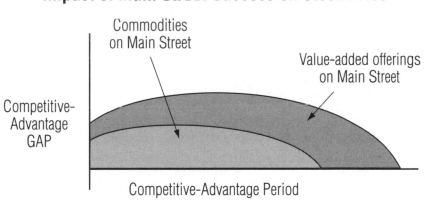

Figure 11.3

GAPs for companies in commodity businesses on Main Street are rarely high. Customer power, which is at its nadir during the tornado, reasserts itself on Main Street to create negotiating leverage. Moreover, since commodities are by definition substitutable, they have relatively low company CAPs as well. (The *category's* CAP, by contrast, is very long—we will have the salt business with us for some time to come.) Progress in such businesses is made by cost-reducing internal processes, particularly in the substructure, but even here, as competitors make the same adjustments, the savings must be passed on to the customer rather than reserved for the shareholder.

Creating value-added offerings through mass customization for end users is the preferred way to resist this erosion in margins. These offers increase GAP modestly—representing the premium end users will pay to get what they really want. They also create modest switching costs—once you get what you really want, it is hard to go back—thereby increasing CAP as well. Both these effects work only up to a point, after which competitive pricing can and will override their influence. Nonetheless, because the volume of sales on Main Street is so high, and the bulk of the business-enabling investment has already been amortized, it is here that most of the profits in any economy are made. And these do go to the shareholders.

Thus it is that blue-chip stocks are created. Decade after decade they are earnings machines, creating modest but predictable growth in both revenues and earnings accompanied by a remarkable lack of volatility in stock price. These stocks, and the New York Stock Exchange, were the bastion of the American economy for the greater part of the twentieth century.

All this value is put at risk, of course, whenever *the next* disruptive technology paradigm appears, reintroducing *yet another* life cycle—but let us not go there. Instead, let us stop, take a breath, and look back over all the ground we have covered in this section.

IMPLICATIONS OF LIVING ON THE FAULT LINE

Consider how many different value-chain permutations we have examined as a technology-enabled market develops through its various stages. To summarize them, here are the four market states in a side-by-side comparison table:

	Early Market	Bowling Alley	Tornado	Main Street
Primary Competitive Advantage	Category advantage	Customer advantage	Industry advantage	Offer advantage
Product Focus	Technology	Applications	Platform products	Consumables
Service Focus	Consulting	Support	Sales	Customer service
Customer Focus	Economic buyer	Department manager	Technical buyer	End user
Stock Price Implications	High GAP, no CAP	High GAP, long CAP (niche)	High GAP, long CAP (mass)	Low GAP, long CAP

The table maps the working out of the competitive-advantage hierarchy over a technology-enabled market's development. The columns lay out the life-cycle phases these markets evolve through. The rows lay out the changes in focus that organizations must make to adapt to this evolution. The first row sets forth the column in the Competitive Advantage Grid that has the most impact during each phase. The next three rows highlight the value-chain elements that create the most impact during the phase because they are best suited to leveraging the type of competitive advantage available. Finally, the last row recaps the stock price result of achieving the competitive-advantage position during each phase of the life cycle.

I hope and trust by now that the logic behind these various combinations is clear. Forces in the marketplace cause them to come about regardless of whether the companies involved want them to. As a result, they lay out the world of "what is."

Even a cursory glance, however, shows that the changes companies have to make to adapt to these forces are dramatic indeed. Moreover, the time allotted to make them is painfully short. As a result, it should surprise no one that few real-world organizations are good at actually keeping their strategies and programs in sync with life-cycle phase changes. Indeed, the larger and more successful a company becomes, the less likely it is to even make the attempt.

It is essentially a problem of inertia. Once you get a certain amount of mass moving in any given direction, the price for changing that direction begins to exceed the return on making the change. Increasingly the logic of trade-offs says let things go forward as they are. Yes, it creates problems, but not as many as trying to change course would. Over time, however, as these problems continue to be left untended, their consequences build, until eventually the cost for *not changing* does indeed exceed the price of change. But by that time things are typically so far out of control, and the time horizon for change has become so immediate, that the inertia-driven organization simply cannot make the turn and crashes into a wall instead.

The rest of this book is focused on helping you avoid that crash. We are going to take it in two parts—"Triage" and "Building to Last." *Triage* is a medical term for the sort of care that MASH units give— real-time prioritization of whom you can help and whom you cannot, followed by immediate first aid given under time pressure. In the triage section we will assume a direct assault in your market by a disruptive innovation and prescribe a short-term course-correction program intended to impact next year's stock price, maybe even this year's. This program is not intended as a substitute for building to last but rather as a prelude to it. The good news is, it does not undermine healthy long-term success. The bad news is, it can be painful.

In contrast to triage, building to last requires changes in culture and behavior that can take years to instill and unfold. Our final section, therefore, is targeted not at improving this year's stock price, perhaps not even next year's, but rather *the stock price for every year thereafter*. The section's premise is that organizations can indeed adjust to the demands of the technology adoption life cycle in real time provided they declare a core culture and maintain alignment with it. It will argue that there are four proven core cultures, any one of which can support long-term competitive advantage and wealth creation for shareholders, and that the primary challenge for the board of directors and the executive team is to choose one and really develop it.

V
TRIAGE

When an earthquake strikes along a fault line, social infra-structure goes into shock, and the first job of the authorities is to get things back up and running. The same holds true when a blue-chip company riding a prolonged wave of competitive advantage suddenly runs smack into a disrup-tive technology that undermines its leadership position in its traditional markets. Stock price crumbles, analysts call, partners defect, employees resign, competitors gloat, cus-tomers hedge, and investors demand action. It is a time for triage.

Triage is the discipline of first aid. It determines what can be fixed in the short term and what cannot, and it focuses all available resources on the former. The goal is to get the company back into the game as fast as possible. It is not to restore it to its former luster, it is not to re-create the past: rather it is to engage the unpleasant truths of the present clearly and deal with them honestly.

Management teams are generally not rewarded hand-somely for doing the work of triage, but it is where they show their true character. If they act with integrity and dis-patch, they build from the crisis strong relationships both inside and outside the company that will be the foundation for success in better times. Conversely, if they flinch from the challenge, there is little chance to recover later on as too many of the key resources perform their own form of triage by simply leaving.

The most useful thing to have in times of triage is an operating manual, a checklist of what to do first and how to proceed after that. In Part V we are going to conduct a fictional case study of a company caught out on the fault line, one that is well established in a technology-enabled market, publicly traded, in the Fortune 500, *and in all likelihood a household name, a company that in an earlier era rode a tornado market to prominence and then subsequently enjoyed a prolonged period of prosperity, a company that now finds itself up against the challenge of disruptive competition.*

The company's name will be BlueChip, and it will trade on the New York Stock Exchange. The goal will be to expose BlueChip to a technology-based attack and explore its options going forward. We will begin by looking at how the company is organized and oriented prior to the attack. Then when the attack hits, we will look at what kind of triage must occur immediately. Finally, we will look at a fundamental change in management behavior that must occur for the company to regain its competitive edge. At the end of Part V, executive teams in similar situations should have at their command a new set of management options and a vocabulary for discussing their merits relative to the challenges they face.

12

EXAMINING THE FOUNDATIONS

To understand BlueChip in its current pre-disrupted state, we need to sort out what happens to a company after it goes through a tornado market and begins to settle down on Main Street. During the tornado, successful companies focus intensely on gaining market share. To do so, they organize operations around line functions, parse out the work, suppress any distractions, and turn the crank as fast as possible. When the tornado market finally subsides, this team crashes into a wall, missing its top-line numbers badly, and the stock takes a big hit.

Now what happens going forward? The company has been shaken to its foundations, and a fair number of people look at their stock options now underwater, look at the next big thing in the market recruiting like mad, and leave to join up. But the rest of the company pulls itself together and begins to sort out life on Main Street. The problem is, there is not as much to do as there once was, and fairly quickly downsizing becomes the order of the day, which the company bravely takes on.

In so doing, however, *it does not reorganize but instead preserves the same line organization and line managers it used to run tornado operations.* This is a serious mistake. Without the pressure of tornado demand forcing these functions to work in harmony, they soon drift out of sync with one another, creating what many have called the *stovepipe effect.* Stovepipes are isolated line functions that optimize for their internal productivity and perform poorly in cross-functional tasks. This organizational structure does not penalize companies inside the tornado because assembly-line throughput is the order of the day. It does, however, penalize them on Main Street, as they are slow to respond to market changes and customer requests.

In technology-enabled markets we typically see five line functions that end up as stovepipes:

- Research and development

- Operations

- Professional services

- Sales

- Finance

Each line function has a characteristic set of attitudes toward the various phases of the technology adoption life cycle. Some are more comfortable at the front end of the life cycle, others at the back, and as soon as the pressures of a tornado market subside, they tend to gravitate back to their comfort zones accordingly. This is by no means all bad. Indeed, by mixing and matching leadership responsibilities among these functions, companies can get reasonably adequate coverage for all but one life-cycle phase. Here specifically is how the various functions self-organize.

R AND D

R and D is the engineering function in high tech. In other technology-impacted markets, where companies may not employ engineers per se, think of whatever function has the charter both to optimize offerings for the current wave of technology and to catch the next wave.

Like all functions in the corporation, when R and D surveys the various market stages created by the technology adoption life cycle, it sees good times and bad times depending on which stage is active. Using icons to represent each stage, here's how this group perceives the life cycle as a whole (see figure 12.1).

R and D

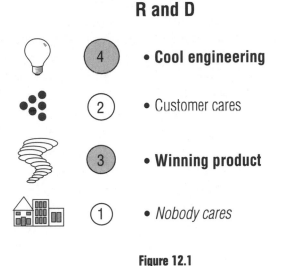

- **Cool engineering**

- Customer cares

- **Winning product**

- *Nobody cares*

Figure 12.1

Ask most engineers where they would like to seek out their next project, and they will answer in the early market. That's where all the cool engineering gets done. Not only is such work great for the résumé, not only does it give them bragging rights around the watercooler (okay, in Silicon Valley it's more likely to be a cappuccino machine), it is just plain fun. This is what you go to engineering school for. So, by way of rating, engineers give the early market their highest score, what we'll represent as a shaded circle with a 4 inside it.

But suppose the company has no early-market projects on the books, now what would the R and D folks prefer? From among the remaining three phases, most will now pick the tornado, revealing that beneath their calm, analytical exterior beats the heart of a ferocious competitor. Outexecuting the competition in a race for best product creates an adrenaline rush that can keep engineering teams running even after the caffeine wears off. So they give the tornado their second-highest rating, which we'll represent by a smaller shaded circle with a 3 inside it.

When it comes to the remaining two phases, enthusiasm begins to wane, but there is still some appetite for the bowling alley. That's because at this stage of market development, although the *pure* engineering problem is subordinated to customer-specific needs, there is usually a pretty interesting *applied* engineering problem to solve. Engineers thrive on problem solving, and so they will give the bowling alley the nod as third choice, which we will indicate by an unshaded circle with a 2 in the middle.

By elimination, this brings us to the one phase in the life cycle that engineers, as a class, loathe—Main Street. Do you know what they call engineering on Main Street? *Maintenance!* Have you ever read a résumé from an engineer that said *seeking forty-year career in maintenance?* No, nor will you. As we saw in the previous chapter, Main Street markets provide no payback for continuing to push the envelope on core system performance. Attention instead is paid to customizing the surface—an important undertaking, to be sure, but a job for marketing professionals not for an engineer. So engineers give this phase of the life cycle their lowest score, which we will represent by a small, unshaded circle with just enough room to contain a lowly 1.

That's how engineers see the technology adoption life cycle as it impacts their lives. Now let's stack their view up against that of the people in operations.

OPERATIONS

Operations in this context covers a range of functions, all of which add up to doing whatever it takes to deliver the promised value to the market. Depending on whether the offering is made up of atoms or bits and whether it consists primarily of a product or a service, this can take on a variety of colorings. Thus in a computer business, operations is anchored in *manufacturing;* in a telecommunications services business, in *systems operations;* in a software business, in *release management;* in a distribution business, in *logistics.* In every case, however, operations acts like the drummer in a rock band, "keeping the beat" for the company, making sure it hits its marks on schedule.

Here's how operations sees the life cycle:

Operations

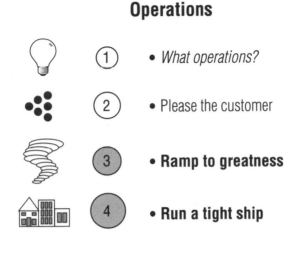

1 • *What operations?*

2 • Please the customer

3 • **Ramp to greatness**

4 • **Run a tight ship**

Figure 12.2

Ask operations people what part of the life cycle they like the best, and they will respond, *Main Street!* Why? Because that's where you can finally get things really under control. Processes are now characterized, control limits understood, continuous improvement programs in place. Our train's on track for six-sigma quality, and that's what gets us bragging rights in our part of town. With any luck we might even get a Baldridge Award for quality. Give Main Street a big 4.

If Main Street is not available, operations will then opt for the tornado. Here, though life is much more of a struggle, operations management is sorely needed. Harnessing all the conflicting demands coming into the pipeline, fusing them into deliverable goods and services, shipping them out to make room for the next batch or wave—it's the stuff of operational heroism. Think of John Henry and his hammer, and give the tornado a 3.

Of the remaining two phases, operations will give the nod to the bowling alley. The customer demands are constraining, to be sure, and typically there is not enough volume to really warrant full-on operational discipline, but there is a legitimate need for the operations discipline called flexible manufacturing, and the resulting output is highly valued. The bowling alley gets a 2.

The one phase operations wants no part of is the early market. Here in a very real sense there are no operations. Everything is still being invented. Procedures are largely nonexistent, and in the rare instances where they have been documented, they are already out-of-date as changing circumstances dictate reinvention. The best thing to do with an early-market project from an operations point of view is to isolate it in a skunk works and not let it corrupt the real work. So the early market garners a 1.

R and D and operations, we can see then, are almost mirror opposites. As we turn to professional services, we'll see that this line function tends to line up more with the R and D crowd.

PROFESSIONAL SERVICES

The term *professional services* is intended to refer to any consulting function in the organization that helps customers implement the company's primary offering and integrate it into their ongoing operations. Its natural opposite is not "amateur services" but rather *transaction services*, the actual outsourcing of the same offering, which would be incorporated under *operations*. Professional services serve as a technology shock absorber, easing early customers into the new paradigm. By contrast, transaction services work as a context outsourcer, taking a fully commoditized function off customers' plates so they can focus their time, talent, and management attention on something more value-creating.

Here's how the professional services function views the life cycle (see figure 12.3).

Note that this is the mirror opposite of operations. The reason why is that professional services add value precisely to the degree that operational procedures are not yet in place. Thus the greatest domain of opportunity is in the early market. Here the new technology challenges everyone, vendor and customer alike, imposing extraordinary demands on systems integration, whether with com-

Professional Services

	(4)	• **Big-ticket projects**
	(3)	• **Profitable business**
	(2)	• Pressure on margins
	(1)	• *Nobody will pay*

Figure 12.3

puter systems, business systems, or cultural systems. Change management is needed everywhere, and that is what professional services offers. Thus the early market gets a 4.

Interestingly, although the early market lets a professional services organization charge its highest fees, it is the bowling alley that offers it the greatest opportunity for profitability. That is because a market is forming around a vertical sector of companies all focused on solving the same problem. As a result, there is greater commonality across projects, captured learning, and thus enhanced productivity. At the same time, the problems are still challenging enough to keep margins relatively high. Ironically, however, the custom-project orientation of professional services organizations often tempts them to overcustomize their offerings during this stage and thus reduce their own margins. Nevertheless, they still make out reasonably well; give the bowling alley a 3.

If the bowling alley is actually better than it looks, the tornado is the opposite. At first blush, the rush of new business opportunities appears hugely positive. But as the tornado unfolds, customers become increasingly sensitive to both cost and time to complete. Firms are asked to show up with a default solution ready to install. This works against the grain of the value-added project model at the core of professional services, and over time such operations must exit tornado markets in favor of earlier phases in some newer life cycle. Color the tornado a 2.

The same forces of commoditization that make the tornado uncomfortable for a professional services organization make Main Street uninhabitable. Markets at this stage expect solutions to be sufficiently well packaged that they do not require consulting to implement. Customers might appreciate the extra services but would not expect to have to pay much for them. Give Main Street a 1.

So if the professional services folks are aligned with the R and D people toward the front of the life cycle, and the operations people are most comfortable on Main Street, who is actually championing the tornado? Need you really ask?

SALES

For the purposes of this exercise let us assume BlueChip is fielding a wide array of both direct and indirect sales channels, with the top executive coming from whichever channel provides the most revenues. Here is how that executive is likely to view the life cycle (see figure 12.4).

I have yet to encounter a sales organization that met a tornado it didn't like. It would be like a bunch of fishermen saying, "Hey, this is no fun, there are just too many fish today!" To be sure, tornadoes attract widespread market attention, so while the game is plentiful, so are the hunters. This makes for a hypercompetitive situation, but that is the way great sales organizations like it. Winning takes aggression, smarts, and stamina—Type A behavior all the way, just the sort of energy that motivated the rest of the corporation to give these folks the sales job and get them out of the building. Give the tornado a 4.

If there are no tornadoes available, salespeople will opt for Main Street, not because it is challenging but because it is such a

Sales

① ② • Cool demo

① • *Quota killer*

④ • **Hottest ticket in town**

③ • **We own this customer**

Figure 12.4

sweet deal. Here the customer is relatively captive, dramatically reducing the competition and increasing sales forecastability. It is a bit like fishing in a stocked pond, but the eating is good. Give Main Street a 3.

Neither of the two remaining phases is particularly attractive to salespeople, but at least the early market is likely to have a cool demo. This has two uses. Occasionally people in the direct sales force can use a cool demo to hook the stray visionary customer and land a major contract. More commonly, however, the entire sales force simply uses the demo as an excuse to have a meeting with their current customers, show them the new stuff, let the techies ooh and aah about it, and then sit down with the conservative managers and sell them a bunch more of whatever it is they already own. For this value-add, salespeople will grant the early market a 2.

That leaves the bowling alley. Now, the first time through the life cycle the bowling alley is not so bad—it is easier to make quota there than in the chasm. But once a company has passed through a tornado and made it to Main Street, the bowling alley becomes a *quota killer*. That is, compared to Main Street market dynamics, sales resistance in the bowling alley is much higher, the solution's complexity much greater, and the sales cycle much longer. In addition, the product-leadership resources needed to succeed at this venture are long gone, either voluntarily out of boredom with Main Street or as part of a cost-reduction exercise in operational excellence. Moreover, your installed base of customers is not the right audience for this offer. They have now become conservatives and are putting pressure on your company to enhance the older stuff, not divert resources into this newfangledness. Even if the sales function were to grant the salesperson quota relief to take on this challenge, there is just too little upside gain for too much downside risk when compared to other possible ways of investing sales time.

So the bowling alley gets a 1, and the reader will not be surprised to learn that this is the phase of the life cycle that will require triage attention. Before looking into that, however, let us first see where the fifth and final function lines up.

FINANCE

In general, finance takes a view of the life cycle that aligns it with operations (see figure 12.5).

For finance teams, Main Street equates to normality. Markets grow at modest but relatively predictable rates. Competition is serious but comes from expected quarters. Improvements are continuous, both in offerings and in operations, all of which lead to incremental gains in productivity that, for the most part, drop to the bottom line, improving earnings per share. Stocks in any Main Street sector are measured by their P/E ratios, so this performance makes investors very happy. Main Street is a land of no surprises, and that is enough to earn it a 4 from finance.

Tornadoes come next. To be sure, by some financial metrics tornadoes might even be better than Main Street, but not when you consider that the added uncertainty and volatility take their toll. The good news is that the top line is robust and growing at

Finance

(2) • R&D tax credit

(1) • *Numbers aren't there*

(3) • **Top-line growth**

(4) • **Predictable earnings**

Figure 12.5

eye-popping rates. The bad news is that losses can show up as often as profits, and cash flow can be a nightmare. However, with the right investors, ones that are more interested in the P/S ratio than the P/E ratio, companies can ride tornadoes to unprecedented valuation heights. Give the tornado a 3.

Interestingly, the early market also gains finance's support. Good finance people know you have to invest in the future to keep a concern going. They know there has to be a protected zone where the burden of profitability is withheld for an incubation period. Besides, R and D earns a tax credit. Thus the early market gets a 2.

But woe again to the bowling alley. From finance's point of view the economics of niche-market investments simply don't add up, certainly not for a company of BlueChip's size. The incubation period is over, and it is time for the new business unit to make a contribution to revenues and earnings, one that can impact stock price. But a niche strategy does not generate sales large enough to make a dent in the overall revenue picture, and the investment of time and focus seems way out of proportion to the return. So finance gives the bowling alley a 1.

END RESULT: STUCK IN THE CHASM—*AGAIN!*

Now when all the line functions are allowed to gravitate toward their natural preferences, companies self-organize in a way that supports three of the four life-cycle phases reasonably well. Here's the overall picture:

Working the Life Cycle

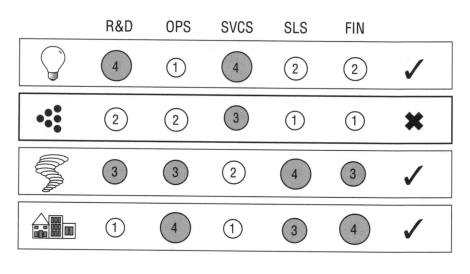

Figure 12.6

The tornado represents the highest scoring phase (15 points if you're counting). Led by sales, the other functions rally round. Indeed, except for highly customized services businesses, it is hard to imagine any company rejecting a tornado call. So, no need for triage here. To be sure, there are challenges, particularly when the company has been out of tornado markets for a while, but like an old warhorse, the spirit can be rekindled.

Main Street represents a close second (13 points), but here ranks are dividing, which has sobering implications, as we shall see later. The good news, though, is that there are two strong lead functions—operations and finance—that are able to pull the organization together. The message goes out: no more Peter Pan, early-market, fly-by-the-seat-of-our-pants stuff. We're adults now, and we have to act accordingly. Thus processes are put in place and procedures followed, people slow down a bit (and organizations put on a little weight), and life goes on. Stellar Main Street performance, to be sure, does require more constructive measures, but from a triage point of view, this ain't broke, so don't fix it.

Interestingly, the early market scores just as high as Main Street (also 13 points) because that is where the other half of the company retreated to when the operations and finance people took over. Engineers, in particular, will gravitate here regardless of what management says. And while salespeople will not actively sell the next big thing (demo it, yes—sell it, no), professional services people can be counted on to step in to help close the deal because one such sale can keep them busy for a long time. Again, stellar performance may not be in the cards, but established organizations are not directly at risk for this phase of the life cycle, so triage rules say don't focus here either.

That leaves us with the bowling alley, and specifically with the challenge of crossing the chasm—making the transition from the early market into the bowling alley. Over and over again, it emerges as the truly broken process in virtually all established organizations. To be precise, the problem is actually *recrossing the chasm* because organizations like BlueChip have made it across at least once before. That's how they got into a tornado in the first place and then later on graduated to Main Street. Now that it is time to reenact this feat, however, *there is no function willing to champion the next crossing.* The people who accomplished this feat last time are long gone, and thus there is no "institutional memory" to rely upon.

The implications of this realization are chilling. If no one will champion the effort, no innovative R and D can cross the chasm. That means all R and D investment in breakthrough technologies is essentially futile. Future disruptive innovations will occur, to be sure, but they will lead to tornadoes for other companies, and BlueChip will be playing catch-up to those market-making efforts, not spearheading its own. In the best circumstances, this means that BlueChip technology can come late to an open-systems market with some chance of becoming a prince and perhaps in the future overthrowing the king. Worst case is, it will come late to a gorilla game with a chimp technology and be crushed by the market's rejection of any standard other than the gorilla's. Neither scenario has much upside.

Combine this observation with the fact that the installed base of customers has become conservative, urging the company to stick to its old knitting, and one generates an environment in which managers learn it is not wise to take technology risk. Indeed, this is the triumph of context—or rather of old core now become context—over core. In such an environment, managers learn not to take any risks at all.

This is the beginning of the end. Good people move on, and with nothing to recruit new good people to join, the team in aggregate gets weaker and weaker, losing its leadership and its savvy. For a while it may appear that all is well because the current set of customers is truly loyal and the offers made to them truly valuable. Sure, one might rationalize, some new customers on the margin are going to the new technology, but that business is not really profitable anyway, and there is still plenty of demand for our established offerings. But sooner or later the next wave of technology does arrive, and with its advent all the frailty of the current position is exposed. This is where triage is well and truly needed.

To state the triage problem succinctly, *the internal line functions of companies on Main Street actively repel adoption of any future disruptive technologies.* As Pogo once observed long ago, "We have met the enemy and he is *us!*" At BlueChip we might imagine it playing out as follows:

1. In line with their predilection for Main Street markets, operations and finance have taken control of the company and instituted management by the numbers. The P&L has become the basis for judging success, and return on assets the key metric when weighing alternative investment decisions. ROA projections, in turn, are judged primarily on short-term, forecastable

sales. This has led to investment decisions that have a high sensitivity to GAP and low to no sensitivity to CAP. Thus CAP has been routinely and often unknowingly sacrificed to GAP. BlueChip has indeed hit its earnings metrics but in part because it has not been investing sufficiently to catch the next big technology wave.

2. When challenged on this point, however, operations and finance deny its validity, pointing instead to the large amount allocated to R and D funding. R and D corroborates this argument. We have sixteen different products in the pipeline, it testifies, and over 40 percent of current sales come from products that were invented in the last three years. We are a healthy and vibrant institution. Moore's criticisms do not apply to us.

3. Marketing, however, intercedes on Moore's behalf (an all-too-often career-limiting move). The new products, it observes, are continuous innovations extending the old paradigm. They do not answer the need to get on the new wave. And speaking of that new wave, the problem is not a lack of new offerings—to R and D's credit they *are* being created—but rather our company's inability to cross the chasm with them. It is additional *market development* investment that is required, not more R and D. All the other line functions, however, interpret marketing's testimony as a thinly veiled attempt to garner more departmental budget, and marketing is asked to sit down.

4. Sales is called to testify. It confidently takes the floor to assure everyone that Moore is indeed off base. Look at the numbers. Revenues are at record levels, and profit margins, although squeezed a bit, are still good. We need to stay on course. (What sales does not say is that this includes supporting a sales compensation plan that continues to pay commissions appropriate for winning market-share battles in the tornado but that is significantly overgenerous for selling into a captive, installed base on Main Street.)

5. Professional services is called to testify. It reluctantly points out that indeed customers are not taking up the new technology as fast as one would like, but it goes on to report that its

own backlog has never been higher, albeit largely from helping integrate other people's technology into the company's legacy systems. R and D and sales both take this occasion to complain that professional services is not helping to promote the new stuff. Services replies, however, that it must maintain a degree of neutrality to keep the trust of the customer and that, after all, selling is sales' job. A round of recriminations follows, brought to a close by the lead executive, who moves the meeting to the next agenda item.

Meanwhile, as this executive staff meeting winds its way through another familiar if long morning, another set of meetings is happening on Wall Street, and these do not bode well for BlueChip.

EARTHQUAKE

While BlueChip's stovepipe functions debate amongst themselves, its investment bankers with their financial analysts are meeting with some start-up championing the next big wave. Both sides at the table are hoping to get together to make an initial public offering, garnering the investment bank a hefty commission for so doing, and the start-up founders and venture-capital backers a big slug of capital gains. In these briefings the financial analysts begin to see from the start-up's business plan just how exposed the current market leaders are. This causes them to make a note to raise the issue at BlueChip's next quarterly conference call.

BlueChip management, not privy to the start-up's briefings, comes to the next conference call prepared to discuss the current quarter's numbers. When the question of market threat from a new quarter is raised, the team is simply not able to respond crisply. Let us get back to you on that, says the CFO. The analysts are actually somewhat tolerant the first time this happens, and so they acquiesce, and the issue is deferred to the following quarter. But after two or three such quarters with no definitive response from BlueChip, one or another of these same analysts breaks ranks and converts the company's coveted Strong Buy rating to a lukewarm

Buy or to an even chillier Accumulate or to a truly frosty Hold—
and the stock price tanks. Even if no analyst breaks ranks, the first
time BlueChip misses any of its numbers, it is devalued some hor-
rific percentage, serving as a kind of catch-up in accounting for
competitive-advantage deterioration.

When the stock market correction strikes, BlueChip management is appalled. How in the world can the market give credence
to these start-ups who have no earnings and precious few revenues
and be so harsh on us who have plenty of both? The question is
rhetorical, of course, for the management team is in complete
denial relative to the true answer. What should be clear to readers
of this book by now, however, is that the market is simply tracking
category competitive advantage. Specifically it is looking at the deteriorating CAP of the older technology and the increasing GAP of
the emerging technology and forecasting a future point in time at
which the lines cross. Beyond that point it is crediting the challenger's category with the advantage going forward and discounting the incumbent's stock to make up the difference.

There is no way out of this box. Accounting for competitive
advantage is as relentless and remorseless as traditional financial
accounting (perhaps more so, in light of recent accounting scan-
dals). The market may be a little slow in balancing its books, but
that only results in more violent adjustments when the correction
comes. In short, a fault line has shifted, an earthquake has hit, and
the company has been dramatically devalued. Now the question is,
how can BlueChip respond?

Going forward, let us assume the best. The management team
is chastened and resolved. It absolutely commits itself to do whatever it takes to restore shareholder value. Now what?

13

TRIAGE IN THE LINE FUNCTIONS

In the short term, there is no time to change course or correct strategy. What matters instead is how quickly BlueChip can shift resources to support its core value-adding functions in the marketplace. Transferring the troops to fill in the value gap is the short-term answer to the emergency. This translates into a fast-paced, hard-edged exercise in determining *core* versus *context*. The question is stark: we must gain traction through increased focus, so what do we save and what do we jettison?

To answer this question, each line-function management team must take a snapshot of its current resource allocations and then determine where to reallocate them going forward. Here's how it plays out.

R AND D TRIAGE

True to its own interests, and those of the shareholders, R and D has kept a major effort going in early-market research. Because of the inability of BlueChip to support crossing the chasm, however, none of these efforts have successfully made it into the mainstream market, and so to earn its keep R and D has split the remainder of its resources between supporting the previous generation of technology, now on Main Street, and doing its best to catch up to other companies' tornado technologies by cloning them as best it can. As a consequence BlueChip has not been first to market with any new wave in so long that it has lost much of the market clout it once had. For some time it has not been able to get in on the best deals nor enjoy the premium margins it once did. As a result, the company's position is more vulnerable to a disruptive innovation than that of a more vital market leader in its category.

From a triage point of view, now that the disruption has arrived, the company has two choices. One, it can decide it is too late for any last-minute chasm crossing and write down all its in-process R and D as scrap. In the short term it will then shift all these early-market resources to the pending tornado based on the competitive new technology, playing catch-up once again. The results will not be first class—this is not BlueChip's forte by any means—but they will blunt the impact of the immediate assault and reassure customers and partners that the company "gets it." Longer term there should be play for a respectable position in the emerging market.

Alternatively, BlueChip can elevate the status of one of its own early-market projects in progress and bet a large chunk of the company's future on creating its own version of the next big thing. Following this course, it will take people off the tornado work on other people's technologies and put them instead on its own disruptive innovation. This is a riskier gambit, to be sure, but if it works, the rewards are much higher. From an objective point of view, however, jumping from worst to first is normally a low-probability bet, and the executive team must be careful not to take this course simply as a move to soothe wounded pride.

Neither of the choices offered is particularly attractive, but that is the price for many prior years of denial. For the purposes of working through the remaining triage scenarios for the other line functions, we will assume that BlueChip has chosen to play catch-up according to the first option. After we are done, we will then go back and show how it can execute a recrossing-the-chasm strategy with the second.

In either case, however, to support the triage shift in resources, ongoing R and D on Main Street technology must be cut back sharply. In general this work must be redefined as context and outsourced with all possible speed. Until management gets it out of the corporation entirely, its inertial weight will inevitably retard all efforts to change course or speed. As part of the transition BlueChip should support initiatives led by marketing and customer service, focused on altering the surface of the offering, and focus the out-sourced R and D efforts on cost-reducing the existing substructure and maintaining its reliability.

R AND D TRIAGE CHECKLIST

• Shoot or promote current early-market initiatives.

• Chase the tornado or race across the chasm.

• Outsource Main Street maintenance work now!

OPERATIONS TRIAGE

The major triage task in operations is to extract the rest of the company from the myriad of context operations into which it has lackadaisically allowed itself to become entangled. The goal is to free up as many resources as possible to focus on core. The tack to take is aggressive, immediate outsourcing.

At this juncture, it is critical to note that the triage challenge cannot be solved either by downsizing or reorganizing. The scarce resources that must be optimized are *time, talent,* and *management attention.* Downsizing or reorganizing do not reduce the demands on any of these elements—indeed, in every case they increase them. So the classic response of a round of layoffs, while providing some immediate running room for cash flow, does nothing to solve the basic problem. Only outsourcing can provide the needed relief.

That said, the notion of *rapid outsourcing* is almost a contra-diction in terms. As we noted in Chapter 2, most context processes are retained because they are mission critical, and these must not be outsourced willy-nilly. Companies must maintain control via systems that ensure work is being done to their standards. They also must maintain visibility into the health of these processes even after their outsourcing since any developing problems are likely to impact them as well eventually. It is a big spec to fill.

Operating in triage mode, BlueChip must assign its very best operations executives to the operations frontiers. They, in turn, should engage with the fewest, most accomplished, and most trust-worthy outsourcers possible. In the short term, work will be trans-ferred without the necessary control and visibility systems, so both sides must be committed to (a) overstaffing the interface functions in the short term to ensure enough human resources to make up for the lack of systems and (b) designing and implementing the necessary systems in parallel, to be put in place as soon as possible.

Needless to say, this is not the cheapest way to handle the transition. Indeed any penny-pinching now will create hesitation and resistance, dire consequences in a time of triage. BlueChip and its outsourcers must function as one team, the former exposing its process to risk because there is no time to solve the problem in a safer way. To keep the outsourcer operating in equal good faith, it must and should pay a premium price for premium resources performing a premium service.

This is tough medicine to swallow. Cash conservation and cost reduction are the order of the day, and here at one of the few places where BlueChip could push for both and get substantive concessions by so doing, it must hold itself in check. Why? Because this is heart surgery, and no matter what, one must not economize.

To be sure, going forward, an outsourcing relationship must provide for the systematic cost reduction of context functions. Those cost reductions will be key to maintaining margins in the older technology, thereby contributing working capital to the next generation of market development. But in the short term, it is more important that outsourcing simply happen quickly and reliably. With so many changes in the wind, the last thing management wants to worry about is the wheels coming off a hygiene operation.

OPERATIONS CHECKLIST

- Drive a core-versus-context exercise across the corporation.

- Manage the outsourcing of context for everything except R and D.

- Focus first on transferring responsibility safely, not cost reduction.

PROFESSIONAL SERVICES TRIAGE

As the consulting arm of BlueChip, professional services finds itself in a peculiar position. There is actually heavy tornado-market demand for its services, but that demand is based on integrating some other company's hot new technology into BlueChip's installed base of legacy systems. Because the company is under attack, management may be so grateful for the revenues this organization can provide that it misses a key point: none of this work does anything to improve the company's stock price. Stock price is a function of securing sustainable competitive advantage—GAP and CAP. That can be achieved only when professional services helps further technology and product offerings coming from BlueChip itself.

The triage problem the services group faces is that BlueChip's own offerings are either too early in the life cycle—stuck on the early-market side of the chasm—or too late in it—stuck out on Main Street—for services to make its most valuable contribution. The systemic correction needed here is better recrossing-the-chasm behavior, a topic we shall turn to later in this section. In the short term, however, professional services needs to put its wood behind BlueChip arrows, wherever they may be.

Thus if the company is playing catch-up inside the competitive technology's tornado, then this group needs to provide discounted services as a way of creating a temporary GAP for a set of product offerings that cannot yet compete effectively on their own. If the company has instead decided to bet on the next big thing from R and D, then the group has to put all its weight behind the chasm-crossing effort needed to make that technology a success. In neither case should the group view maximizing its own revenues and earnings as the appropriate goal or correct metric.

Professional services, in other words, should treat itself as a fungible resource that can be configured to support virtually any competitive-advantage strategy the company undertakes. Its critical metric in this light is to make sure it puts its resources to work on core work and not on context. To put this as clearly as possible, as we stated earlier, *nonbillable work on core* will create more shareholder value than *billable work on context*.

In particular, what professional services must guard against is being co-opted by a sales organization under intense pressure to make quota and unable to do so with the current lineup of BlueChip products. In such a situation, sales teams will often resort to offering "random acts of service," selling early-market projects in support of some other company's disruptive innovations. This is bad business.

It is almost never profitable for the services organization, it does not contribute to the company's competitive-advantage position, and it may well enhance the position of a potential future competitor. Of course, such projects are flattering to the services folks, and the revenue numbers will be hungrily eyed by the finance department, but the truth is, this is toxic revenue and must be shunned.

PROFESSIONAL SERVICES ORGANIZATION TRIAGE CHECKLIST

- Identify the top corporate market initiatives and focus all resources there.

- Reset performance metrics based solely on the success of these initiatives.

- Do not get lured into pursuing revenues or margins as a primary goal.

SALES TRIAGE

When the earthquake hits, of all the functions sales is typically the one most in need of realignment and yet most resistant to change. Its misalignment is that it has the bulk of its resources dedicated to Main Street, but BlueChip needs to reallocate them to more competitive customer-acquisition efforts earlier in the life cycle. The resistance is a function of an organizational structure and a sales compensation program that has not kept pace with value migration.

The triage fix is to migrate mature offerings from a higher-cost channel to a lower-cost one and correspondingly to migrate top-talent sales teams from the task of customer retention to that of new-customer acquisition. Depending on the scope, severity, and urgency of the need to change, sales management chooses from the following escalating series of interventions:*

---

*I am indebted to Mike Meisenheimer and Jim Triandiflou, executives at Ockham Technologies Inc., a sales management software company in Atlanta, Georgia, both for this escalation model and for their general framework for managing sales organizations through the various stages of the technology adoption life cycle.

1. *Tell.* For minor changes, just tell people what the desired new behavior is and then monitor their performance for compliance to the new directive.

2. *Measure.* For more significant offers, where the consequences are important, but the scope of the change does not merit a new channel or a revision in compensation, measure the current channel's sales success against the desired new behavior. Use rank-ordered public reporting against success measures as the prime motive to drive the new behavior.

3. *Compensate.* For still more significant offers, but where a channel change is still more work than it is worth, change the compensation program to reward the new behaviors and penalize persisting in the old ones.

4. *Redefine the job.* This is effectively what happens in a channel change. The existing team members can keep their current jobs and change products or keep their current products and change jobs. What they cannot keep is the status quo.

5. *Replace the person.* This is what happens when a member of the sales team simply cannot handle the previous choice.

Conducting this escalation is the job of sales management. One reason it is so challenging is that the sales executives in charge typically owe a lot of their personal success to the people they are managing. It can easily happen that they have too many "relationship debts" outstanding for them to hold strictly to this line. When that's the case, BlueChip executive management must step in and change the team at the top.

Again, this is nothing personal—it is simply a matter of stock price. Don't change the team and the existing channel will block access to the customer and withhold support from any new offers. Other companies not hobbled by such a channel will get in behind the BlueChip team, build up a new market around the new paradigm, and stick the company with a legacy customer base and an aging product line. In the long run nothing is gained and nobody is served.

SALES TRIAGE CHECKLIST

- Redefine Main Street metrics and compensation and match staff accordingly.

- Charter a new team to tackle the new-customer-acquisition challenges.

- Where needed, change the channel of distribution to drive change.

- Where needed, change the people doing the job to gain traction.

FINANCE TRIAGE

The first triage activity of finance is to help BlueChip realign its goals and metrics by changing the tools and feedback it gives to executives to help them manage for shareholder value. A prolonged stint on Main Street has institutionalized a P&L orientation, but in addressing the new triage challenge, that viewpoint is counterproductive. Instead finance must help the executive team focus on the competitive-advantage crisis, in large part by communicating Wall Street's interpretation of the change in the category. GAP and CAP charts, and indeed the entire discussion of finance in Part I, are intended to provide a foundation for this discussion.

At the same time, all the while this is going on, another group within the finance department should be working internally with those parts of the business that will stay on Main Street. This group must retain an emphasis on standard P&L metrics for several reasons. First of all, the better the quarterly bottom line, the more forgiving investors will be of BlueChip having fallen temporarily behind in the new competition. Second, the more that Main Street operations can contribute to working capital, the better, since at the moment investor enthusiasm for providing that same capital is waffling. And third, by holding Main Street operations' feet to the fire, finance will actually help accelerate the outsourcing of context that is so key to their role in getting the company on track to recross the chasm. One final note: the finance team must support the outsourcing of context, first to shed inertia and second to reduce costs. That is, despite all temptation to the contrary, it must not force a cost-reduction agenda too soon.

FINANCE TRIAGE CHECKLIST

- Reset the internal orientation from P&L to GAP/CAP.

- Relax financial controls on change initiatives.

- Tighten financial controls on Main Street operations.

- Don't force immediate cost-reduction goals on context outsourcing.

WRAP-UP

So much for triage. These are practical steps designed to stop the bleeding. They are intended to buy time for BlueChip to address its recrossing-the-chasm effort more directly. Like all forms of first aid, the sooner they are applied, the better for the patient. At the end of the day, however, despite its immediate criticality, triage within the line functions solves no long-term problems. All it can do is take the company out of range of crisis and buy it some time to regroup and redirect its efforts. In technology-enabled markets, this means BlueChip must sooner or later sponsor its own disruptive innovations and get them across the chasm to compete for mainstream market share. For that we must turn to the next chapter.

14

RECROSSING THE CHASM

Recrossing the chasm is the essential act of renewal needed for corporations to sustain themselves across multiple technology adoption life cycles. The program for so doing is organized around four cornerstone behaviors the company must adopt:

1. Get the board of directors focused on renewal as the real challenge.
2. Construct a dedicated chasm-crossing team focused on appropriate goals and metrics.
3. Deconstruct lingering resistance.
4. Don't stop with the first pin.

This chapter is dedicated to describing these behaviors in more detail.

GET THE BOARD OF DIRECTORS FOCUSED ON RENEWAL AS THE REAL CHALLENGE

Ninety percent of success in triage lies in prioritizing the right problems to address. Well, we just did that. We've flat-out said, *It's recrossing the chasm, stupid!* Surely that is enough to get everyone focused? Fat chance.

The inertial forces behind business as usual are huge. They routinely overpower even the most well-articulated management agenda, independent of manager rank. So even if you're the CEO, you need powerful allies, beginning with the board of directors.

To get the board of directors engaged, begin with this reminder: if anyone is the steward of stock price, it is the board. Disruptive innovations—when they cross the chasm—have dramatic impact on the stock price of every company in the sector. Therefore, the current status of such innovations, be they yours or someone else's, is a board-level issue that deserves board-level attention annually at minimum, and in rapidly changing markets more like twice a year.

In this review, the entire domain of discontinuous technologies should be laid out—the company's internal bets, the bets of competing companies, and the status of each relative to the chasm. Management must lead here in terms of which bets are best to make, but the board must lead in ensuring that alternative bets are not ignored and that contingency plans are in place in case the other guys' bets win instead of yours. In particular, if you are unable to get your technology across the chasm in time, what is your fallback position if you have to adopt their technology? The fates of Wang, Lotus, and Digital Equipment Corporation—all of whom bet their companies on some competitor's technology not succeeding and then lost their companies when in fact it did succeed—should keep boards alert during this session.

Please note that the focus here is not on technologies in the early market but rather on technologies crossing the chasm. Therefore, instead of getting reports from R and D on the latest cutting-edge projects, which is how boards typically engage this issue today, they need to get reports from marketing on market development. Specifically, they need to get a *technology-adoption report*.

The key questions the board must see answered in the technology adoption report are as follows:

1. *Have any of our new technologies proven themselves in the early market?*

   The answer to this question is yes when one can point to a handful of visionary customers who have deployed the technology successfully and are referenceable. And if the company's own professional services organization has helped in the process, that is a big plus, for it is likely to have captured key lessons that will help in crossing the chasm.

2. Is it time to cross the chasm?

The answer to this question is yes if management believes, with the help of partners, the company could field a replicable solution to a thorny problem that a niche of customers is clamoring to see solved. By contrast, if early-market deployments have revealed that such a solution is not currently feasible or that the benefits envisioned for it simply are not sufficiently compelling, then the candidate technology either retains its early-market status and seeks out additional visionary customers, or it gets scratched from the list.

3. What is the target beachhead segment?

Assuming it is time to cross the chasm, the answer to this question must call out a single vertical market segment, defined in terms of geography, industry, and the department or profession of the system's end user. It should further be delineated by a list of target customer companies that represent all the significant players in the segment. Absent a single definitive list, segmentation-based programs cannot be held properly accountable. And finally, management must identify to the board the *broken, mission-critical business process* in the target segment that it intends to fix.

4. What are the metrics of success?

The primary success metric is the number of sales of the new technology to companies on the target list. This is measured against sales by any other company of any competing disruptive innovation in the same prospect base. The market share of established technologies is not the issue, as that represents the legacy, not the future. Sales outside the target segment are also not relevant, as they do not help generate adoption momentum to cross the chasm.

5. What is the goal to which compensation rewards are tied?

The goal is to dominate sales of the new technology to the target segment. Recall the rule of thumb that if a company wins 30 percent of these sales, it is *a leader;* 50 percent and it is *the leader;* 70 percent or more and it is *the dominator.* In crossing the chasm the goal is to dominate the first segment, be the leader in the next one or two, and then be a leader from there on out. Executive compensation programs should be reshaped to reflect the top board-level priority given to these goals.

6. What is the status of the chasm-crossing program today?

Once a chasm-crossing program is initiated, members of the board should inquire into its status every occasion they have to speak with management. After a while even the most resistant manager capitulates under this single-minded treatment. Nothing is more motivating than knowing the question you are going to be asked and knowing that if you do not have a good answer, you're going to look like an idiot.

Most important of all, however, the board needs to hold executive management accountable *as a team.* This forces them to work as a united force to directly engage the inertial forces of business as usual. Anything less than that simply will not turn the boat.

To ensure this behavior, the entire team's compensation and recognition should depend upon chasm-crossing success. That is, no individual member of the team should be allowed to win big if the chasm is not crossed—not the VP of sales, even if the sales organization beats quota; not the VP of professional services, even though it turns in record revenues; not the head of R and D, despite that the company won several product awards; not the VP of operations, who achieved six-sigma quality; not the CFO, whose accounting folks lowered days sales outstanding by fifteen days. Why? Because every one of those achievements ignores a triage crisis in the making.

Finally, to put all this in perspective, chasm-crossing assaults are not the stuff of every year's plan. Moreover, when they do arise, only a small number of people are actually assigned to make them happen. Everyone else is simply expected to help out, if only by not resisting. The entire action is expected to be brought to a conclusion within a year or two. Indeed, if it is not, the risk increases dramatically that it will never be accomplished at all. So we are not asking for a major revolution in board oversight, management compensation, or even business as usual. All we are asking for is the simple recognition that *the entire company's stock price is at stake, and all its members should act accordingly.*

CONSTRUCT A DEDICATED CHASM-CROSSING TEAM

Because, as we have seen, no natural leadership emerges from the line functions for recrossing the chasm, it must be artificially constructed in the form of a heavyweight, cross-functional chasm-crossing, team. The team should be led by a *senior executive sponsor.* This person is not an active agent in the process but rather a highly placed connection who can help power through any resistance from lower-level line functions to the niche-market initiative.

Without this kind of sponsor it is all too easy for the business-as-usual coalition on Main Street to prevail. Indeed, that is also why it is so important to get the board of directors focused on the problem and to tie the entire senior executive team's compensation to chasm-crossing success. Visibility and consequences at the very top of the organization are key to ensuring this initiative never gets lost in the shuffle.

The chasm-crossing team itself must be cross-functional because the effort requires coordination across all of the line functions. The team should be led by an *industry marketing manager* who has strong domain expertise in the target customer's vertical market. Because there is no time to do market research, this person has to know the customer requirements from the outset. He or she leads the rest of the company by identifying and characterizing the problem to be solved, helping the marketing communications organization target the right audiences with the right messages, and holding the rest of the company accountable for delivering the complete solution to the customer problem, either through internal offerings or from partner contributions.

Three key team members must work closely as lieutenants to this leader. The first of these is a *sales manager* in charge of a dedicated sales team focused exclusively on sales into the target niche. The goal here is to create not a separate sales organization but rather a separate sales territory that reports in parallel to the other, typically geographically organized, territories. People on this team must get a deep orientation to the target vertical, its general industry dynamics, the specific dynamics of the broken mission-critical process, and the likely job description for the department manager who is the target customer. Until the company reaches dominator status in the vertical niche, this sales manager will spend all his or her time either teaching or conducting consultative sales sessions within the target domain. Once dominator status has been reached and the company's market position is solidly in place, then this manager will oversee the migration of sales responsibility to an indirect channel that has more strength in demand fulfillment than in demand creation, and the redeployment of the direct sales resources to focus on the next niche market in the bowling alley.

The second key team member is a product marketing manager responsible for delivery and quality of the whole product. At the Chasm Group we like to call this person the *whole product manager* to make sure that everyone understands that the job does not stop with what your company makes and delivers but rather extends to managing every other component of the solution as well, regardless of whether it comes from a partner or even from the customer. End-to-end integrity of what is an emerging value chain is this person's fundamental focus, and he or she is the point of control for solution accountability. Once market momentum is achieved, the whole product becomes self-correcting as more and more players compete to improve its quality. At this point the job reverts to a more traditional form of product marketing, with the whole product management task migrating to some other individual responsible for building the solution for the next niche market.

The third and final core team member is a *professional services manager* whose sole assignment is to support sales and to provision project teams focused on bringing the whole product into existence in the target segment customer's environment. At the outset this person's role leans more to the sales side as the early customers seek reassurance that their needs will get met. Once market momentum is established, the focus shifts to the delivery side of the equation, emphasizing knowledge capture, whole product component reuse, interface simplification between solution components and the partners who provide them, and training of newly deployed teams on lessons already learned. Over time, much of this function can migrate out of professional services into field sales support, at which time the resources can be released to support penetrating additional niche markets.

The remainder of the crossing-the-chasm team consists of liaisons to the line functions of R and D, operations, and finance. In each case the goal is to regulate interaction with the function so as to minimize disruption to business as usual and to restrict the impact of Main Street inertia on the chasm-crossing effort. The key principles here are as follows:

- *With R and D,* the team needs to isolate market requirements for vertically specific functionality. The trade-off is whether to build workarounds outside the product, either through a partner or professional services, or to engage with R and D to modify the product to incorporate them. The latter does more to secure power within the niche, but it opens up the program to Main Street inertia, putting the request in the hopper with every other enhancement request. The ideal solution here is for R and D to split off a vertical release team to build vertically specific modules that plug into a standard architecture.

- *With operations,* the team needs to isolate and bundle niche-specific exception requirements from the standard operating procedures and to work through their resolution in an organized fashion. It is important to involve the other solution partners in this process (a) because they can explain the particulars of the exceptions they require, and (b) because they may be able to provide alternatives that can relieve the stress on inside operations. If the conflicts are found to be inherent and deep, outsourcing chasm-crossing operations is a legitimate alterna-

tive. This decision can stimulate Main Street resistance, however, hence the need for executive sponsorship as a backup.

- *With finance,* the team needs to build an accountability model for
meeting time-sensitive market-development objectives, so that it
is not evaluated simply as another profit center contributing to
the P&L. This will seem odd, to say the least, because the group
will in fact generate revenue with attractive margins, albeit with
modest volumes. But the company must stay focused on the key
competitive-advantage issue, which is that breaking through into
the mainstream marketplace will create future revenue opportunities far greater than those of the initial target niche market.
Therefore, the company wants to optimize this effort for time, not
for money, and must provide financing, metrics, and oversight to
support that end.

DECONSTRUCT LINGERING RESISTANCE

Regardless of how important top management determines recrossing the chasm to be, large segments of middle management in
threatened context positions will resist the effort. The notion that a
company could somehow clean house all at once, once and for all,
is neither practical nor desirable. Such reengineering would shock
the culture to its core and would typically be fatal to the organism.

Instead, the winning behavior is simply for management to act
like a snowplow and clear the path. That is, it must make it unmis-
takably clear that in any conflict between a chasm-crossing effort
and an established Main Street institution, the latter will lose. As
in all such things, the breakthrough communication does not happen until the favored side wins an argument it really has no right
to win. That is, until everyone can see that the contest is blatantly
rigged, some players will continue to try to resist. So best executive
behavior is to demonstrate favoritism early and often.

Once this favoritism is made clear, the organization actually
rebounds in the other direction, and many individuals inside the
company compete to join the vertically focused chasm-crossing
efforts, while others in horizontally oriented organizations com-

plain their teams need more vertical focus. When this happens, you know you are well on your way. The only danger in it is that, as these other organizations adopt the protective coloration of vertically focused chasm-crossing efforts, management will actually take them at face value and think it has multiple target markets under development. Almost certainly this is not the case. Instead, we have set up the dynamics for a final state of jeopardy—stopping bowling alley strategy after knocking down only one pin.

DON'T STOP WITH THE FIRST PIN

As we have just noted, niche-market domination, once it gets going, is self-reinforcing. The results get better and better within the niche, and the organization as a whole gains enormous confidence about its market development acumen. But then a funny thing happens. It comes time to transition from the headpin to the next couple of bowling pins in the market development sequence, and all of a sudden every lesson that was learned seems to fly out the window. The organization announces its next two target niches, each of which is not a niche at all but a wholly separate bowling alley. Then, when it goes after these new markets, it forgets all about broken mission-critical processes, or even bent ones, and reverts to product-centric selling. In short, even as the company is congratulating itself on its terrific grasp of vertical niche marketing, what it is actually doing is shedding the behavior as fast as it possibly can.

What has happened is that, as the Main Street organization saw the privileges granted to the chasm-crossing group's vertical niche approach, it took on the lingo and dressed up its other offerings in similar clothes. Management took these representations to be the fully developed constructs created in the first niche and planned for their success accordingly. But in fact they were nothing of the sort. They were instead all talk, no walk.

The consequence of this behavior is that the wheels start to come off. The first niche is fine, but none of the other efforts deliver. The managers complain that they aren't getting the support the first niche got, but the executive team doesn't see it that way, preferring instead to blame the team. In the marketplace, meanwhile, the company starts to get a single-niche reputation. This causes both partners and people inside the company to polarize, either wanting to join the winning niche team or to move on to something completely different. Now executive management is faced with two unattractive choices—become a single-niche player forever or transition back to being a purely horizontal competitor from a position of weakness.

The correct path instead is to leverage one's initial niche victory by seeking out one or two more pins *within the first bowling alley*. These will be niche markets from the same vertical sector but with different applications. Because of the credibility gained in the first niche, the numeric target for new sales wins in these follow-on pins can be lowered from 70 percent domination to 50 percent leadership. At the same time, one can target a second bowling alley if it has a 70 percent dominatable headpin. But that's the limit, regardless of how big or global your company is. It is just too easy to forgo niche ways in a publicly owned, successful corporation.

However, once you have multiple pins falling in one bowling alley, and the headpin knocked over in a second one, you can seriously undertake a broad horizontal attack on the market. The key here will be, have you discovered a killer app? That is, is there some use of the new technology that has broad common-denominator appeal and is sufficiently compelling to cause the pragmatists here to stampede en masse. If so, then you will change strategy once again, moving to a tornado approach, and leaving behind this bowling phase, albeit continuing to enjoy a special status in the niches you have already won. If not, you will continue with a bowling-alley-forever strategy.

WRAP-UP

This section has laid out in detail the challenge of renewal, of recrossing the chasm, for an established *Fortune* 500 company. While giving deep and due respect to the breadth and depth of this challenge, it has also laid out a prescription for facing it down. In other words, this is not a time to give oneself excuses. Investors, as well as all the other constituencies in the corporation's universe, are watching; action is required.

That said, the strain such actions put on established cultures is so severe, and the resistance those cultures can mount is so powerful, that simply stating the necessary actions is not enough. Managers need a better guide as to what moves business cultures to act, especially when the actions called for are unfamiliar and threatening.

And so, to close out this book on dealing with the fault line and its disruptive impacts, we are going to turn to an examination of business culture itself in search of leverage to support the changes we are all being called to make.

VI

BUILDING TO LAST

To live on the fault line—to embrace the challenges of the technology adoption life cycle and manage for shareholder value in any economy—one must, in the words of Jim Collins and Jerry Porras, build to last. *What we have learned from the study of earthquakes is that buildings with rigid structures fare the worst when the ground underneath them shifts. By contrast, buildings engineered to sway with the wave of force restore themselves to balance safely. Similarly, corporations need to find points of balance that can absorb and survive the shocking changes in market dynamics when innovations disrupt established market positions. That balance is to be found in* culture.

At a high level, a business culture provides unifying values and practices that equate to "how we like to get things done around here." Like the stars to ancient travelers, these help orient navigation. They do not purport to get you across town, but they do propose to get you across large bodies of water. Culture in this sense is a global proposition.

Below this level, culture is deliberately unspecific. That is, instead of specifying procedures, it prescribes a style of action—a set of basic questions to use in sizing up a new cir-

cumstance, a set of preferred strategies and tactics from which to craft an appropriate response, and a core set of values for judging outcomes. Rather than being a set of rules, a culture is a rule-making framework that enables its members to cope with unpredicted and unprecedented circumstances.

Businesses benefit from this sort of capability at all times but particularly so in the current era, when deep changes in market dynamics are occurring with such disturbing frequency. This is not an era for the one-minute manager. These are not problems that can be solved by the twenty-two immutable laws of anything. We are all being asked instead to reach deep into ourselves to come to grips with new business models and find ways to align ourselves and our organizations with them. How we do this individually is largely a matter of personality. How we do it collectively is largely a matter of culture.

In the next chapter we are going to examine four distinct types of business culture, each of which takes a significantly different approach to the challenge of managing for shareholder value. All four have proven their ability to support sustained excellence in business, and thus no one of them is to be preferred to any other. Nonetheless, because they define themselves in part through opposition to one another, it is important to pick one if people in your company are going to be clear about "how we like to get things done around here." Without this choice and the commitment it implies, everyone in the corporation will fundamentally be in doubt about which way is north.

This poses a challenge for executive management, and frankly most teams duck it. Each of the four cultures described has characteristic virtues that make it attractive to incorporate, so ruling out any one of them is hard, and ruling out three of the four is virtually impossible. Indeed, coming to the challenge with the mental framework of ruling out *makes it highly unlikely one will get anywhere. Instead, the right thought is* place above. *The key question to ask throughout the entire next chapter is, when the pressure is really on, and the cultures give very different feedback on how to proceed, which one of the cultures will you and your team encourage everyone in the company to place above the other three?*

In the interests of maintaining diversity, you should understand that all companies have multiple cultures operating within them all the time. That is, because companies are organized at multiple levels, the corporation as a whole can have one culture while particular departments, line functions, or business units can have others. Indeed, as we shall see, this property of culture and organizations can be exploited to help meet the varying demands of an evolving technology market. So we do not want to exterminate such diversity within the corporation.

But cultural flexibility can be carried too far. When different cultures interact, a kind of "import/export tax" is placed upon intercultural commerce, as each group translates the issues and values of the other into its own frame of reference. In relatively benign times, this tax is worth paying just to gain the flexibility of capabilities it enables. But in crisis, this same tax causes bottlenecks in execution that result in lost competitions wherever speed of response is required. By contrast, companies that can automatically resolve such conflicts by falling in line with a preestablished, unifying global culture have a huge advantage in execution.

As we have seen, living on the fault line calls for repeatedly executing rapid cross-functional changes in market development strategy. There is simply no time to negotiate a sequence of intercultural exchanges while putting these changes in place. The company has to be prewired to fly in formation. That is what making an abiding commitment to any one of the business cultures described in the next chapter can deliver.

15

MODELING BUSINESS CULTURES

FOUR BASIC CULTURES

To support executive teams in selecting their culture of choice, there is an extremely useful model described by Bill Schneider in *The Reengineering Alternative: A Plan for Making Your Current Culture Work*, which divides the cultural landscape into four differentiated choices:*

We are going to look into each of these four cultures in detail, but first we need to orient ourselves to the set as a whole. Each culture derives its characteristic identity from a fundamental human motivation that drives people in business as well as in the rest of their life. That characterizing motivation is where the core energy that drives and unites each culture comes from, and we can follow the varieties of culture by keeping in mind Abraham Maslow's hierarchy of needs.

---

* William E. Schneider, *The Reengineering Alternative* (New York: McGraw-Hill, 1994). I have taken some liberties with the book's diagrams, so while Bill should be credited with the value they provide, he should not be blamed for any errors I insert. I am also indebted to Brad Spencer of Spencer Shenk Capers, an organizational-development consulting firm, for drawing my attention to Schneider's work and for pointing out the parallels to Treacy and Wiersema's *The Value Disciplines of Market Leaders*, which I discuss later in this chapter.

- At the base of the hierarchy, people value *order and security*. This is the most broadly felt of all the needs, and it is the motivating force behind *control culture* which, not surprisingly, is the most scalable of the four.

- If order and security are not at risk, people move up the hierarchy to *affiliation*, the desire to belong to an encompassing entity, to be a part of the team. This is the driving force behind *collaboration culture* which excels, again not surprisingly, at teamwork and team building.

- When order and security as well as affiliation can be taken as givens, people move their focus to individual *achievement*. This is the driver for *competence culture*, which excels at competition.

- And finally, if all the lower levels can be taken as givens, people move their focus to *self-actualization*, the realization of their best self. This is the driver for *cultivation culture* which has the most success in generating breakthrough or breakaway innovations.

Schneider's improvement on Maslow is to take the hierarchy out of the relationship among these four motives and cultures. This is key, as hierarchy implies superiority, whereas experience shows no one of these is necessarily better or worse at creating business success. Instead of a hierarchy, he shows us a 2-by-2 matrix (thereby endearing himself to consultants everywhere) (see figure 15.1).

The matrix derives from two sets of dipoles that have characterized Western culture from its onset. The first of these asks us to weigh our allegiance to *the individual* versus our allegiance to *the group*. In competence and cultivation cultures, the balance comes down on the side of the individual; in collaboration and control cultures, on the side of the group. But we need to be clear here. No culture is denying the value of the opposing pole; each is simply stating a bias toward one or the other side. This bias helps organizations expedite working through thorny questions that would otherwise take prolonged negotiation to resolve.

The other dipole in operation here is between *form* and *sub-*

Four Cultures Model

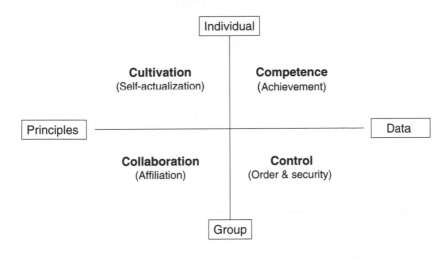

Figure 15.1

stance, *ideas* and *facts*, or as we put it in the diagram, between *principles* and *data*. The issue at stake is, on what basis will the organization make its tough decisions? Along this axis competence and control cultures come down on the side of *measurable data*, tying their key decisions wherever possible to quantifiable changes in observable metrics that can be *externally verified*. By contrast, cultivation and collaboration cultures gravitate toward *operating principles*, looking to representative examples and anecdotes to reveal the essentials of good decision making that can be *internally validated*. The distinction between *verification*, and *validation*—the one examining fit with data, the other fit with ideals—is another expression of the root distinction between these two approaches. Again, no culture denies the existence or the validity of the opposite pole; each simply states a bias toward one side or the other. The purpose of this bias is to foster consistency across multiple decisions and decision-makers operating simultaneously and independently of each other—to allow, if you will, the corporation to fly in formation.

The four culture choices that emerge from pairing these elements in different combinations are all sufficiently rich and flexible to support a global business culture that scales. Their value is a function of their stability over time. When people have history with a culture and can internalize its norms, they can unite smoothly and spontaneously when swift changes in direction are required. Thus customer service reps can "know" what to do based on the norms of their group. They can also "know" how the corporation as a whole is going to respond. This kind of knowing is what permits swift, unified action in times of rapid change.

And with that thought in mind, let us turn to a closer look at each culture in isolation, beginning with competence culture and working our way clockwise around the model.

COMPETENCE CULTURE

Competence culture celebrates individual accomplishment as verified by objective data. Its essence and spirit are to harness the *achievement* motive, creating great work products out of the desire in individuals and teams to excel. Implicit in excelling is the notion of beating the competition, and outperforming competitors is a prime motivator of competence cultures, not always to their benefit. At their best, however, these organizations are marvelously adaptive in their strategies and awesome at execution.

Competence cultures begin with the question *how*. That's because competence itself is all about knowing how. People in this culture want to know *the best way*. They instinctively seek out the most efficient means to get anything done, even something as simple as the shortest route between two points, and will debate that issue strenuously. They love data, specifically quantifiable, observable metrics, as a means for calibrating and corroborating such discussions.

Leadership in a competence culture is a function of demonstrable expertise and a proven ability to execute, and authority must constantly be renewed on this basis. Leaders, that is, must communicate their proposals clearly and persuasively, and anyone is permitted to challenge them as long as it is on the merits of the argument. Expertise is the currency of legitimacy, not job title or seniority.

The resulting organization is typically a work-centric meritocracy where people are organized around projects—a client engagement, a product launch, or a caseload—and promoted based on their ability to execute the tasks assigned to them. The element of consistency in the system is the work itself, with people being shifted from one group to another as work demands. Its key to success lies in hiring the best people and then holding them to a high standard going forward. Standards are set deliberately high, but not unattainably so, and are often reinforced via internal competition. Performance management typically incorporates forced ranking of people, with exceptional rewards going to the top performers and pink slips to those at the bottom. This can raise hackles when interacting with cultivation and collaboration cultures, both of which reject such behavior as dehumanizing.

When it comes to reacting to shifts in market dynamics, competence cultures rely on individuals to detect the change, analyze it, propose a modified course of action, and provide metrics by which both the change and the response to the change can be tracked. The strength of a competence culture is the competitive intensity its members bring to this task, which translates into an unmatchable ability to act quickly and decisively. Its weakness is a tendency to burn out its people, particularly by forcing sustained intensity when the market's dynamics no longer require it. Competence cultures tend to know one speed only.

Microsoft and Cisco are notable examples of companies with competence cultures. At Microsoft, in particular, prospective employees are put through a grueling interview during which the company makes no effort to sell the virtues of the company but instead focuses exclusively on testing the competence of the candidate. People who don't like this process are typically not a good fit for the culture. On the other hand, people who have a high achievement motive actually thrive on this stuff, making them a good match not only for the test but the company as well.

Within corporations with other cultures, the line functions of engineering and sales tend to enact local competence cultures. Both disciplines have a fundamental emphasis on concrete and tangible results—ship the product on time; get the P.O. before the end of the quarter—that measure and validate superior performance. Managers from these organizations love the clarity that such measures create and tend to denigrate the "soft disciplines" of human resources and marketing because they lack any such definitive metrics for excellence.

CONTROL CULTURE

Control culture celebrates achieving a plan as verified by objective data. Its essence and spirit are to harness the desire for *order* and *security*, using the discipline of planning to gain mastery over a changeable world. Here leader and follower alike live by the same credo: *Plan the work—work the plan.* Accountability to the plan of record is the fundamental mechanism for achieving success in this culture.

It is a marvelously reliable system with a proven capability to create large-scale operations that endure. At the same time, more than any other culture, the weaknesses of control culture are brought to light by the challenges of a technology-enabled economy. Specifically the fault line's recurrent demand for rapid changes in strategy and execution—sometimes even *within* a given planning period—violates the fundamental discipline and rhythm control culture relies upon. Thus, to contemporary eyes, this culture is the most problematic of the four, and more than one management guru has made a living mocking and deconstructing its principles.

Control cultures begin with the question *what.* Its members are expected to seek clarity and find security in well-articulated missions, goals, objectives, assignments, job descriptions, and task definitions. Data is highly valued, both as a metric and as a means for classifying things properly. At its best, this clarity around classification is what allows these organizations to scale so effectively. At its worst, it can degenerate into a nightmare of red tape.

Leadership in control cultures is a function of authority, and decision-making is tied closely to title and role within the organization. Leaders call the shots, with the rest of the organization chartered to supply them with the relevant data and issues. This creates the single greatest point of failure in the culture, since underlings can manipulate decisions by slanting or withholding data inputs.

The resulting organization is typically a hierarchy of command organized around distributing work across a system of line functions, one into which first people and then work are fit. The organization is galvanized into action by a commitment to achieve the metrics in the annual plan. Standards derive from the plan, which creates another potential weakness, as they can be set artificially low to ensure "success." If the market as a whole outperforms the metrics in the plan, a company can beat its plan and still fall behind. Such behavior alienates members of cultivation or competence cultures, both of whom see this is as an inexcusable "dumbing down" motivated by lack of self-confidence. Nonetheless, control culture is virtually unstoppable when it comes to executing its plans—and as long as the world does not change on it in the meantime, this creates dominant advantage.

Staffing in a control culture is based on finding people who have demonstrated success in meeting previous plans and who present well to upper management. Hiring and promotion, therefore, are at risk of becoming politicized, resulting in too much energy being diverted into the internal politics of "looking good" and too little on doing whatever it takes to create success in the outside world. Risk taking and personal commitment are frequent casualties in this process.

When it comes to managing changes in marketplace dynamics, control cultures rely on the system to detect the change and to plan and execute an appropriate response to it. The strength of a control culture is its ability to execute such plans efficiently and with high quality over a large-scale operation. Its weakness is its inability to cope with phenomena that change faster than the planning cycle or, worse, that require changes in the planning process before they can be addressed at all. Control cultures, like the *Queen Mary*, find it hard to turn sharply.

IBM, General Electric, and Motorola are all examples of highly respected control cultures. In each of them planning is the cornerstone of management activity. As long as this maintains an external focus, as Jack Welch was able to achieve at GE, it is powerful indeed. When it becomes internally focused, however, when plans worry more about cannibalizing or being cannibalized, when managers worry more about their place in the hierarchy than about getting things done—as happened at IBM during the late 1980s and early 1990s—then things become grim indeed.

Within technology-oriented companies, the line functions of manufacturing, logistics, and accounting all tend to have local control cultures. That's because their disciplines readily translate into procedural systems that run best when exposed to a minimum of creative disruption. Such systems drive people from cultivation and competence cultures to distraction as they need to push against the norm, not reaffirm it.

COLLABORATION CULTURE

Collaboration culture celebrates the ideals of teamwork as validated by subjective feedback from customers and partners. Its essence and spirit are to harness the *affiliation* motive, accomplishing great outcomes through many working together as one. Unlike competence and control cultures, collaboration culture puts people and relationships ahead of the work per se, trusting that by nurturing the former the latter will take care of itself. It is particularly good at incorporating diverse talents and points of view, including reaching outside the company to involve suppliers, partners, and customers. More than any other culture, collaboration culture excels both at serving others and allowing others to serve it. In this sense it provides a superior platform for the core-specialized *virtual organization* that the financial markets are driving us all toward.

Collaboration cultures begin with the question *who*. People in this culture make an effort to get to know the others around them, spending what looks to advocates of other cultures like an inordinate amount of meeting time on introductions and icebreakers. Data is nowhere near as interesting to this culture as are insights, especially pertaining to its ideals, hence its recurrent focus on stories and anecdotes, for these better communicate the essence of its value. At its best this culture engenders the kind of trust and devotion that makes great deeds possible. At other times, it can degenerate into a complacent and self-indulgent social club.

Leadership in a collaboration culture is role-based, not expertise-based nor title-based, and authority is situational. Thus, for example, the role of team leader is central and constant, but who that leader will be is allowed to shift with the situation. Stability comes from process, and decisions are reached through working the process until consensus is achieved. The goal is to allow the natural expertise of individuals to come to the fore in those situations for which they are best suited to lead. Used immoderately, however, consensus decision-making creates analysis paralysis and a culture in which all members believe they are entitled to participate in every decision. Thus collaboration cultures need to restrict their use of consensus process to matters that are core and delegate context decision-making to executive functions.

The natural organization of a collaboration culture is cross-functional teams aligned to go after specific market opportunities. Quality and effectiveness are achieved by keeping teams intact even as work assignments come and go—essentially the dead opposite of a competence culture. Standards and metrics are calibrated to the outcomes of the team, not individuals. This can create "hiding places" for less competent team members, something that drives members of cultivation and competence cultures crazy, both of which thrive on individual accountability. Team culture, however, is impressively powerful in building a new value chain to penetrate a new market. There the marketplace power gained from forming new linkages outweighs the gains achievable from superior performance within any one link. On the downside, collaboration culture tends to become inefficient whenever market dynamics reward performance within line functions more than cross-functional coordination.

Staff in a collaboration culture is recruited based on people's ability to get along well with others. The goal is to maximize synergy across functions, getting superior results through teaming behaviors. Team players, therefore, are highly valued and get promoted. Conversely the organization is leery of prima donnas and superstars, who are better suited to competence and cultivation cultures.

To manage changes in market dynamics, collaboration cultures rely on the team to detect the change and work out an appropriate course of action. The strength of the collaboration culture is its ability to adapt to change by leveraging diversity. This makes it exceptionally good at accommodating the interests of others in its own internal plans. At its worst, however, collaboration culture fails to weed out its mediocre performers and thereby loses its ability to compete effectively.

Nokia and HP are prominent examples of collaboration culture in the technology sector. In particular, HP's culture—the HP Way—has often been called out both for its virtues, which were widely hailed in the early and middle 1990s, and its weaknesses, which have been the focus of more recent attention. There is a wonderful story from the early days of Bill Hewlett taking a fire ax to a locked supply cabinet one weekend when employees were in working and could not replenish their supplies—very much the sort of "people first" kind of anecdote that collaborative culture thrives on. More recently the culture has been overwhelmed by size and bureaucracy—effectively, too many resources devoted to context rather than core—something that collaboration cultures struggle with as they wish to honor everyone's contributions. In 2002 this has led to its worst traits being exposed in a fight over a merger with Compaq.

Within corporations with other cultures, marketing and customer support tend to be local collaboration cultures. In both cases a conscious attempt is made to embrace and reconcile multiple points of view, a task for which members of competence and control cultures have little appetite. It is no accident that neither engineers nor salespeople tend to have much time for marketing.

CULTIVATION CULTURE

Cultivation culture celebrates the ideals of the individual human spirit validated by the personal insights of its wisest members. Its essence is to harness the desire for *self-actualization*, the complete fulfillment of one's human potential, individuals unleashing capabilities they did not know they had. It brings its members together by articulating a compelling vision of a possible future and then calling on them to turn that vision into reality.

Like a collaboration culture, cultivation culture puts people first, but as individuals rather than as teams. Teams, in its view, are too likely to compromise and accept the actual instead of stubbornly pursing the ideal. Cultivation culture is inherently iconoclastic and attracts maverick individuals with high creativity and a low tolerance for external control. More than any other culture, it succeeds at producing breakthrough innovations that simply could not come from planned, measured, or collaborative approaches.

Cultivation cultures begin with the question *why.* This serves as a two-edged sword, both as an outward-facing challenge to existing orthodoxy and as an inward-facing challenge to oneself to drive to a deeper level of understanding. As with collaboration cultures, anecdotes take priority over data in this realm, but here they are valued not for their common touch but rather their ability to capture and transmit breakthrough insights, as in the example of Zen koans or parables.

Leadership in a cultivation culture comes in two forms—highly visible charismatic leaders who attract willing troops or absolutely invisible administrators who create sanctuaries for misfits. In both cases the leaders are motivated by a deep and abiding vision that they recognize cannot be achieved by ordinary means. As a result they eschew objective measurement and supervisory control and substitute for them loyalty and devotion to a common goal. Power gravitates to people in the spotlight who perform brilliantly. At its best this creates hugely refreshing novelty—at its worst, unmatched arrogance and increasingly tedious egotism.

The natural organization of a cultivation culture is antiorganizational. That is, the culture seeks to celebrate the individual and resists structurally subordinating any member to any other member. Titleless organizations are therefore commonplace. Work worth doing is perceived as a self-organizing system that will recruit and deploy talent spontaneously, without the need for externally applied infrastructure. Standards are often set impossibly high, not with the thought that they will be achieved but rather to provide a target to aspire to, very much along the lines of Browning's "A man's reach should exceed his grasp, / Or what's a heaven for?" This can cause problems, however, when interacting with competence and control cultures, both of which define closure as hitting targets, not simply aiming at them.

Staffing with only the best and the brightest is the key to success in cultivation culture. The good news is that these best and brightest are attracted by the privilege of working in such an atypical environment, and they are hard to recruit away for the same reason. Promotion should never be an issue, as there is nowhere to promote anyone to. Compensation is also a second-tier concern. The only form of discipline is based on controlling access to the resources needed to do one's work. Weaker members of the culture are eliminated through snubbing: when their funding runs out, they are simply not invited into the next round of projects.

When it comes to managing changes in market dynamics, cultivation cultures rely on individual insight both to detect the change and to capitalize upon it. The strength of a cultivation culture is that it can anticipate and react to changes long before any of the other cultures even detect them. That is because the insight of brilliant individuals activates well in advance of any substantive corroborated evidence. This capability, however, also underlies the culture's most serious weaknesses, a tendency to chase phantasms or "false positives" well past the point of diminishing returns and to defend that practice with self-indulgence, righteousness, and insularity.

The premier example of a cultivation culture is the Silicon Valley start-up, founded by a pair of twenty-somethings, glorying in brilliance and unconventional behavior. The original prototype for this was the Apple Computer of the early 1980s during Steve Jobs's first tenure. Steve is a superb example of both the strengths and weaknesses of a cultivation culture leader. He is phenomenally charismatic and can motivate people during even the most trying times armed with the most improbable of value propositions. At the same time, he drives those oriented toward control or collaboration cultures to distraction, continually overruling decisions that have been made by the person or the process in authority, thereby making it virtually impossible to scale an organization beyond his personal boundaries.

In corporations with other cultures, skunk works R and D groups are the most prominent localized manifestation of cultivation culture. These typically form around genius designers and architects who are able to recruit and retain others like them, with everybody else just tiptoeing around the outside for fear of disturbing genius at work. In general, however, as corporations scale, they become increasingly hostile to cultivation culture, as it actively defies the norms by which the other cultures negotiate—accountability to the plan of record, subordination of the individual to the team, measurement relative to specific, quantifiable objectives. Thus it is no accident that breakthrough innovation tends to happen at the periphery of established institutions, not at their cores.

WRAP UP

To summarize the preceding, consider the following table. Like all things human, cultures do not really lend themselves to being pigeonholed, but the various comparisons and contrasts should help executive teams navigate where their own culture fits.

	Competence	Control	Collaboration	Cultivation
Cherishes	Achievement	Order & security	Affiliation	Self-actualization
Celebrates	Top performers	Making the plan	Teamwork	Creativity
Prioritizes	The work	The system	The people	The idea
Asks	How?	What?	Who?	Why?
Leads by	Expertise	Authority	Process	Charisma
Organizes as	Work projects	Hierarchy	Persistent teams	Little as possible
Recruits for	Competitiveness	Loyalty	Trustworthiness	Brilliance

As we look over this table, each of the four cultures should seem sufficiently attractive in its own right that a corporation would want to embrace parts of each. However, to react swiftly to the shifts in market dynamics that characterize living on the fault line, management must privilege one culture above all the rest. What that entails is the subject of the next and final chapter of this book.

16

MANAGING CULTURE FOR SHAREHOLDER VALUE

The power of a culture clearly defined is that it prescribes a general approach to take to all unspecified challenges. As such it allows individuals unbeknownst to each other to tackle the same problem and discover somewhere down the road that their independent work efforts reinforce each other. Grounded in common principles, even dramatically different tactics can be reconciled and unified into an overall plan of attack.

The opposite is the case when multiple work efforts have been incubated in different cultures. Here it can be challenging to reconcile and unify work that appears to be precisely on the same track. The problem is there is no agreement on common underlying values, hence no basis for trust. Fierce debates erupt over the most trivial issues and will continue to rage until a common culture is established and the individuals involved opt in or move on.

The destabilizing shocks created by disruptive technologies inevitably spawn multiple independent work efforts as various parts of the corporation seek to reestablish their positions in the market. If the disruption amounts to a minor tremor, it can usually be contained within a single group, and all is well. But larger shocks demand cross-functional and pan-organizational responses which must be orchestrated under a common set of principles and practices. Lacking a common pre-established culture, this is all but impossible. In addition, in technology-enabled markets, to keep up with the rapid pace of innovation, successful companies are resorting more and more to mergers and acquisitions. The logic of these actions is above reproach, but the results have all too often been below expectations. At The Chasm Group, we believe this is primarily a function of not managing the cultural evolution required to put things on a common footing going forward.

This is simply bad management, and it needs to stop. Executive teams need to explicitly confront the subject of culture, examine it through the lens of some set of models—if not this one, then some other—and make choices about the kind of foundation they want to provide. It is a bit like determining the default language for a global corporation: the intention is not to prevent the use of other languages but to have one common underpinning when all must work as one.

SELECTING A CORPORATE CULTURE

Challenging as this process is, there is some good news here: it is usually already under way by the time executives decide to engage. That is, while it is rare to find companies with strong single-culture roots, it is also rare to find companies equally attracted to all four. The first task of management, therefore, is to take the cultural temperature of (a) its own members and (b) the organization as a whole to see the hand it has been dealt.

Testing for culture is remarkably similar to testing for personal traits—if you have ever taken a Myers-Briggs test and found out you were (in my case) an ENTJ, then you will find culture tests almost the same. And by taking the test—personally, as an executive team, and then as a pan-organizational effort—you will learn the same kinds of lessons: people are different, groups are different, and you did not know yourself quite as well as you thought.

Most importantly you will most likely see that the company has already gravitated toward cultural preferences. In some cases a default monoculture may already be in place: Microsoft *is* a competence culture, GE *is* a control culture, and the like. The primary issue management teams face here is keeping that culture in balance, something about which we will have more to say shortly.

For most companies, however, at least two cultures are vying for the tiller. In these cases, the first step is to recognize that it is not the other two. That is, the other two cultures can and should be deprioritized. In looking to the remaining two, it matters a great deal whether they are *adjacent* or *diagonally opposed* on the culture grid.

Adjacent cultures share a common element which can become the focus for initial work. Thus competence and control cultures share a common interest in measuring themselves by *objective data,* whereas collaboration and cultivation cultures seek to validate their decisions through *shared values.* Similarly, cultivation and competence cultures share a common tendency to privilege the *individual,* control and collaboration cultures, the *group.* Just knowing this much about an organization can help determine the most effective ways to communicate, motivate, and manage during times of exceptional change.

By contrast, shared commitment to diagonally opposed cultures implies a core tension that is inherently unstable and must get resolved before the organization can proceed with dramatic change. Cultivation cultures are by nature in rebellion against control cultures, who in turn see cultivation cultures as in violation of business's fundamental rules. Similarly, competence cultures fear collaboration culture will either dumb them down or slow them down, while the latter see competence cultures as having lost all sense of humanity and true values. Diagonal dipoles tend to develop whenever a dominant culture has grown out of balance, become too full of itself and, thereby called into existence its antidote. But because the cultures have no common ground upon which to interact, the end result is increasingly dysfunctional.

As both the time and need to choose a culture looms, please understand there is no one left make the call but you. That said, here are some principles to guide you at this time.

1. *Choose a culture for which you have a leader.* Seems obvious enough, and yet more than one company has gone awry on this point, typically by identifying its diagonal culture as the answer, only to find no one suitable to lead that culture exists in or is willing to be recruited into their company.

2. *Favor reforming an existing culture over migrating to a new one.*
    Changing culture is wrenching and disorientating. Reform-
    ing culture is also wrenching, but it is reinventing. That is, as
    people get back to first principles, they find familiar friends
    and this makes it easier for them to align with the new re-
    formers.

3. *Favor migrating to an adjacent culture over crossing the diagonal*
    for all the reasons we have been discussing. Use the common
    element in the adjacency as the anchor point for driving
    change.

4. *Treat the decision for what it is—something that requires the
    total commitment of every leader involved for the next year.*
    Every major program launched in the next year, be it within
    function or cross-functional, becomes an instrument for fur-
    thering the culture change. This is what we mean by *declaring* a
    culture.

DECLARING A CULTURE

Once a culture is selected, it must be *declared*. Declaration is what
activates a culture. It is not a matter of *saying* anything, although that
is clearly part of what is involved. Rather it is a matter of focusing the
corporation on the core activity that defines the culture. That is, this
is where *core* as investors define it and *core* as cultures define it inter-
sect. It becomes the highest-level abstraction of the company's most
abiding competitive advantage strategy.

   In this light, each culture has a natural core, as follows:

Cultivation culture	**Shared vision**
Competence culture	**Measurement and compensation**
Control culture	**Business planning**
Collaboration culture	**Customer focus**

Each culture believes that its natural core provides a foundation upon which its members can build a great and lasting company.

Declaring the culture makes one of these four principles the centerpiece of the change-management initiative. Management communicates the declaration by consistently and continually incorporating this particular emphasis into all major activities. It takes every occasion to bring it up, talk it up, relate present circumstances to it, and explain success or failure in its terms. It does not have to actively suppress any of the other three; it simply must obsess on the fourth.

This is most easily seen in the management of local cultures. Most sales cultures are competence cultures. How do we know? Because most sales managers are always talking about quota and compensation. Most financial cultures are control cultures. How do we know? Because they are always referring to the business plan and variances from it. Similar observations can be made about marketing cultures and their emphasis on customer focus or about R and D lab cultures and their interest in sharing vision.

To meet fault-line change management challenges, the executive team must take this kind of declaration up to a global level, giving the corporation a distinctive personality, one that employees, customers, partners, and investors can all rally around. To make the needed adaptation, people must be absolutely clear about "how we do business around here." They *know* that General Electric is a control culture. They can count on that. If they want serious attention, they know they have to relate their issue to the business plan. Similarly, people at Charles Schwab *know* it has a collaboration culture. If they want serious attention, they know they have to relate their issue to a burning customer concern. These are hugely useful frames of reference.

In essence, what we are prescribing is an intense, company-wide marketing program on behalf of the new culture. Like all things related to marketing, this should not be misunderstood as one-way communication. In fact, it is much more important to listen and respond than to simply preach the gospel. By listening, we allow anxieties and frustration to surface, and by responding we model how the new culture expects its members to deal with such things. For we must be clear on two fronts: first, we respect everyone's right to feel uncomfortable about any major change, and second, there is no chance we are going to revisit this choice of direction anytime soon. Thus, it is not a time to entertain other choices or to get back to people later on something. This is the declarative moment, and while some people may not appreciate it, they should not be confused about it.

DEVELOPING A CULTURE: INTEGRATING, BALANCING, AND COMPLETING

Even as the new culture is being declared, it needs to be systematically developed. In *The Reengineering Alternative*, Schneider lays out three steps to this end, the first of which is *integration*. Here one reviews and, if need be, reconstructs all of the corporate systems to ensure they conform to the values and style of the selected culture. By corporate systems we mean all of the non-line functions that serve as the cartilege that helps orchestrate the movements of muscle and bone:

- Organization
- Information systems
- Planning
- Compensation
- Human resource management
- Public relations
- Legal
- Facilities
- Security

The power of these systems is that they seep into every cranny and corner of the corporation. Thus if they are well and truly aligned with the new path forward, that message will get repeated thousands of times every work day.

Do not miss the power of symbolism here. Every element of the business takes on a different coloration depending on the culture, even something as seemingly mundane as facilities or security. That is because all acts have overtones, and the job of executive management is to orchestrate those overtones to communicate a common cultural theme. What would it say about a cultivation culture if everyone had to wear badges? What would it say about a control culture if executives did not? What about a collaboration culture where all the line functions are housed in separate buildings? How about a competence culture where everyone has to punch a time clock and merit raises are limited to 3 percent? Nothing is nonsymbolic. Everything communicates.

The value of integration is that it allows the culture to recognize and realize its true self. In so doing, it reinforces the style and strength of the culture, all of which is rewarded by stronger competitive advantage in the market—when the culture's propensities are in phase with the demands of the technology adoption life cycle. The challenge comes when the market and the culture go out of phase. How can a company respond when the market wants to reward the culture that is the diagonal opposite of the one it selected? It is here that one must learn the second discipline of culture management, what Schneider calls *balance.*

The key to balance is to achieve the effect of the opposing culture without abandoning one's own. To do this it must adopt the *principles* of the diagonal culture but avoid adopting its *practices.* Thus, for a collaboration culture inside the tornado, it must achieve the effect of a competence culture—intense competitive behavior in an all-out winner-take-all battle—without forsaking its collaborative roots. To do this, it *collaborates to become competent.* That is, it competes, but as a team, not as a set of individuals. Similarly, a competence culture crossing the chasm is called to collaborate, but it must not try to adopt some touchy-feely approach to "getting closer" to the other party, giving up its competitiveness for some greater good. That is unnatural in a competence culture. Instead, it must leverage the competitiveness of its people, say through a contest to see who can score highest on a set of specified customer satisfaction metrics. In other words, it must use its competence to mimic collaboration and achieve its ends. It's a bit like Amazon.com. There customer service software isn't *really* customer-intimate, but it succeeds in making you feel that way.

This brings us to Schneider's third and final step in cultural development, the move to *completeness*. Up to this point, our discussion of culture has been focused exclusively on company culture as a monolithic whole. But as we have already noted several times, subcultures exist at every level of organization. That is, each division, each line function, indeed each department or work group, is sufficiently local and self-organized to sustain an internal culture independent of the corporate culture, if it so chooses.

This creates an environment within which a global culture can learn to embrace the behavioral capabilities of its two *adjacent cultures*. It is accomplished not by any systemic change but rather by simply drawing attention to the accomplishments of one or another of the local cultures. The tactic is to celebrate some accomplishment in that organization that is "countercultural" and yet has clearly contributed to the health and well-being of the company. The goal is to keep the company from becoming Johnny One Note, to stretch beyond playing every song in the key of C.

Stepping up to this last growth objective is key to getting consistent sustainable performance across the entire technology adoption life cycle. The world is just too varied to be "solved" by any one equation. But in seeking out these complements, it is important not to call into question the commitment to the global culture. That is why local cultures are the appropriate place to celebrate these virtues, and why work on completeness comes after work on integration and balance.

To sum up, developing an integrated, balanced, complete culture is a journey, not a destination. In our Darwinian world, any level of accomplishment is sooner or later challenged to reinvent itself. That being said, in a business environment with an emphasis on growth through acquisition, this need for reinvention tends to come sooner than expected.

MERGERS AND ACQUISITIONS: WHEN CULTURES COLLIDE

As we mentioned in the opening of this chapter, many of the most successful corporations in high tech in recent years have turned to mergers and acquisitions to keep themselves current with the market. Despite all the work done by M&A advisers, however, not to mention the high premiums paid in boom years to acquire companies, the sad truth is that most mergers and acquisitions simply do not work out well. That is, one discovers that, after a couple of years to shake out, the shareholder value of the new entity has gone down, not up.

Our claim, stated there and reiterated here, is that most mergers fail when the cultures of the two companies conflict and the executive team does not resolve the conflict swiftly. What is required instead is to reset the culture counter to zero, assemble the decision-making body, and replay the sequence of identifying, declaring, and developing a global culture for the new combined entity.

There are shortcuts, of course, the simplest of which is to assert the current global culture of the acquiring entity. This is the way Computer Associates successfully managed a whole series of acquisitions in the 1980s and early 1990s. It had a control culture, and it made no bones about it. The acquired company was stripped bare to only its products and a core of supporting engineers, which were then assimilated into the corporation. Everyone else was sent packing. Draconian, to be sure, but effective and, I would argue, fair.

Cisco Systems has taken a different approach to its successful acquisitions. It operates as a competence culture. It plans to retain the R and D and product marketing of its acquisitions—indeed it must if it is to continue to compete across an increasingly broad line of network equipment technologies. So it does not try to assimilate those teams but instead encourages them to remain autonomous. At the same time, it immediately works to assimilate all the other functions—sales, support, manufacturing, logistics, finance, and human resources, all of which are expected to conform to the Cisco culture.

Consider, by way of contrast, several acquisitions that back-

fired. In the 1980s IBM, a control culture, acquired Rolm, a cultivation culture. For a while it vowed to let the Rolm folks do it their
way, but undeclared cultural shifts led to miscommunication and
mistrust, and soon the IBM folks came in to assert their control
culture. This led to mass defection by the key Rolm engineers and
ended ultimately with IBM exiting the business.

A similar saga played out when HP, a collaboration culture,
acquired Apollo, a competence culture. HP was confident its adaptive style would win over the Apollo engineers, but in fact the latter
perceived the company as dumbed down by a consensus culture
they wanted no part of. As a result, the alliance that was supposed
to overthrow Sun did nothing of the sort, and HP ended up refocusing its UNIX business on commercial servers instead.

The point of these tales is not to assign blame but to point out
that culture management is a critical success factor, and that it
takes more than lip service to bring it about. In every M&A go-forward plan there simply has to be an assigned task to identify and
declare the new culture. To ignore this work is to put the combined
organization at risk to no purpose. Even if it is known going in that
the plan is to assert the acquiring company's culture, that assertion
will play out differently depending on the culture of the acquired
company. Talking through the issues and building the right transition can save millions of dollars, perhaps even billions of dollars,
in shareholder value.

AGING CULTURES: WHEN *CONTEXT* OVERTAKES *CORE*

In any culture, when the mass of activities that we have termed
context exceeds in volume the mass of activities that we have
termed *core*, culture begins to transform from a source of vital
energy into a set of confining rituals. This happens more easily
than one might think.

Think of context tasks as organisms seeking to survive, if for no
other reason than that the people who do them want to keep their
jobs—or even expand them. How do they get the resources to do
so? *By masquerading as core!* They dress themselves up in the language of the culture in order to fool the corporate immune system

into thinking they are friends when they are, in fact, foes. But peer beneath those covers, and it is painfully obvious no real competitive advantage is being created.

Whenever a culture loses it core resources to context tasks, it becomes a parody of its best self. The results are ludicrously obvious to outsiders but are virtually invisible to longtime members of the culture. So it helps to know what to look out for. By way of helping executive teams stay on their toes, we'll close this chapter with a review of what each culture looks like when it becomes at risk.

CULTIVATION CULTURE AT RISK

When context overcomes core in a cultivation culture, the result is a *cult*. You can see the trappings anywhere. What used to be inspired bits of whimsy—say, a Ping-Pong table in the lunchroom or a fireman's pole to slide between floors—start to become fetishes. People *require* the right to bring dogs to work, the right to dress sloppily even though a customer is coming that day, the right to send a flaming e-mail if they think it is warranted. Whereas in a vibrant cultivation culture hard at work on its core mission, any one of these behaviors could, and probably should, be overlooked; when they become the very stuff of work, then the culture is in deep trouble. It happened in spades at Apple. It happened at any number of dotcoms after they went public. It is at risk of happening at the research labs of IBM, Lucent, HP, and Xerox. And of course, high tech has no monopoly on this sort of thing; it is clearly happening routinely at any number of advertising agencies, investment banks, and Hollywood agencies.

The disease these companies fall prey to is *unbridled extension of the ego*. Because their culture eschews metrics—metrics being artifacts of an obsolete worldview that they have long ago transcended—its leaders fall prey to the vice of denial. No event or result can cause them to self-correct their entrepreneurial willfulness because they can simply choose to ignore it. Boards of directors in such cases are often intimidated by these charismatic leaders and typically lack the will, although not the inclination, to replace them. It is a death spiral that has one attribute unique to it—it tends to end with a bang, not a whimper.

Cultivation cultures gone awry cannot be reformed. They have to be abandoned and then reconstructed elsewhere. Once the magic is lost, "reconstructing" it is like trying to reconstruct a romance—it is just not in the cards. What makes Silicon Valley such a great breeding ground for cultivation culture is that it is so easy to abandon failure, to simply walk away from it and start over. There is a dark side to this, something that might be approximated by a twist on Jack Nicholson's great one-liner from the movie *As Good As It Gets:* "When I want to imagine a charismatic entrepreneur, I just think of an engineer and then take away reason and accountability." In the end, however, Silicon Valley actually does enforce accountability by denying future access to capital—hence the ongoing vitality of its ecosystem.

COMPETENCE CULTURE AT RISK

When competence culture gets caught up in context rather than core, it devolves into a *caste system* ruled over by an aloof and increasingly cynical elite. All the trappings of a meritocracy remain, but the metrics that drive the competition for rewards become inwardly focused with less and less impact on the outside world. The culture continues to subject its members to innumerable tests and measurements, but at the end of the day they do not correlate to creating gains in competitive advantage or increases in shareholder value. They do, however, correlate to promotion within the culture, and so they are vigorously pursued. The result is a tightly controlled guild—law, medicine, and accounting have all fallen into this trap—training its members to master reams of data and procedures while failing to prepare them for the changes that really matter. Why does this happen?

In a competence culture, the metric acts as proxy for the goal—it ceases to be questioned and is simply made the focus of achievement. Get the new product into the market in time for the Christmas season. Ratchet up the megahertz on the next microprocessor. Reach the next lower price point with the new printer. As long as these goals are in line with what the marketplace values, all is well. But when when the marketplace no longer values the behavior, all this core becomes context, and the culture has no mechanism for detecting it. It thereby falls prey to missing the next new thing, persisting instead at becoming *ever more competitive* at a performance that has *ceased to be relevant*. This is the price of focusing on old competitors instead of new customers, and unchecked it will marginalize the company's offerings going forward.

CONTROL CULTURE AT RISK

If we look at a control culture, its parody takes on a familiar form: *bureaucracy*. Indeed this condition is so familiar to us we tend to treat it like dandruff, but it is much more like the build-up of cholesterol—slow acting but ever deteriorating to quality of life, and ultimately fatal in consequence.

Bureaucracy is the application of the processes and procedures of control culture to context tasks that are unworthy of them. Control processes are industrial-strength phenomena requiring enormous expenditures of time, talent, and management attention to deploy. When they are directed toward context instead of core, they divert the bulk of an organization's resources into inconsequential projects, sapping the energy so desperately needed for creating real value. Thus a large part of business's frustration with government is not that its agenda is wrong, not that its intentions are ignoble, not that the targets of its programs are unworthy, but simply that so much bureaucracy is mandated by law that too few resources ever get applied to the problem at hand.

But before business takes government to task, it behooves it to look considerably more closely at its own operations. Bureaucracy build-up around context tasks is the number one cause of failure to recross the chasm. The new innovation is not only starved for resources because the bureaucrats have sopped them up, it is also called upon to waste additional resources by sending representatives to an endless stream of meetings, not one of which has any hope or intent of improving stock price. And should the new group refuse to comply, it will be ostracized and denied the political allies it needs to win its next battle for resources. Thus any initiative that might actually change shareholder value is quickly tamed and taught that context, not core, is the way we really do business around here.

As we have already noted, neither downsizing nor reengineering solves this problem. Both only add to the tax on time, talent, and management attention. The only way forward is to do an aggressive core-versus-context housecleaning with major out-sourcing of context functions. Every day you put this off allows the bureaucracy to siphon a little more vitality from your corporation.

COLLABORATION CULTURE AT RISK

Collaboration cultures find it easy to succumb to context because just by assembling a team to do any task—core or context—it ful-fills its primary motive of affiliation. Thus a collaboration culture can feel great about itself for an extended time, all the while mak-ing no contribution to shareholder value. But when the stock price finally reflects this performance, then the culture goes into a funk, realizing belatedly that it has let one of its prime constituencies down.

A collaboration culture overrun by context becomes a *club*. Each member is allowed a say even when (a) it is not their busi-ness, and (b) the thing isn't worth talking about in the first place. That's because the culture so honors the individual and his or her place in the community that it hesitates to call out—or cull out—inappropriate or mediocre performances. The result is that all action becomes subject to a paralyzing web of review. At the time of this writing, HP has fallen prey to this problem and is learning painfully it is not the sort of thing one can quickly fix. Digital Equipment Corporation fell prey to it in a prior decade and lost its independence altogether.

To reform a collaboration culture the directive must come from the top, but the performance must come from the middle. That is, in this culture middle managers collectively have more power than top executives because the culture "happens" in meet-ings, and middle managers attend a lot more of them. To get out of the context trap, top management must personally reorient and even retrain the middle to be more selective in its use of meetings, to be proactive in disciplining members who are abusing this priv-ilege, and to weed out members who are holding back perform-ance. This task cannot be delegated—else it becomes just another piece of context—hence the true enormity of the task, considering who has to do it and what other tasks are also calling for their attention.

CLOSING ON CULTURE

For as long as I have been engaged with business, culture has been relegated to that class of things that are both terribly important and hopelessly unmanageable. (You know the class; it's where you also put rekindling the romance with your spouse, keeping up with the music that your teenager listens to, and getting your local NFL franchise into the Super Bowl.) The occasional inspired CEO manages to create great effects, but for the most part culture has been more talked about than taken care of.

The problem with this strategy of benign neglect is that when markets are disrupted by a fault line, it simply won't work. Two emerging trends have brought the issue to a head:

- The need to respond swiftly and globally to the shifting dynamics of technology-enabled markets.

- The need to supplement organic growth with mergers and acquisitions.

Neither of these needs can be met successfully without actively managing culture. The goal of this chapter has been to offer a framework and vocabulary within which executive teams can approach this task. The ultimate deliverable is to identify, declare, and develop a culture that enables your corporation to compete successfully given its heritage, its core competence, its position in the marketplace, and the talents and aspirations of its executive team.

The discussion leading up to this decision needs to be initiated at the board level. Here the board should act in an advisory capacity to the executive team, letting it explore various possibilities, providing it advice and counsel. Then once the go-forward culture has been identified, all hands, board and executives alike, must join as one to declare the culture via sustained emphasis on that culture's defining activity.

There is nothing in this call to action that is radical *except the insistence that it no longer be ignored.* I am making the claim that explicit, engaged management culture is a direct determinant of shareholder value and that it is the fiduciary responsibility of the board and the executive team to see that this declaration is appropriately managed. Them's fightin' words, so either dispute the claim or get on with the activity. Your call.

Epilogue

SHEDDING CONTEXT, EMBRACING CORE

As this book reaches its end, it seems to me we have come full circle, where, as T. S. Eliot put it, "the end of all our exploring / [is] to arrive where we started / and know the place for the first time." In our case, where we started was with a notion that, to manage for shareholder value, organizations must shed context to embrace core.

From that vantage we said *core* was any activity that could raise stock price, a claim that drove us into a discourse on shareholder value, the main point of which was that stock price is an indirect measure of competitive advantage (Part I). To raise stock price, we realized, meant one had to increase competitive advantage, leading us to describe the discipline of managing for shareholder value (Part II). That in turn led us to build a more complete model of competitive advantage (Part III) and to explore how it evolves through different stages over the technology adoption life cycle (Part IV). What we learned is that competitive-advantage strategy has to change much more frequently and dramatically than most organizations are prepared to support. When organizations do not rise to this challenge, the result is a series of default behaviors that culminate in the innovator's dilemma. We explored these behaviors (Part V) and then outlined a program of triage for correcting them. Triage, however, is only a temporary expedient, and so (Part VI) we described a platform of four cultures, any one of which, if properly declared and developed, can support the kind of ongoing adaptations required.

It remains for us to validate this last claim by exposing it to the test set forth at the outset of this book—how do each of these cultures meet the challenge of shedding context and embracing core? By now we know the short answer—*differently!* But by way of bringing this book to a close, I would like to at least sketch out the four paths forward, leaving it to you and your team to pick the one most to your liking.

Cultivation cultures have the easiest time shedding context—they simply walk away from it. Often this behavior is described as absentminded, but I assure you it is nothing of the sort. It is instead the same atavistic mechanism by which teenagers everywhere evade cleaning up their room, an innate response that keeps them true to their messy cores despite every parental encouragement to the contrary. The result in cultivation cultures is a kind of spontaneous outsourcing in which a supporting cast, managed by one or more invisible administrators, simply takes up the discarded work so that the geniuses can attend to whatever it is that genius attends to, or the work simply does not get done at all.

This mechanism works perfectly well provided it is monitored at some level by a genius. Because it is so blatantly subject to abuse, it must continually be vetted by someone who can discriminate between the real stuff and a fraudulent imitation. Think of this individual as an art director, someone whose taste instinctively discriminates between what is truly fresh and new and what has become stale or derivative. It is a role that Steve Jobs has played quite visibly at Apple and that venture capitalist board members play on many a board—the person who keeps the organization climbing up the down escalator, always moving it out of its comfort zone to the edge of innovation. People not climbing fast enough or high enough are goaded to go higher and faster or to withdraw from the field (or have their funding withdrawn from them). This brutally Darwinian mechanism must be fully exercised if cultivation culture is to keep itself relevant to the world.

Competence cultures can also keep themselves on track through constant testing and proving of themselves, but instead of letting their core be defined by the subjective insights of an art director, they objectify it in observable, measurable outcomes. Context can overtake core in these cultures in two ways. In the first, the overall goal itself becomes context. This occurs whenever competing institutions have already reached the goal so that it no longer provides competitive differentiation.

In such instances competence cultures can shed context simply by raising the bar. But in so doing they must actively manage the growing accumulation of context work by systematically outsourcing it. If they do not, they will increase the burden on their talent pool beyond tolerance, burning people out with work they should really not be doing. One tactic here has been to assign context work to temporary employees and contractors, but social and governmental resistance has now blocked this path. The only sustainable response is to reconstruct the workload into an outsourced/insourced workflow and proceed accordingly. Because competence cultures are so proficient with observable metrics, they are able to design highly effective service-level agreements with outsourcers and thus are well positioned to succeed in this effort.

The more insidious threat to competence cultures occurs when the metrics it has targeted no longer reflect true progress toward the end goal. Metrics, after all, are simply representative outcomes intended to signal change relative to a larger scheme. When they instead become enshrined as goals in themselves, competitive individuals find shortcuts to achieving them that meet the letter of the challenge but violate its spirit. Alternatively, management setting the objectives can fall into the trap of simply replaying the old metrics blindly instead of rethinking goals anew and constructing new metrics in light of changed conditions. The signature characteristic of competence cultures is that you get what you pay for. Thus management must vigilantly assure itself each year that it is indeed paying for the right things.

Competence cultures keep in touch with what is truly core through a healthy paranoia. They navigate, in other words, by keeping a safe distance between themselves and their competitors. If they exhaust the current set, they must take on a more ambitious one or in the absence of a suitable external opponent find ways to compete among themselves. This incessant competing and testing sloughs off most context work because people quickly see it does not lead to winning. The risk instead is that in its focus on outperforming a competitor, competence culture mistakenly directs its own core down a wrong road simply because that's where the other guy went. Thus the final competence required is the ability to navigate by a higher goal as well, defining core as an alignment between the company's internal competitive motivations with external value-creation activities that serve an end customer.

Control cultures shed context incrementally through quality improvement programs that prune and adapt workflows to accommodate gradual drifts in business processes. Their biggest challenge comes when disruptive technologies enable new market paradigms calling for wholesale deconstruction and reconfiguration of the incumbent value chain. At such points all the inertia and history of the old configuration resists transition to the required new state. The instrument for overcoming this resistance is the business plan. But instead of having it percolate up from the bottom of the organization, as it should in years of incremental change, in times of discontinuous change it must be formulated at the top and driven down through the organization over the objections of middle management.

Under this direction the culture must first plan how to shed context and then execute that plan. The plan is built around (1) conducting the core-versus-context exercise at the executive level, (2) identifying the largest chunks of context that can be outsourced, (3) assigning a team and an executive sponsor to each chunk, (4) having them plan the search for, selection of, and transition to an outsourcer, and (5) executing that plan. Once this plan is under way, the part of the organization that is not being outsourced should also be taught the core-versus-context exercise so that, in its own planning functions, it can work through the exercise during its next planning cycle.

More than anything else the key to control cultures successfully negotiating shedding of context is for the executive team to really "get" the new core. Mike Vance, a creativity consultant, tells a great story about helping the Mayo Clinic board get over such a hump. They wanted to know what was the key to becoming a more creative and flexible institution. Vance told them the one thing that all creative organizations have in common is that the people who work in them are cool. *Cool?* queried the board. Vance, sensing an uphill battle, had an inspiration. The board had assembled in preparation for a three-day off-site to review and approve the five-year operating plan. Vance proposed that he be allowed to approve the plan on the spot. The chairman, caught a bit off guard, acquiesced. Vance promptly announced, "You've just allowed a complete outsider to come in and approve your five-year plan—*now that's cool!*" The board went on to its off-site, spent three days talking about everything in the Mayo Clinic's future but the five-year operating plan, and the only standard they used to continually challenge each other was "Yeah, but is that cool?" So for control cultures, when it comes to stepping up to the task of embracing core and shedding context, that is the prescription: be cool.

Finally, **collaboration cultures** shed context and embrace core by continually renewing their focus on the customer to ensure their efforts are adding true value. In stable markets, however, this mechanism can lose touch with the market whenever "the customer" comes to stand for the entity immediately downstream in the value chain. An internal group can determine that its customers are another internal group, which in turn could have as its customers yet another internal group, and so on. This leads to more and more energy going into creating customer satisfaction for colleagues or partners, not end customers. It also leads to far too cozy a system with neither motive nor mechanism to pare this context away from core. Thus the first recourse of collaboration cultures must be to redefine customer focus as referring to the end customer only and to treat every intermediary in the value chain not as a surrogate customer to whom value is due but rather as a partner who must add value to the end customer or else lose its place in the chain. Without this change in frame of reference, collaboration cultures become paralyzed when faced with the need to reengineer value chains to eliminate unnecessary middlemen, a key step to ensuring sustainable competitive advantage in maturing markets.

The biggest challenge for collaboration cultures, however, comes when a disruptive innovation forces the wholesale abandonment of the old value chain. This runs completely counter to the affiliation-based motives of collaboration itself, and those among this culture tend to remain loyal to established relationships long after they have ceased to provide value. The most extreme example of this problem occurs when the disintermediation happens inside the customer organization, so that the old "end customer" is displaced by a new one, as happened in the telephony industry when phone and fax no longer reported to the office manager were was repositioned instead under the IT department.

At such times collaboration cultures must return to their roots by recommitting to true and unwavering customer service. More than any other culture, they are likely to bring the right attitude and the greatest domain expertise to the new challenge. It is simply a matter of reframing their understanding of the market in light of a new end customer who needs a new whole product that will be supplied by a new value chain—in essence, a matter of recrossing the chasm. The challenge is in letting go of the old and letting go of what feels like self-interest (but which in fact is simply inertia headed on a dangerously wrong course). Such radical shifts in momentum, as always, must come from the top down, not the bottom up. There are simply too many local loyalties to overcome piece by piece in anything like the time available to make the transition.

In conclusion, each of the four cultures offers excellent prospects for shedding context and embracing core, what might be termed in aggregate *organizational renewal*. In every case, as long as innovation is continuous within existing market frameworks, incremental renewal can be expected to bubble up from below, leveraging the natural attraction to quality as defined within that culture. Here management's primary role is simply to reinforce the natural actions of the culture. But whenever disruptive innovations arrive, whether they come from outside the organization or, even more challenging, when they come from within, they demand disruptive responses. To navigate such a transition, it must be driven by timely, unambiguous intervention from the top down. In these cases management must make itself highly visible and act courageously outside the organization's familiar norms to reposition it onto the next technology wave.

The goal of this book has been to enable that act of leadership. The models and metaphors offer a common vocabulary by which executive leadership interacting with the rest of the management team can accurately describe changes in the marketplace and definitively prescribe actions in response.

At the end of the day, it may come down to a matter of courage. Specifically, for companies that have thrived on Main Street for decades, that have not seen a disruptive innovation in management's memory, these new market forces are intimidating indeed. The thought I would leave you with is simple: If we say that leadership requires courage, we should recognize that courage is not required except in the presence of fear. If you are not scared, you are not leading.

Best wishes and God speed.

Geoffrey Moore
April 2002

INDEX

Page numbers in italics refer to diagrams.